Deer Hunters' 1994 Almanac

FROM THE PUBLISHERS OF DEER & DEER HUNTING MAGAZINE

Published by:

**krause
publications**

700 E. State Street • Iola, WI 54990-0001
Telephone: 715/445-2214

Library of Congress Number: 92-74255

ISBN: 0-87341-275-3

Printed in the United States of America

Contents

❖ Thoughts on Deer ❖

Deer hunting is much more than statistics, success stories and new gadgetry. Deer hunters are linked by the philosophies, experiences and observations of others who preceded them in the woods. In many cases, they never knew their predecessors personally, nor shared a cabin with them in the November woods. Still, they feel a kinship with these deer hunters of bygone days.

Many of those feelings are expressed in writing, thereby ensuring they'll be passed on to new generations of hunters. In fact, some of the nation's favorite outdoor literature revolves around deer hunting. Well-known deer hunting tales have come from such writers as Aldo Leopold, Gordon Mac-Quarrie and William Faulkner. And although entire books have been written on deer hunting, in many cases the writer captured the hunt's mood in a paragraph or two. What follows are some examples of that rare talent of taking a deer hunt and boiling it down to its essence with a few bold strokes of the pen.

Dreaming The Buck

Joel M. Spring

How many seasons had he hid in these woods, which I thought were so familiar? How many times had he lay motionless as my blaze-orange coat passed within 50 yards?

Heaving breaths break the misty silence of opening morning. The does have long since passed through the low spot in the stone fence on their way back from a night of feeding in the orchard. They passed 30 yards from my hiding spot on the wall, never detecting me.

I had passed the first test. Next was the forkhorn I had seen regularly during my week-long bow hunt in October. A broken right antler confirmed this was the same little deer. He had looked sickly during the bow season but now wore a sleek, dark-November coat, obviously having overcome what had ailed him. He paused briefly in the fence opening. For a moment, he glanced my way, perhaps hearing the safety click off when I first saw antlers over the fence. Either way, he quickly dismissed the danger he may have felt and walked into plain view, taking a moment to chew a few grasses

that had survived two hard frosts. He spent no more than a moment or two in the meadow's little finger that extended down through the beech trees.

When I was sure he was out of sight, I eased the safety back on. That's when I heard the grunting.

Most of the does had come silently up the hill, escaping my notice until they were at the fence opening. Even the forkhorn was fairly quiet, although I thought I heard a low grunt just before he appeared. But what I was hearing now just positively had to be the big buck I had awaited. For four long years.

The buck strolled into the opening, nose to the ground, not pausing at all, but following the forkhorn's steps. He was hot on the trail of the does, and was letting his little scout make sure his route was safe. I waited for his head to swing away from me and I raised the rifle, feeling confident. The deer froze at the safety's click. But for once he wasn't fast enough. As he crouched, readying for flight, the crosshairs settled behind his shoulder and my finger touched the trigger's cold metal.

That scene has played itself over and over again in my mind. And I'm hoping this is the year it really happens.

I first saw that buck four years ago on opening day, crossing in that same clearing, but my stand was more than 100 yards from the trail. He ran out on the heels of a lone doe, but was in and out of the meadow before I could raise the rifle. The brief sighting burned the impression of the heavy-racked buck into my mind. We hunt in a deer-rich area, but what we have in numbers we lack in quality. A deer like that buck is rare, not one to be quickly forgotten. I moved my stand closer to the opening but the buck never showed again. I was convinced he was killed by one of the hunters on the neighboring property.

It wasn't until a year later that I saw him. Again, it was opening day. Even though I thought the big buck had been shot, I set up my stand near the opening. It was a pleasant place that always produced deer sightings, so I had nothing to lose. I arrived at the stand around daylight on opening day and was settled in against the fence when the first rays of sun appeared on this unusually warm November day. Around 8 a.m., a loud rustling in the leaves behind me suddenly made we worry that I had misplaced my stand. Shifting slowly around on my rock seat, I craned my neck just enough to make out

a small flock of turkeys pecking in the leaves. Walking in a loose bunch, they slowly and noisily worked their way into the deeper woods. Another rustling got my blood pumping, but again turned out to be a turkey. A lone tom.

I turned back to watch the woods where I expected the deer to appear. Fifteen minutes passed. I settled in against the stone fence, trying to get lost in the rhythm of the woods. I knew I was trying too hard. I closed my eyes to concentrate. Behind me, the sound of the turkeys grew more faint. I turned my head to watch, this time with the measured slowness so vital to deer hunting. What I saw was the hind end of the large-racked buck disappearing into a thick tangle of blown-down birches. I quickly shifted my weight, trying to get the rifle up. The motion was detected by another deer, much closer than the big buck. A loud snort sent the buck crashing off through the woods as the sound of the other deer's escape echoed in the other direction. I felt sick.

Later that morning I killed a nice 6-pointer that was preparing to chase off a young spike buck. Each time I look at that 6-point rack, I think of the buck that could have been.

Last year, the big buck showed on the season's third day. Once again he was chasing a group of does, and briefly appeared in the opening, running at full speed. I started thinking about where to move the stand. I needed a place where I could catch him when he wasn't moving so quickly. Maybe in the creek bottom. Maybe up in the blowdowns Or maybe ...

Boom!

My heart leapt briefly into my throat before becoming lodged in my stomach. The shot was straight below me. My ears rang from its concussion.

It was over. I knew he was down. And it was probably someone from my own gang who got him. Breaking the agreement of not bothering the other hunters before 11 a.m., I quickly packed up and went down the hill. One of our party's older members was getting up from his seat. He had been not 200 yards away.

"Did you get him?" I yelled, praying under my breath.

"I saw him come down, but he was movin' too fast," the man replied. He had only managed to get one shot. I told him I would follow the track into the thick hemlocks in the creek bottom. The does had run back up the hill.

"He ain't hit, but go ahead."

It was fairly easy to see where the deer had begun to sprint, probably at the sound of the shot. No blood or hair was anywhere to be found. I followed his sparse trail through the leaves down toward the creek. Where the beeches melded into the hemlocks, the single set of tracks was easy to follow. The deer had slowed once it entered the shadowy woods' protective cover.

Two main deer trails run through that stretch of woods,

and I had hunted them both with some success. We called this place "The Bowl," and it was always a favorite for drives. But I wasn't familiar with the trail the buck had taken. Often taking the less convenient route around obstacles, the buck's trail bobbed and weaved, doubled back, cut across the creek and did just about every other thing it shouldn't have.

Somewhere along the trail, the buck's track simply evaporated. The chest-high hemlocks prevented much tracking. He was gone. I decided to stay on this unexplored trail to see where it led.

A few minutes later, the trail made a sharp uphill turn that had me huffing and puffing before leveling out in an unfamiliar stand of 6-inch thick white pines. I let out a loud breath of air, not from the exertion of the climb, but from what was before me. About every 20 feet, the pines were brutally rubbed. Two distinct rub lines arrowed deep into the pines. In some places the ground was heavily scarred where the deer's hooves had dug in while he battled the trees. To my right, a single impression in the brown needles betrayed where he would lie and watch down the hill. After three years of chasing this buck, I felt as if I had discovered the King Tut's Tomb of buck lairs. I could imagine him up here, listening to the gunfire rip across the hills. How many seasons had he hid in these woods, which I thought were so familiar? I had probably driven the hill below him a dozen times. How many times had he lay motionless as my blaze-orange coat passed within 50 yards of him? It sent a chill up my spine to imagine such things. Only one day left to hunt, and then it was time to head home. I was elated and disappointed all in one. I hated to go, now that I had unlocked a couple of this deer's secrets.

But I knew where I would set up next year.

Bow season passed without one sighting of the big buck. I planned it that way, though. I was plenty happy with the 5-pointer that I killed down on the orchard. But when rifle season comes around (13 days, 10 hours and 12 minutes from now), I plan to celebrate my fourth anniversary with that buck by meeting him at a certain low spot in the stone fence. This year he's mine.

Sure he is. Keep dreaming.

On The Cusp Of Autumn

Greg Miller

My truck rolls steadily down the highway toward Winnipeg, Manitoba. It's not a long, exhausting drive from my home in Wisconsin. If all goes as scheduled, I should arrive sometime late this afternoon after 10 hours on the road. I'll rest tomorrow, and then Monday I'll sneak through "the bush," bow in hand, trying to move on a white-tailed buck.

It's shortly after dawn in the third week in September. The leaf change along my northbound route is at its peak. Vivid yellows, golds and reds are splashed across the trees everywhere I look. At this hour, only the leaves in the uppermost branches brilliantly reflect the sun's touch. I can't imagine a man-made sight to equal this early-morning art show.

As if the show of autumn leaves isn't enough distraction, I snatch glimpses of wildlife, and torture my neck for one last peek before the truck carries me out of sight. Waterfowl have taken up temporary residency on every lake, pothole, river and creek within sight. Occasionally, I spot the familiar chevron of geese flying toward winter food and warmer climates.

And how about those deer? They stand on the edges of the rare alfalfa and oat fields in this region, grabbing a last bite before returning to the safety and solitude of their bedding areas. A few deer even slow my progress, causing me to brake to allow them safe passage across the pavement.

Can anything match the sights, the feel, the wonder of this time of year? The sounds and fragrances of autumn are unlike those of any other season. The air, which just a fortnight ago seemed heavy, warm and dank, is replaced by a lighter, crisper, fresher atmosphere. We suddenly awake to scattered dawns where lawns and truck windows sparkle with frost.

Now, is it just me, or does the mood of many people seem to change in autumn? Instead of being short- and ill-tempered, as is often the case in summer, most folks become more passive and easy-going in September. No doubt about it. This is a unique time of year.

I remember the problems that autumn's onset created in school. The teacher stood in front of the class, striving to help us unravel the vagaries of verbs, nouns and dangling participles, or telling us how, to decipher theorems and sniff out the value of "x." She could well have saved her breath on me. Although I attended in body, my mind was wandering through the nearby fields and forests of west-central Wisconsin. I was gone with a casual glance out the classroom window. I was well-schooled in imaginary forays, searching for grouse, rabbits, squirrels or, better yet, a thick-racked whitetail.

The years haven't changed me much. My mind still journeys to the deer woods as I sweat and toil at the construction sites where I work. On early-October mornings I'll bend over to put the finishing touches on freshly poured concrete. Suddenly, off in the distance, comes the hrronk-hrronk of Canada geese. I'll straighten up and look to the north, trying to detect the calls' source. Straining my eyes a bit, I'll scan the bluebird sky and eventually locate a straggling line of geese. A slight wind will brush my face. It's one of those trademark cool, fresh breezes of autumn.

In seconds, I'm off again. Now, however, I harbor few thoughts of grouse, rabbits, squirrels or other small game. Nearly all of my imaginary forays are centered on one thing: whitetails.

Fortunately, I have a tolerant boss, both at work and at home.

Occasionally, I'll return to Earth to find my construction taskmaster staring at me, He'll smirk and ask, 'What was it this time? An 8-, 10- or 12-pointer?' There's no use denying it. We've worked together too many years. He knows all the warning signs of a mind set loose by falling leaves. Getting back to work I mutter about a certain 10-point buck that has lived in my thoughts lately. He grins again and shakes his head.

The one rap on autumn is that September, October and November never pause for breath. Wet, sloppy springs bog down under their own weight. And hot, sticky summers move slower than a porch swing. but when fall arrives, it turns and slips away faster than a spooked buck. So many things to try, so may ideas to test, so many deer to hunt.

Suddenly, it all must wait till next year.

Before getting too down, I remember a new hunting season is near. The leaves and frost say this is so. I'm halfway to Winnipeg. In two days, my bow season will start with a chase for Canadian whitetails.

That brief magical time is just beginning.

October Cadence

Al Cornell

The quartz crystal vibrated another 32,768 times and the second hand jumped again in the modern clock. It joined the others at the 12, and October officially began. At this point the frenzied quartz crystal lost its significance. October time can't be reckoned in ordinary pieces.

October time pulses to its own devices. Leaves changing color and falling from top down on maples and bottom up on aspen gauge the month's transition. Crystal structures, forming from the night vapors, greet morning sun rays with increasing determination. White-tailed bucks, responding to internal fires, paw and thrash, scent-mark and search.

The hunter, refreshed by the prevailing coolness, emerges in the dawn, reads the wind and slope, and ascends a chosen tree. Once on stand, a need finds its satisfaction. Not a subsistence requirement watered or fed, but something inside that longs to be filled with an essence of wholesomeness.

The uninitiated feel shock at the thought of time without earphones and motion pictures, or places to run and people to alternately cheer and boo. The October woods rebel against such melancholy madness. They offer a block of time that need not be disturbed by motion, but that can burst into steaming nostrils and flashing antler tines. That block can remain unsevered by ticking and chiming, or be split unequally by honking from a south-bound flight.

October may change from the bite of a northwester to the balm of Indian summer, or pull a unique day from among the infinite. Such is leaf-fall day. On the cold night before, ice crystals broke the normal hold that the petiole had on the branch. However, the crystals themselves briefly hold the leaf firmly to the branch. This new, seemingly tight grip, betrays its promise in the warmth of the morning sun, and October unleashes its special shower as a commitment to the humus and nutrient recycling. The motion of leaf-fall day may disquiet the whitetails, yet the hunter imbibes its fascination.

October offers us a chance to

share in a way of life that continues to drift away on society's stream. Herein we sense a bond to life and matter that hunting and gathering people knew daily. We ponder age-old values and perceive that not every aspect of being progressive enriches life. Nowhere else is the extravagance of the warm end of the light spectrum shown forth equally to October's sunlit hardwood hillsides. Being part of it establishes an unbreakable bond, but causes frequent longing through the rest of the year.

Ah, to good health. The joy to laugh from seeing and hearing. The wit to sense the approaching buck. The strength to climb, to sit, to wait, to draw the bow. And, eventually, the wisdom to find solace by weeping among old oaks. October's way restores quality lost to anxiety.

The realm of view, from a perch above the deer trail, captivates. Few places exist where one would want to catch every sound and capture every movement. Awareness here is learned. More events unfold within the zone of perception for the one seasoned by Octobers past. Trained senses and a knack to not disturb the wild things combine to increase the spectacle. However, remember the seasoned hunters were simply beginners who overcame their early blunders and melted into October's rhythm.

Some things transpire but once in a lifetime. They may comprise pages with asterisks inside a diary, or they may simply live on within a vivid memory. Perhaps you saw the buck deftly paw an intruding leaf from his bare patch of ground. Maybe you learned the meaning of kinglet by viewing, at arm's length, a golden crown on a tiny feathered object. Or, possibly, you saw a gray fox sit and yawn beneath your tree before resuming his evening venture. Repeatedly, scenes against the October backdrop make indelible memories and refresh the one who visits.

Within this unique character of October time, there exists an opportunity to contemplate the meaning and purpose of it all. In this mode, I can recall and ponder Loren Eiseley's dictum: "In the world there is nothing to explain the world ... It is as if matter dreamed and muttered in its sleep." I sense his longing for a better explanation in much that he wrote. But my meditations, from the leisure of a tree stand, find more substance in Aldo Leopold's words from A Sand County Almanac: "What value has wildlife from a standpoint of morals and religion?" The concluding sentence in his answer quotes from Isaiah, a 27-century-old fountain for lovers of this creation, who suggests that we "... may see, and know, and consider, and understand together, that the hand of the Lord hath done this."

October adds its own evidence.

The Hunt Continues

Bob Traun

Dear Doug, old friend,

I think I know how you feel today, on the eve of your first deer season without your father, your son Brian's grandfather. I lost my father 11 years ago and, although it hasn't been the same, I am struck now with mixed feelings and perhaps a different perspective than I had in November 1980.

I knew it would be tough that first year, but the older generation of hunters in our camp, my dad's friends, really, helped me remember him in a way that brought some good memories. And on that opening day, my younger brother, Jim, shot his first deer and suddenly I became the father. I was so proud for him! For the first time in my life I understood how Dad must have felt when I shot my first deer in 1968.

Some year, maybe this one, you will have that same opportunity with Brian.

I will always remember the first time my dad called me a man, and treated me as one. It was my 16th year, my first time in the deer camp. I realized that I was being invited into this close fraternity of Dad's friends, and their sons, and it was something special. I began then to understand the unique bond that deer hunting partners feel for each other.

Today I can acknowledge that the loss of a parent is a natural thing, perhaps as difficult to accept as it is inevitable. You were the child, and now the parent. You hunted with your grandfather, and he passed on. Now Brian's grandfather has passed on. This is the first year Brian will hunt alone in a stand. You see, he's growing to be a man, too.

As you feel the loss, think of how your dad would have wanted you to react. Probably not with much sadness, but rather a celebration of his life, the traditions of deer camp, and hunts long past. Would he expect you to carry on in these same traditions? Absolutely. So have fun, tell a few deer stories, and remember days forever gone.

You may also find comfort in thinking about it this way: The way I figure, our dads met last spring up there in the Great Deer Shack, and have been swapping lies and making plans for the fall hunt ever since. So while you and I are freezing in the cold November woods, our fathers will be sitting in their deer stands, where the winds blow gently, the snowflakes fall softly, and where some day, we can all hunt together again.

Your friend,

Bob

CLASSIFICATION AND
DISTRIBUTION OF THE WHITE-TAILED DEER

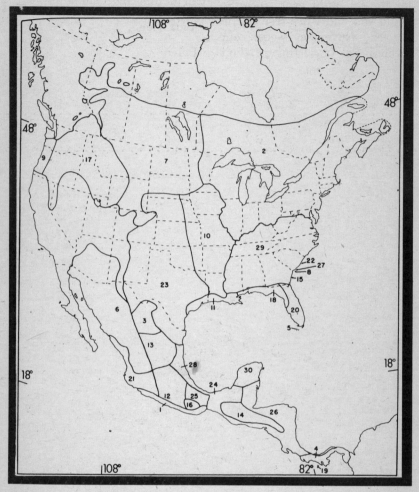

FIGURE 10. Distribution of white-tailed deer (*Odocoileus virginianus*) subspecies in North and Central America

1. *O. v. acadpulcensis*
2. *O. v. borealis*
3. *O. v. carminis*
4. *O. v. chiriquensis*
5. *O. v. clavium*
6. *O. v. couesi*
7. *O. v. dacotensis*
8. *O. v. hiltonensis*
9. *O. v. leucurus*
10. *O. v. macrourus*
11. *O. v. mcilhennyi*
12. *O. v. mexicanus*
13. *O. v. miquihuanensis*
14. *O. v. nelsoni*
15. *O. v. nigribarbis*
16. *O. v. oaxacensis*
17. *O. v. ochrourus*
18. *O. v. osceola*
19. *O. v. rothschildi*
20. *O. v. seminolus*
21. *O. v. sinaloae*
22. *O. v. taurinsulae*
23. *O. v. texanus*
24. *O. v. thomasi*
25. *O. v. toltecus*
26. *O. v. truei*
27. *O. v. venatorius*
28. *O. v. veraecrucis*
29. *O. v. virginianus*
30. *O. v. yucatanensis*

*From **White-tailed Deer: Ecology and Management**, 1984: Courtesy of the Wildlife Management Institute.*

❖ SKELETON ❖

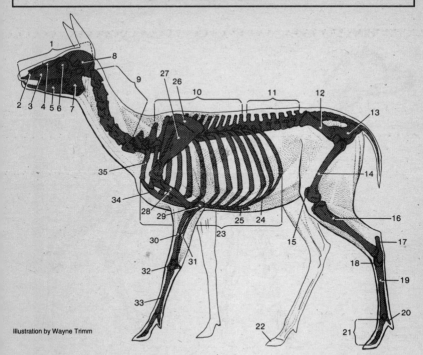

Illustration by Wayne Trimm

1. Skull
2. Os incisivum
3. Maxilla
4. Os nasale
5. Manible
6. Orbita
7. Mandibular condyle
8. Os temporale
9. Cervical vertebrae
10. Thoracic vertebrae
11. Lumbar vertebrae
12. Illium
13. Ischium

14. Femur
15. Patella
16. Tibia
17. Tuper calcis
18. Tarsus
19. Os temporale
20. Dew claw of phalanges
21. Phalanges
22. Hoof
23. Rib cage
24. Rib cartilages
25. Xiphoid cartilage

26. Scapula cartilage
27. Scapula
28. Humerus
29. Olecranon
30. Radius
31. Ulna
32. Carpals
33. Metacarpal
34. Sternum
35. First Rib

*From **White-tailed Deer: Ecology and Management,** 1984: Courtesy of the Wildlife Management Institute.*

❖ MUSCLES ❖

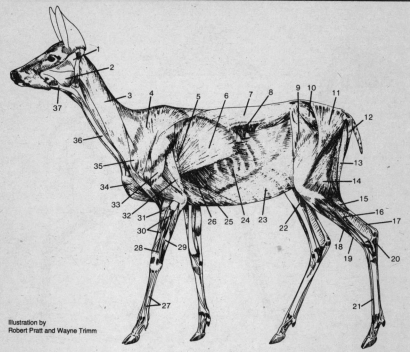

Illustration by
Robert Pratt and Wayne Trimm

1. Arcus zygomaticus
2. Masseter
3. Brachiocephalicus
4. Trapezius
5. Tensor fasciae antebrachii
6. Latissimus dorsi
7. Lumbo-dorsal fascis
8. Serratus ventralis
9. Tensor fasciae externus
10. Gluteus medius vertebrae
11. Trochanter major
12. Semimembranosus
13. Semitendinosus
14. Biceps femoris

15. Gastrocnemius
16. Deep flexor tendon
17. Tendon of Achilles
18. Lateral extensor
19. Long extensor
20. Superficial flexor tendon
21. Anterior tendon
22. Flexor digitorum (pedislongus)
23. Aponeurosis
24. Obliquus abdominals exterrnus
25. Deep pectoral
26. Serratis ventralis

27. Flexor tendons of metatarsus
28. Tendon of extensor digiti
29. Extensor carpi (ulnaris)
30. Extensor digiti
31. Extensor carpi (radialis)
32. Triceps
33. Deltoid
34. Superficial pectoral (brisket)
35. Shouldler-transverse process Muscle
36. Sternocephalicus
37. Sternomandibularis

*From **White-tailed Deer: Ecology and Management**, 1984: Courtesy of the Wildlife Management Institute.*

16

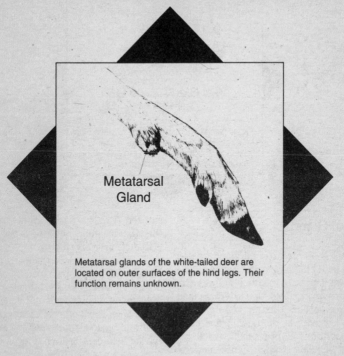

Metatarsal glands of the white-tailed deer are located on outer surfaces of the hind legs. Their function remains unknown.

Metatarsal Gland

This gland is not well understood. The metatarsals are located on the outer hind legs between the toes and heel. All deer possess these glands from birth. Many wildlife biologists suggest that gland size, in some cases, can have taxonomic value between species. The mule deer has the largest metatarsal glands, followed by the black-tailed and white-tailed deer. Although smallest in comparison to other deer species, the gland is clearly visible on the whitetail and is noted by a light, tannish-colored circle of hair against the more dominant colors of reddish-brown or gray. The light-colored cluster is actually the hair that surrounds the gland. A closer examination of the gland reveals an area lacking hair, rib-shaped, and not a true external gland. (A true external gland has a surface opening or duct.) The metatarsal glands, actually located below the skin surface, are technically known as sebaceous (sweat) and sudoriferous (scent-producing) glands. This gland secretes very small amounts of scent, but its intended purpose has not been proven. Knowledge of its physiology then is minimal.

Some speculators claim that when a deer lies down the glands rub the ground and leave a scent. Another possibility is that through change and adaptation, the metatarsal gland could be a rudimentary vestigial gland that had a more significant purpose at one time in the evolution of deer. We see this fact evident concerning dewclaws. Dewclaws are remnants of what used to be functional toes.

Tarsal Gland

Tarsal glands on the inner surface of the hind legs of white-tailed deer produce a scent unique to individual deer and are involved in rub-urination and marking behavior.

Tarsal Gland

This is a true external gland located inside both hind legs at the foot/heel junction and is present in both sexes at birth. We know more about this external gland than any other. Clearly visible on all three deer species, the tarsal gland plays an important role in reproductive activities as well as social dominance and communication.

Through years of research, biologists discovered many relevant facts concerning this gland. They know the tarsals are a deer's most important scent gland. Tarsal glands are concealed in hair and measure about four inches in diameter. The hairs associated with the gland have the ability to stand on end or flair out should an unusual or excitable situation arise, putting the deer "on guard." In the excited state, the hairs can be seen at fairly long distances and at this time the gland releases scent that clings to the hairs and acts partly as a warning signal to nearby deer. Wildlife biologist D. Mueller Schwarze states that the active olfactory components in the tarsal gland are lactones. He mentions that lactones are both age and sex specific and that the hairs used to deposit the urine and scent (pheromone) mixture are termed "osmetrichia." These lipid-covered hairs are spe-

cialized scent hairs. It can be assumed then that one function of the tarsal glands is that of survival behavior.

During the mating season males, females, and fawns rub-urinate on their tarsals for several reasons. Bucks do it as a means of displaying social dominance. Males smell each other's tarsal glands in determining dominance ranking. Females rub for self-identification. Fawns depend partly on this when they become separated from the does. Fawns also rub-urinate, possibly for identification purposes. L.W. Bouckhout revealed that the more socially dominant males rub-urinate more frequently than do males of lesser dominance. K. Ralls, C.C. Shank, and C. Barrette state that the odor of tarsal glands is stronger in dominant males due to the frequency of urination. Young males and females have been know to lick their tarsal glands after rub-urination more so than older males. This act would seem to remove scent, as an expression of lesser dominance perhaps.

Deer hunters should know that the tarsal gland is associated only externally with deer. The need to remove the gland prior to field dressing or meat cutting is necessary only if a hunter feels he will come in contact with the glands. If contact isn't made, the gland will not spoil or ruin the flavor of the meat.

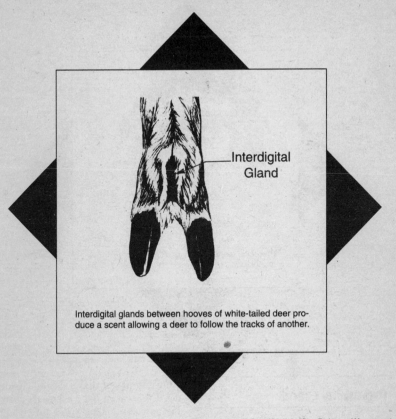

Interdigital
Gland

Interdigital glands between hooves of white-tailed deer produce a scent allowing a deer to follow the tracks of another.

Interdigital Gland

Interdigital glands are located between the toes of each foot on both sexes. These glands, functional from birth, are used by deer to track one another. Each deer carries a specific odor from the gland. The interdigital gland is covered with hair and not readily seen with the naked eye. Close examination reveals a duct or opening between the toes, visible only when the toes are spread and the hair parted. The largest interdigital glands are found on white-tailed deer.

An active gland, the interdigital emits scent each time a deer takes a step. Use of the scent differs between sexes. Females rely on the scent to track their young, while males use it to track females during the rut.

An amazing aspect of wildlife ecology is an animal's ability to follow only one particular scent. Many kinds of wildlife, especially the female and her offspring, can distinguish an individual's scent no matter how many animals are in an area or how many scents there are to differentiate. Since deer rely primarily on scent for positive identification, this gland seems especially important.

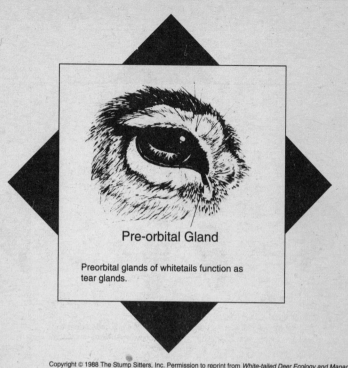

Pre-orbital Gland

Preorbital glands of whitetails function as tear glands.

Pre-orbital Gland

Located below the eyes on all deer, the preorbital gland is not well understood. Characteristics of the gland include a small canal or duct by which small amounts of scent trickle. Easily visible and largest in mule deer, the purpose of the glands is believed to be that of a scent marker.

One theory claims that habitats reflect use of the gland. White-tailed and black-tailed deer would probably make best use of this gland since they inhabit areas of more dense vegetation, whereas mule deer inhabit open plains having little vegetation upon which to rub the gland. It seems unusual that a marking gland would be so near the eye since it is so vulnerable. Sharp twigs and forest debris could impair vision should the animal unknowingly rub near sharp objects.

Another possibility is that through doe/fawn contact the doe smears some of her own scent on her young through nuzzling. This may be beneficial when the fawn wanders out of the doe's sight.

Conclusion

Presented here are some facts as well as assumptions. Each year new information is published concerning glandular activity among deer. We will probably never know all the reasons deer do what they do, but through future studies and new findings, we may see the gap of the unknown slowly close.

❖ DEER TRACK IDENTIFICATION ❖

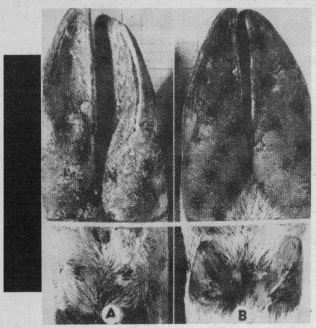

Dr. Frederick Weston

Experts often disagree whether it's possible to positively identify a deer's sex by the tracks it leaves. Leonard Lee Rue III, for example, believes most people who say they can make a positive ID would stop making the claims if they ever saw many of the deer that made the tracks.

That being said, other experienced hunters believe it's sometimes possible to tell a deer's sex by its tracks. Myles Keller, for example, says tracks measuring 3 to 3.25 inches were likely made by a trophy buck. Keller also says a mature buck's rear hooves will usually land short of imprints made by their front hooves (Figure 1).

Here are some other indicators:

• A doe's track usually meanders while bucks maintain a purposeful, fairly straight line. Because of a doe's pelvic structure, her hind hooves will overlap and land outside

the front imprints.

• All deer make drag marks in deep snow, but only bucks drag their hooves in leaves or light snow. During the rut, drag marks reach their maximum lengths.

• Heavy-bodied bucks with swollen necks and large antlers tend to walk with their front hooves more splayed, turned out and wider apart am does and yearling bucks. This puts more pressure on the tips of their hooves, which causes them to dig in and become rounded.

Most bucks, however, are shot as yearlings in much of the country. Therefore, few live long enough to display those tendencies. Also, hard or rocky ground tends to round off the hooves (Figure 2).

Like the fingerprints of man, deer hooves have individual characteristics that can distinguish one deer from another. For instance, the hoof on the left is concave and has a partial break

The tracks of a walking doe usually appear along an imaginary straight line with the tracks of the hind hooves ahead of the front hooves.

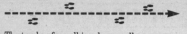

The tracks above indicate a mature buck in good condition. Note that the toes turn out from the center line rather than follow a straight line and that the tracks of the hind hooves appear behind the tracks of the front hooves.

Figure 1

Experts disagree whether it's possible to positively identify a deer's sex by the tracks it leaves.

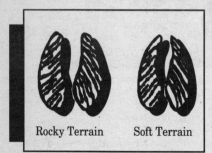

Rocky Terrain   Soft Terrain

Figure 2

in one toe.

• Does hunch back and urinate in their tracks, often with a wide and irregular spray. A buck's urine typically comes straight down and perforates unbroken snow. Also, bucks often dribble urine while walking, while does do not.

Illustration: Buck tracks during the rut

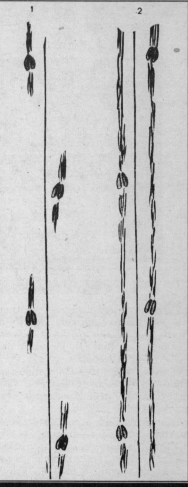

(1) The track of a white-tailed buck before and after the rut. Notice how the toes pointing outward from the center line.
(2) During the rut the drag mark almost extends from step to step.
— Josef Bunner,
   1909 *Tracks and Tracking*

❖ THE DOPE ON DEER DROPPINGS ❖

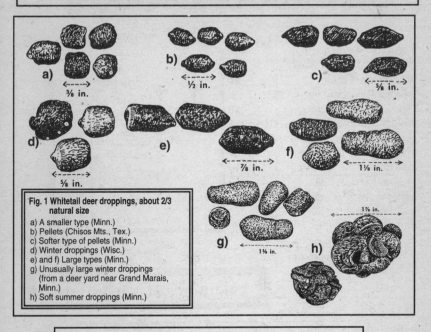

Fig. 1 Whitetail deer droppings, about 2/3 natural size

a) A smaller type (Minn.)
b) Pellets (Chisos Mts., Tex.)
c) Softer type of pellets (Minn.)
d) Winter droppings (Wisc.)
e) and f) Large types (Minn.)
g) Unusually large winter droppings (from a deer yard near Grand Marais, Minn.)
h) Soft summer droppings (Minn.)

Deer pellets might be the best scouting tool the hunter can find.

Deer pellets might be the best scouting tool the hunter can find. They help indicate bedding and feeding areas, forage preferences, and the deer's movements and whereabouts.

In addition, pellets give a general idea of how many deer are present in your area and whether they've been there recently. Just be sure not to base your evaluation on areas where deer yard in winter.

Deer droppings vary greatly in shape, color and form at various times of the year and under different food conditions. In winter, when deer feed on browse, the pellets are hard and become harder as the winter progresses. Their color is various shades of brown, and they're about three-fourths of an inch long. In summer, when deer feed on soft vegetation, their droppings form into soft clumps.

Sometimes, however, summer droppings consist of individual pellets.

Research verifies that more droppings are found by nighttime beds than daytime beds. Unlike urination, deer defecate while going about their daily routines. Rarely do they interrupt what they're doing while dropping their pellets. Deer also defecate the most shortly after rising from their bed. On average, they defecate about 13 times a day, with the number of pellets per defecation varying from 42 to 320. The frequency of defecation depends on the quantity and succulence of the forage.

While you generally can get some feel for the deer's size by the size of its pellet, this isn't always true. The type of food ingested may play a larger role than the animal's size or age.

SEASONAL CHANGES

Figure 1. Sequence of velvet loss among males by number of antler points as observed by David H. Hirth of the Welder Wildlife Refuge. N is the number of males of each antler class examined during the shedding season. Vertical lines indicate range of velvet loss dates and the horizontal bars show the mean velvet loss dates. (From *The Southwestern Naturalist*, 1977)

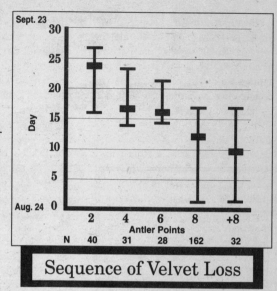

Sequence of Velvet Loss

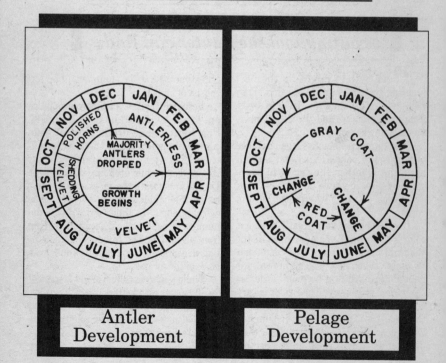

Antler Development

Pelage Development

❖ PEELING VELVET ❖

In August, in our northern areas, antler growth is completed, and the velvet-covered skin which nourished it now becomes shriveled. The buck presents a ludicrous picture when the peeling velvet sometimes hangs in fluttering ribbons from the rack.

The velvet from antlers is not always shed bit by bit in a slow peeling and drawing process. On this I have some first-hand information, for once I found the complete velvet case from a single antler of an eight-point buck. It was during the middle of August, and I happened across the strange object which looked like a piece of dark suede leather. The soft velvet was shed in one entire piece, and it split along the outside length of the beam to free itself from the prongs. The fuzzy growth was about an eighth of an inch thick and was substantial enough in body so that the projections covering the points of the antler stood out firmly on the discarded casing.

The curio was found in an open spot where the pasture grass was closely cropped. There was nothing nearby which the buck might have rubbed against in an attempt to free himself from this skin growth. The soft, damp condition of the casing caused me to believe it was shed that very day.

I brought it home in some sort of triumph, but the next day it was already beginning to shrivel and dry, and in a few days it lost its shape and the mummy-like skin was reduced to something that looked like a withered and twisted leaf. In this aged condition, it might not have caught my attention had I passed over it and only the eyes of a naturalist could have identified it when found. I would guess that at least some velvet shedding takes place in this manner. Most bucks seen at this time are either in or out of velvet, and only in the few is there an indication of a gradual peeling off of the velvet.

There has always been considerable controversy over the manner in which the buck rids himself of the peeling skin, yet there need be no argument. Buck rubs do not normally occur in the northern states until October, at a time when the antlers have been free of velvet for a month or more. In short, the bush fighting is a sex urge building up in the males at the approach of the rut, and if any velvet is worn off or antlers polished in this process, it is an incidental occurrence at best. Anyone in deer country during the months of September and October can make this simple observation.

— George Mattis

❖ HOW DEER REACT TO HUNTING PRESSURE ❖

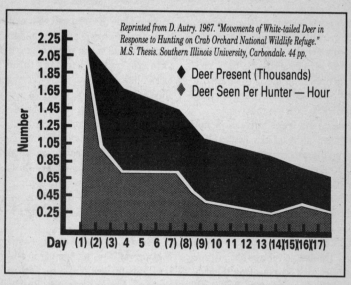

Reprinted from D. Autry. 1967. "Movements of White-tailed Deer in Response to Hunting on Crab Orchard National Wildlife Refuge." M.S. Thesis. Southern Illinois University, Carbondale. 44 pp.

◆ Deer Present (Thousands)
◆ Deer Seen Per Hunter — Hour

Numbers in parentheses indicate the days of the hunt. The gradual increase in deer seen during the closing days of the hunt occurred as a result of several supervised deer drives.

In most studies of deer tracked by radio telemetry, deer seldom leave their home range, preferring instead to sit tight in heavy cover. A deer's knowledge and familiarity with its home range enable it to survive hunting pressure. This is especially true of mature bucks.

Most studies found that hunting pressure caused yearling bucks to move significantly farther than mature bucks, probably making them more vulnerable to hunters. Bucks that remained in their beds, moving only when flushed at extremely short distances, tended to survive.

After the initial surprise of opening day, mature deer adjust their feeding activities, avoiding open areas, and sitting tight until darkness. The impression that bucks move great distances to sanctuaries

or remote regions was usually not confirmed by the studies. After the season's first day, the deer's wariness doubled or quadrupled, and remained at this heightened state the rest of the season.

Deer tend to elude hunters by circling and seeking patches of heavy cover within their home range. Their escape is often triggered not by a hunter's appearance, but rather his disappearance. They allow a hunter to walk by, and then sneak out behind with great evasive maneuvers.

Some researchers have also found that deer in areas open to public hunting are more skilled at eluding hunters than those in areas where hunting pressure is controlled.

❖ PLANT & BROWSE PREFERENCES ❖

Most hunters know that agricultural crops like rye, corn, alfalfa, soybeans and other legumes are high on a whitetail's menu. What about natural browse? Which wild-growing foods do white-tailed deer prefer?

The accompanying charts show some of the more common deer forage that's found in woods or clearings. Remember, though, that a plant's availability varies by region. Not all of these will be found in your area.

And don't forget hard and soft mast such as acorns, apples and persimmons. In addition, look for freshly fallen trees or branches, such as maples or white cedars. Large windfalls become deer magnets with their bountiful supply of buds or succulent leaves. Deer will also munch on lichens, so take note of recently fallen dead trees.

Woody Plants		
White cedar	Red Osier (Dogwood)	Sweetbay
Hemlock	Jack Pine	Poison sumac
Maples	White Pine	Aquatic plants
Poplar	Black Spruce	Berry bushes
Birch	Vines	Ferns
Sumac	Honeysuckle	Cypress
Viburnums	Wax myrtle	
Willows	Bay	

Herbaceous Plants — Species		
Joe-pye weed	Sheep sorrel	Bedstraw
Early goldenrod	Hop clover	St. John's wort
Spotted jewelweed	Bluegrass	Panic grass
Woodland goldenrod	Butter-and-eggs	Pearly everlasting
White wood aster	Grassleaf goldenrod	Field horsetail
Giant goldenrod	Wild geranium	Blueflag iris
Elecampane	Canada bluegrass	Liveforever
Sensitive fern	Clover	Wood sorrel
Virgin's bower	Wild oat grass	Yarrow
Bracken fern	Sweet vernalgrass	White snakeroot
Whorled loosestrife	Strawberry	Ragweed
Goldenrod	Common wintercress	Indian Jack-in-the-pulpit
Water averns	Wild carrot	Thistle
Timothy	Common St. John's-wort	Small purple
Oxeye daisy	Oldfield cinquefoil	fringed orchid
Wrinkled goldenrod	Pussytoes	Rush
Redtop grass	Vetch	Indian tobacco
Hawkweed	Speedwell	Bugleweed
Buckhorn plaintain	Common plaintain	Blackseed plantain
Buttercup	Fowl mannagrass	Purple milkwort
Fleabane	Sedge	Arrow leaved tearthumb
Argrimony	Avens	Dock
Selfheal	Virginia bugleweed	Silver goldenrod
Aster	Bulrush	
Red clover	White wood sorrel	

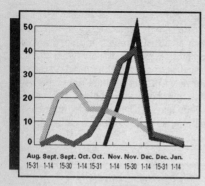

	Breeding
	Scrapes
	Rubs

Rubs, Scrapes and Breeding Chart

The frequency of rubbing, scraping and breeding activity of white-tailed deer in the Georgia Piedmont during two-week periods.

Reprinted from T.L. Kile and R. L. Marchinton, 1977. "White-tailed Deer Rubs and Scrapes: Spatial, Temporal and Physical Characteristics and Social Rule." American Midland Naturalist, 97(2):263.

Rubs and scrapes provide vital clues to a buck's home range. Contrary to popular belief, bucks usually don't start rubbing until weeks after their velvet drops off. Rubbing peaks shortly before the actual breeding season. Fewer rubs are made as the rut progresses and deer open and maintain scrapes.

Rubs tend to be found in clusters and often occur near scrapes. Myles Keller, a well-known bow hunter from Minnesota, believes a high density of rubs indicates the buck's bedding area is nearby. Keller thinks that if a buck beds in a relatively small area, he needs frequent exercise to tone his muscles. He gets this by vigorously rubbing trees.

Georgia researchers offer an additional thought: On several occasions they saw dominant bucks make rubs when encountering other bucks. Because the bucks also snorted and took intimidating stances, the researchers concluded that rubs play a major role in marking a buck's territory and maintaining his social rank.

Bucks prefer to rub smooth-barked trees with few low branches. Most prefer pines or other resinous, aromatic trees. Scientists generally agree that bucks deliberately rub their foreheads on debarked trees to leave their scent, which lasts several days. Because does also sniff, lick and even mark buck rubs with their foreheads, rubs appear to be a form of communication between the sexes.

However, in heavily hunted areas where the herd has a high percentage of does and a young-buck age structure, the role of rubs and scrapes diminishes.

Research shows that even though does participate in scraping, bucks carry out more activities at the scrape. One study showed that the average number of different types of behavior performed per visit for each age class was 2.4 for bucks, 2 for juveniles and 1.8 for does.

Recent evidence indicates scrapes aren't territorial markers. For one thing, various deer of all ages and both sexes repeatedly use the limb overhanging the same scrape. Secondly, all ages of bucks have been observed at the same scrape, and even at the same time.

Researchers also have found that the amount of mutilation on the overhanging limb is a better indicator of visitation frequency than the scrape's size. In many cases, smaller scrapes get the most attention.

❖ RUT SEASON ❖

A PHEROMONE IS — a chemical or a mixture of chemicals which is released to the exterior by an organism and which, upon reception by another individual of the same species, stimulates one or more specific reactions.
— H.H. Shorey, "Pheronomes." 1977 In *How Animals Communicate* (Indiana University Press) edited by Thomas A. Sebeok.

Types of behaviorial events observed and number of each.

Behavior	Total (63)	Bucks (18)	Does (36)	Juveniles (9)
Limb Events				
Smell Limb	40	10	24	6
Lick Limb	23	4	16	0
Rub Preorbital on Limb	2	2	0	0
Rub Forehead on Limb	1	1	0	0
Totals - Limb	**66**	**17**	**40**	**9**
Ground Events				
Smell Scrape	41	13	22	6
Paw Scrape	9	5	2	2
Urinate in Scrape	8	6	1	1
Auto-erotic Behavior	2	2	0	0
Totals - Ground	**60**	**26**	**25**	**9**
Totals	**126**	**43**	**65**	**18**
Average No. of Events/Visit	**2.0**	**2.4**	**1.8**	**2.0**

Michael E. Graham

Find an intensely used overhanging branch for rubbing and licking in July and/or August and you will have found a major dominance area. Sit tight. During the summer months you will be able to view firsthand the expression of dominance — the establishment of a dominance hierarchy via rubbing, sniffing, and licking the overhanging branch. Many deer hunters overlook this pre-season scouting tool.

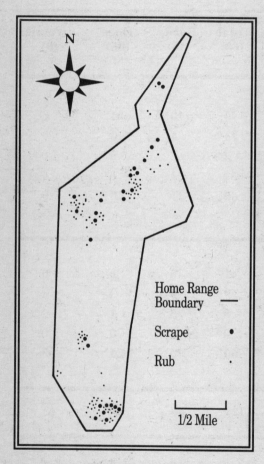

N

Home Range Boundary —

Scrape •

Rub ·

1/2 Mile

Reprinted from W.G. Moore and R. L. Marchinton. 1974. "Marking Behavior and its Social Function in White-tailed Deer." Page 452 in The Behavior of Ungulates and its Relation to Management. IUCNN, Morges. Switzerland.

HOME RANGE ACTIVITY MAP

FIGURE 1. The distribution of rubs and scrapes made by one Georgia white-tailed buck between Oct. 14 and Dec. 5. Note the clumped distribution or centers of rubs.

In populations with a high percentage of does and a young age-structure among bucks (typical of many heavily hunted populations), the communicative role of rubs and scrapes may be less signigicant. In open habitat, direct visual cues have relatively greater importance than signpost communication. The function of rubbing and scraping in white-tailed deer social behavior is not fully understood. This is highlighted by the recent discovery that does also make scrapes on occasion, and that this behavior among does is not limited to the breeding season.

— *Larry Marchinton and David Hirth, White-tailed Deer: Ecology and Management, 1984*

REPORTED BREEDING SEASONS OF WHITE-TAILED DEER

STATE	BREEDING DATES	PEAK OF THE RUT	SOURCE, YEAR
Alabama Northeast	Mid-Nov. to Late March Late Nov. to Early Jan.	Varies by Region	Lueth, 1967 Adams, 1960
Arizona		Early to Mid-Feb. Feb. to Mid-March	Nichol, 1938 O'Connor, 1945
Arkansas	Early Oct. to Mid.-Jan.	.	Donaldson & Holder, 1951
Colorado	Oct. to Mid-Dec.		Warren, 1942
Connecticut	Late Sept. to Early Jan.		McDowell, 1966
Florida	Varies by Region		Harlow & Jones, 1965
Georgia	Varies by Region Mid-Oct. to Mid-Dec.	Nov. 15-30	Downing & Whittington, 1964 Kile & Marchinton, 1977
Iowa		November	Haugen, 1958
Kansas	Nov. 8 to Dec. 20 Sept. 6 to March 8		Anderson, 1964 Queal, 1964
Kentucky	October to January		Gale & Meyers, 1954
Louisiana Avery Island Delta Refuge Evangeline GMA Jackson-Bienville GMA Red Dirt GMA Tensas Parish West Bay GMA	Sept. 26 to Dec. 9 Nov. 15 to Jan. 18 Oct. 18 to Oct. 31 Dec. 2 to Jan. 26 Oct. 22 to Jan. 25 Dec. 10 to Feb. 26 Sept. 27 to Dec. 9	October 1-31 December 14-29 October 18-31 December 1-15 November 1-15 January 1-15 October 16-31	Robertson & Dennet, 1966
Maine	Oct. 20 to Dec. 28	Mid-November	Banasiak, 1961
Massachusetts	Oct. 31 to Jan. 29	November 10-25	Shaw & McLaughlin, 1951
Michigan	Oct. 9 to Dec. 5	November 16-22	Haugen & Davenport, 1950
Minnesota	Mid-Sept. into Feb.		Erickson et al., 1961
Mississippi	Dec. 5 to Feb. 24	December 18-31	Noble, 1960
Missouri	Oct. to Early Dec.		Robb, 1951
Montana	Nov. 7 to Dec. 10		Allen, 1965
Nebraska	Oct. 21 to Mar. 1		Havel, 1963, 1964
New Hampshire		Mid-November	Silver, 1957
New Jersey	Late Oct. to Jan.		Mangold, 1958, 1963
New York	Sept. 22 to Feb. 22 Oct. 28 to Dec. 28	November 10-23 November 10-30	Cheatum & Morton, 1946 Jackson & Hesselton, 1973
North Carolina	Early Oct. to Early Nov.		Weber, 1966
Ohio	Oct. 22 to Dec. 9		Gilfillan, 1952
Oklahoma		November 2-26	Lindzey, ?
Pennsylvania	Late Oct. to Mid-Dec.	Mid-November	Lang et al., 1971
South Carolina		Nov. 17 to Dec. 13	Payne et al., 1966
Tennessee	Oct. 29 to Feb. 9		Lewis, 1972
Texas		December 15-24	Illige, 1951
Vermont	Early Nov. to Mid-Dec.		Day, 1964
Virginia	Oct. 1 to Late Nov.		Anon., 1948
West Virginia	Oct. 13 to Jan. 11		Chadwick, 1963
Wisconsin	Oct. 1 to Jan. 8	November 10-29	Dahlberg & Guettinger, 1956

AGGRESSIVE
Behavior of Deer

Aggressive Behavior:
Bucks and Does

Walk Toward
Aggressor walks toward another deer. Lowest intensity aggressive pattern exhibited by deer.

Ear Drop
Deer presses ears back alongside neck with the orifices directed away from the neck. Low intensity, frequently used aggressive pattern.

Head High Threat
Deer stands erect, holds head high, tilts nose upward, and lays back ears. A seldom used threat.

Head Low Threat
The aggressor lowers the head and extends the neck toward the aggressee with the ears laid back along the neck. Sometimes termed "Hard Look."

Lunge
The deer abruptly jerks its head forward toward the recipient and back without contact.

Head Raise
The head, oriented toward the recipient, is quickly snapped up and backward, then brought back to a resting posture while the ears are held out horizontally.

Front Leg Kick
Dominant deer strikes out at subordinate with a forefoot one or more times. Forefoot does not necessarily make contact with subordinate. Also termed "Strike."

Charge
Deer runs rapidly at another from a distance of three to fifteen feet, but stops before making contact. Deer usually performs another threat at the end of charge.

Chase
Subordinates that do not respond to lower level aggressive displays are sometimes chased by the dominant. Head low threat posture frequently used during the chase.

Rake
Used by dominant deer to displace subordinate from bed. Deer lifts a foreleg about eighteen inches above the ground and scrapes foot across back of the bedded deer.

Poke
One deer contacts another with its nose. Commonly used to direct group movement or supplant another deer.

Head Shake
The deer lowers its head and separates stiff forelegs to lower the anterior portion of the body while shaking the head from side to side with ears relaxed. A high intensity threat performed at a distance from the recipient.

Body Push

The aggressor approaches from the rear and pushes its front shoulder against the flank of the recipient while laying its throat on the back.

Sidle

Sidling deer stand with broadsides toward each other in head high threat posture and move slowly together. A buck usually turns head and body approxi-

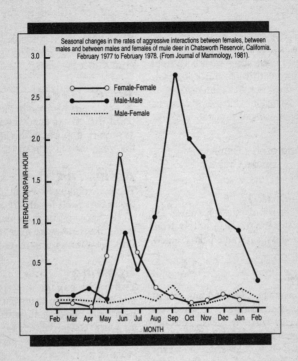

Seasonal changes in the rates of aggressive interactions between females, between males and between males and females of mule deer in Chatsworth Reservoir, California. February 1977 to February 1978. (From Journal of Mammology, 1981).

Aggressive Interactions For White-tailed Deer at Winter Cuttings

			TERMINATING AGGRESSIVE ACTION (percent frequency)				
INTERACTION	TOTAL NUMBER	Ear Drop/ Hard Look	Strike	Rush	Sidle	Snort	Flail
Buck over Buck	39	28	18	36	5	3	10
Buck over Doe	84	32	33	22	1	7	5
Buck over Fawn	59	41	41	12	0	6	0
Doe over Buck	20	15	35	40	0	10	0
Doe over Doe	98	21	40	26	1	7	5
Doe over Fawn	85	21	47	24	0	8	0
Fawn over Fawn	28	15	46	32	0	0	7
Fawn over Doe	4	0	75	0	0	0	25
Total	417						

From Journal of Wildlife Management (1972)

mately thirty degrees from his adversary. If neither deer retreats, sidling usually followed by flailing or a rush.

Rear Up

A deer rears up on its hind legs into a vertical position. Usually preceded by a head high threat.

Flail

Adversaries stand on their hind legs and strike out at each other with both front feet. Flailing continues until one deer submits to the other. Most intense form of aggressive behavior exhibited by does and bucks without polished antlers.

Aggressive Behavior:
Bucks Only

Nose Licking

The buck constantly licks his nose. He protrudes the tongue alternately from each side of the mouth and flicks it quickly upward.

Crouch

The buck lowers his head and tilts antlers toward opponent. Involves a hunched posture; hind legs partially flexed, shoulder and elbow joints also partially flexed with the combined effect of lowering the height of the buck. Erector pili effect frequently used. The walk is slow, stiff and stilted. The crouch is a dominance display performed only during the breeding season by high-ranking bucks.

Circling

The aggressive male slowly circles his opponent while assuming the crouch position.

Rut-Snort

Mule-deer: Snort occurs while buck circles in crouch position. Buck extends neck almost parallel with ground. The upper lip is raised upwards at each side beneath the nostrils. Nostrils held tightly closed.

Snort is five to ten second expulsion of air through nostrils, causing them to vibrate. Neck muscles bulge, back may arch slightly, hairs stand erect over entire body, and the tail is held outwards or upwards stiffly with the tip turned down. White-tailed deer; Rut-snort not as loud as that of mule deer and performed rarely.

Black-tailed deer: Rut-snort more loudly than mule deer and add series of loud grunts after the snort.

Antler Threat

A buck lowers his head so that the antlers point directly toward the rival. If the adversary duplicates the antler threat, the "rush" normally follows.

Antler Thrust

The buck rapidly lowers his head so that the antlers point toward the rump or side of the opponent then abruptly raises the head. Directed toward males and females. Does not always result in contact.

Sparring

Two bucks engage antlers and push and/or twist their heads back and forth. Relatively non-violent contests. Bucks of all antler sizes participate. Bucks frequently remain in close proximity after sparring.

Rush

This rare form of aggressive behavior involves hostile combat between two, usually large, males. Both bucks lunge at each other in a violent antler clash from a distance of about six feet. Buck may attempt to pull opponent backwards or swing him sideways. Erector pili effect frequently present. Usually of short duration, the rush terminates when one buck turns and bolts. No major differences observed in rushing behavior of white-tailed, mule or black-tailed deer.

❖ DEER AND THE WIND ❖

Generally speaking, deer activity decreases as wind speed increases. Calm and light winds produce more deer sightings while moderate and gusty winds reduce them. The dividing line seems to be somewhere around 15 mph.

However, some researchers and hunters have documented an increase in buck activity during strong winds and less buck activity during calm winds.

Deer tend to group up and become excitable in high winds. During cold months, high winds cause deer to seek shelter on the lee slopes of hills and in dense coniferous woodlands. Conifer stands reduce wind speeds by up to 50 to 75 percent.

Research proves that even though deer will move in all directions in relation to the wind, they'll move directly into the wind whenever possible. Deer trails closely match the prevailing wind direction and traditional wind changes. Wind fits two basic patterns:

Pattern A — Occurs during stable, high-pressure weather systems with clear or partly cloudy skies. This pattern brings little or no wind at sunrise and sunset, and maximum wind speeds in mid to late afternoon.

Pattern B — Occurs during changing weather conditions. This pattern brings constant wind speeds throughout the day with frequent gusts reflecting atmospheric turbulence.

Thermal winds — Thermal currents move uphill as the air temperature increases in the morning. Thermals move downhill as air cools toward evening.

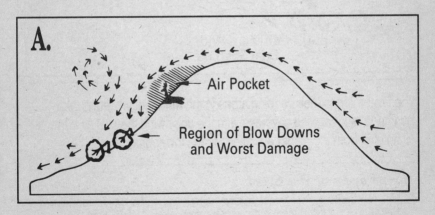

A.

— Air Pocket

Region of Blow Downs and Worst Damage

Gale winds force deer to pick sheltered bedding sites in the air pockets on the lee side of slopes and ridges approximately one-third of the way down from the crest.

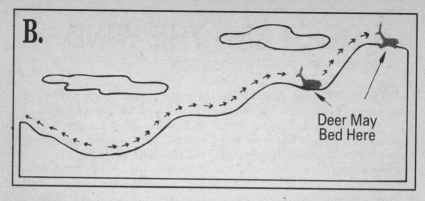

B.

Deer May
Bed Here

Whitetails prefer to bed on slightly higher ground when the terrain permits.Consequently, when they move down-slope toward their feeding area in the afternoon, they experience ideal wind coverage on their trails with the thermal air currents still moving upslope.

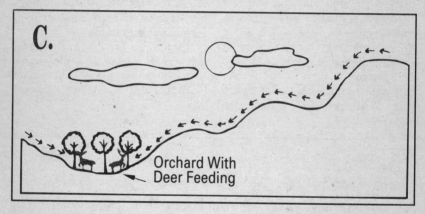

C.

Orchard With
Deer Feeding

When returning to their bedding areas in the morning, whitetails take advantage of ideal wind coverage with the downwind thermal air currents still holding from the higher elevations to the lower ground.

Tips for Judging Wind Speeds:

* **Calm, less than 1 mph** — Smoke rises vertically, leaves on tree remain motionless.
* **1 to 3 mph** — Smoke drifts but wind vanes stay motionless.
* **7 to 10 mph** — Flags extend and leaves are in constant motion.
* **11 to 16 mph** — Small branches move, dust blows and loose paper flies.
* **17 to 21 mph** — Noticeable motion in tall tree tops, and small trees with leaves sway.
* **22 to 27 mph** — Large branches in motion, whistling in wires.
* **28 to 47 mph** — Tar paper pulls off your shack's roof, and whole trees are in motion.

A GOOD DEER WATCHER

By Richard Prior

Deer study, no matter what your particular field may be, becomes more and more fascinating as experience builds up. If by degrees you find that you can think like the deer, anticipating their movements and trying to understand their way of life, it will become a challenging battle of wits — human brains matched against their finer senses. Never forget the consideration which these lovely animals are due. To us it is just a hobby — to them a life or death struggle for survival in a very hostile world. Much of their ability to survive stems from their ability to watch us without our being aware, and to act accordingly. A good deer watcher should always try to do the same.

THE WIND CHILL FACTOR

ACTUAL THERMOMETER READING (F°)

| 50 | 40 | 30 | 20 | 10 | 0 | -10 | -20 | -30 | -40 |

EQUIVALENT TEMPERATURE (F°)

	50	40	30	20	10	0	-10	-20	-30	-40
Calm	50	40	30	20	10	0	-10	-20	-30	-40
5	48	37	27	16	6	-5	-15	-26	-36	-47
10	40	28	16	4	-9	-21	-33	-46	-58	-70
15	36	22	9	-5	-18	-36	-45	-58	-72	-85
20	32	18	4	-10	-25	-39	-53	-67	-82	-96
25	30	16	0	-15	-29	-44	-59	-74	-88	-104
30	28	13	-2	-18	-33	-44	-63	-79	-94	-109
35	27	11	-4	-20	-35	-49	-67	-82	-98	-113
40	26	10	-6	-21	-37	-53	-69	-85	-100	-116

Over 40 MPH (little added effect)	LITTLE DANGER (for properly clothed person)	INCREASING DANGER	GREAT DANGER
		(Danger from freezing of exposed flesh)	

WIND - AVERAGE SPEED (MPH)

DATA THROUGH 1990	SEP	OCT	NOV	DEC	JAN
BIRMINGHAM AP, AL	6.4	6.2	7.3	7.8	8.2
HUNTSVILLE, AL	6.9	7.5	8.6	9.5	9.4
MOBILE, AL	7.9	8.2	9.3	10.1	10.4
MONTGOMERY, AL	5.9	5.7	6.5	7.1	7.7
FORT SMITH, AR	6.6	6.8	7.8	8.1	8.2
LITTLE ROCK, AR	6.7	6.8	8.0	8.2	8.6
COLORADO SPRINGS, CO	9.5	9.6	9.5	9.5	9.5
DENVER, CO	7.9	7.9	8.3	8.5	8.7
GRAND JUNCTION, CO	8.9	7.9	5.9		5.6
PUEBLO, CO	8.0	7.5	7.6	7.9	8.0
BRIDGEPORT, CT	11.2	11.9	12.7	13.0	13.2
HARTFORD, CT	7.3	7.8	8.5	8.7	9.0
WILMINGTON, DE	7.8	8.2	9.2	9.4	9.8
APALACHICOLA, FL	7.8	8.0	8.0	8.0	8.3
DAYTONA BEACH, FL	8.3	9.2	8.6	8.5	8.9
FORT MYERS, FL	7.6	8.5	8.2	8.0	8.4
GAINESVILLE, FL	5.9	6.6	6.2	5.9	6.9
JACKSONVILLE, FL	7.6	8.1	7.7	7.8	8.2
KEY WEST, FL	9.9	11.3	12.1	12.0	12.0
MIAMI, FL	8.3	9.4	9.7	9.3	9.5
ORLANDO, FL	7.7	8.6	8.6	8.6	8.9
PENSACOLA, FL	7.6	7.9	8.4	9.0	9.0
TALLAHASSEE, FL	5.9	6.3	6.1	6.4	6.8
TAMPA, FL	7.8	8.5	8.4	8.5.	8.6
VERO BEACH, FL	7.6	8.9	8.9	8.1	8.7
WEST PALM BEACH, FL	8.7	10.2	10.3	10.1	10.0
ATHENS, GA	6.4	6.8	7.4	8.0	8.5
ATLANTA, GA	8.1	8.4	9.1	9.8	10.5
AUGUSTA, GA	5.5	5.7	6.1	6.6	7.1
COLUMBUS, GA	6.5	6.5	6.5	6.9	7.3
SAVANNAH, GA	7.2	7.4	7.5	7.9	8.5
BOISE, ID	8.2	8.3	8.4	8.1	8.0
POCATELLO, ID	9.1	9.3	10.4	9.9	10.8
CAIRO, IL	7.0	7.3	9.1	9.3	9.8
CHICAGO, IL	8.8	9.9	11.0	11.0	11.6
MOLINE, IL	8.2	9.3	10.9	10.7	11.0
PEORIA, IL	8.4	9.4	11.0	10.9	11.2
ROCKFORD, IL	8.5	9.5	10.6	10.5	10.6
SPRINGFIELD, IL	9.0	10.4	12.5	12.5	12.7
EVANSVILLE, IN	6.4	6.9	8.7	9.0	9.3

WIND - AVERAGE SPEED (MPH)

DATA THROUGH 1990	SEP	OCT	NOV	DEC	JAN
FORT WAYNE, IN	8.3	9.2	10.9	11.2	11.6
INDIANAPOLIS, IN	7.9	8.8	10.4	10.5	10.9
SOUTH BEND, IN	8.6	9.6	11.1	11.4	11.9
DES MOINES, IA	9.5	10.4	11.5	11.4	11.7
SIOUX CITY, IA	9.8	10.4	11.3	11.0	11.4
WATERLOO, IA	9.1	10.2	11.2	11.2	11.6
CONCORDIA, KS	11.6	11.9	11.9	12.1	12.3
DODGE CITY, KS	13.7	13.5	13.8	13.5	13.6
GOODLAND, KS	12.1	11.8	12.0	12.0	12.4
TOPEKA, KS	8.8	9.2	10.0	9.9	10.0
WICHITA, KS	11.6	12.0	12.2	12.1	12.2
JACKSON, KY	6.1	6.7	8.2	8.4	8.1
LEXINGTON, KY	7.6	8.3	10.1	10.7	10.9
LOUISVILLE, KY	6.8	7.2	8.9	9.3	9.7
PADUCAH, KY	6.2	6.9	8.9	8.9	9.3
BATON ROUGE, LA	6.7	6.7	7.8	8.3	8.9
LAKE CHARLES, LA	7.2	7.7	9.1	9.5	10.0
NEW ORLEANS, LA	7.3	7.5	8.7	9.1	9.4
SHREVEPORT, LA	7.2	7.4	8.6	9.0	9.3
CARIBOU, ME	10.4	10.9	11.1	11.5	12.4
PORTLAND, ME	7.8	8.4	8.8	9.0	9.2
BALTIMORE, MD	8.0	8.7	9.3	9.3	9.7
BLUE HILL, MA	13.5	15.2	16.4	16.8	17.4
BOSTON, MA	11.3	12.0	13.0	13.6	13.9
WORCESTER, MA	8.6	9.4	10.2	10.9	11.9
ALPENA, MI	7.1	7.8	8.5	8.6	8.9
DETROIT, MI	8.8	9.8	11.2	11.5	12.0
FLINT, MI	8.8	9.8	11.3	11.4	11.8
GRAND RAPIDS, MI	8.3	9.4	10.4	10.8	11.4
HOUGHTON LAKE, MI	8.0	9.1	9.9	9.6	10.1
LANSING, MI	8.3	9.3	10.8	11.3	11.9
MUSKEGON, MI	9.4	10.8	11.9	12.1	12.6
SAULT STE. MARIE, MI	8.6	9.2	9.9	9.7	9.8
DULUTH, MN	10.4	11.1	11.7	11.3	11.6
INT. FALLS, MN	8.7	9.3	9.5	8.8	8.9
MINN.-ST. PAUL, MN	9.9	10.5	10.9	10.4	10.5
ROCHESTER, MN	11.8	13.1	13.7	13.8	14.6
SAINT CLOUD, MN	7.1	7.8	8.3	7.7	8.2
JACKSON, MS	6.4	6.5	7.6	8.5	8.6

WIND - AVERAGE SPEED (MPH)

DATA THROUGH 1990	SEP	OCT	NOV	DEC	JAN
MERIDIAN, MS	5.3	5.2	6.2	6.9	7.1
TUPELO, MS	6.5	6.2	7.7	7.9	7.5
COLUMBIA, MO	8.5	9.5	10.6	10.8	11.0
KANSAS CITY, MO	9.5	10.5	11.4	11.3	11.5
ST. LOUIS, MO	8.1	8.8	10.1	10.4	10.6
SPRINGFIELD, MO	9.3	10.1	11.3	11.6	11.7
BILLINGS, MT	10.2	11.0	12.1	13.1	13.1
GLASGOW, MT	11.0	10.6	9.5	9.8	10.1
GREAT FALLS, MT	11.3	13.2	14.6	15.6	15.3
HELENA, MT	7.4	7.1	7.1	6.8	6.8
KALISPELL, MT	6.4	5.3	5.7	5.6	6.0
MISSOULA, MT	6.0	5.0	5.1	4.8	5.2
GRAND ISLAND, NE	11.0	11.3	11.8	11.7	11.8
LINCOLN, NE	9.7	9.9	10.3	10.2	10.1
NORFOLK, NE	10.8	11.1	11.9	12.2	12.5
NORTH PLATTE, NE	9.7	9.6	9.6	9.2	9.3
OMAHA EPPLEY AP, NE	9.5	9.8	10.9	10.7	10.9
OMAHA (NORTH), NE	8.4	8.9	9.9	9.9	10.4
SCOTTSBLUFF, NE	9.4	9.6	10.2	10.5	10.8
VALENTINE, NE	9.6	9.3	9.6	9.2	9.4
CONCORD, NH	5.5	6.0	6.7	7.0	7.2
MT. WASHINGTON, NH	28.9	33.7	39.6	44.8	46.2
ATLANTIC CITY AP, NJ	8.4	9.0	10.5	10.6	11.0
NEWARK, NJ	9.0	9.4	10.2	10.8	11.2
ALBANY, NY	7.4	8.0	9.1	9.3	9.8
BINGHAMTON, NY	8.8	9.8	11.0	11.3	11.6
BUFFALO, NY	10.3	11.1	12.8	13.4	14.3
ISLIP, NY	7.5	8.3	9.9	9.4	9.7
NEW YORK (C. PARK), NY	8.1	8.9	9.9	10.4	10.7
NEW YORK (JFK AP), NY	10.6	11.2	12.5	12.9	13.4
ROCHESTER, NY	8.0	8.7	10.2	10.8	11.7
SYRACUSE, NY	8.2	8.8	10.2	10.4	10.8
ASHEVILLE, NC	5.6	6.8	8.1	8.9	9.7
CAPE HATTERAS, NC	10.5	11.1	11.0	11.5	12.1
CHARLOTTE, NC	6.7	6.9	7.2	7.4	7.9
GREENSBORO, NC	6.6	7.0	7.5	7.6	8.1
RALEIGH, NC	6.8	7.1	7.6	8.0	8.5
WILMINGTON, NC	7.9	8.1	8.1	8.5	9.1
BISMARCK, ND	9.9	10.0	9.9	9.5	10.0
FARGO, ND	11.9	12.6	12.8	12.3	12.7
WILLISTON, ND	10.0	10.1	9.1	9.7	9.9

WIND - AVERAGE SPEED (MPH)

DATA THROUGH 1990	SEP	OCT	NOV	DEC	JAN
AKRON, OH	8.0	9.1	10.9	11.4	11.6
CLEVELAND, OH	9.0	10.0	11.8	12.2	12.3
COLUMBUS, OH	6.5	7.5	9.2	9.6	10.1
DAYTON, OH	8.1	9.0	11.0	11.2	11.5
MANSFIELD, OH	9.0	10.6	11.9	12.7	13.4
TOLEDO, OH	7.6	8.7	10.2	10.5	11.0
YOUNGSTOWN, OH	8.1	9.3	11.0	11.4	11.7
OKLAHOMA CITY, OK	11.1	11.9	12.4	12.5	12.8
TULSA, OK	9.2	9.7	10.4	10.3	10.5
ALLENTOWN, PA	7.2	8.2	9.7	10.0	10.5
ERIE, PA	10.0	11.3	13.1	13.5	13.4
HARRISBURG, PA	6.1	6.6	7.8	8.0	8.3
PHILADELPHIA, PA	8.2	8.8	9.6	10.0	10.3
PITTSBURGH, PA	7.4	8.4	9.8	10.4	10.7
AVOCA, PA	7.3	7.9	8.7	8.8	8.9
WILLIAMSPORT, PA	6.2	6.8	8.2	8.6	9.0
BLOCK IS., RI	8.0	9.3	12.6	11.8	12.7
PROVIDENCE, RI	9.4	9.7	10.6	10.9	11.2
CHARLESTON AP, SC	7.8	8.1	8.1	8.5	9.1
COLUMBIA, SC	6.1	6.1	6.4	6.7	7.2
GREENVILLE, SC	6.1	6.5	6.8	7.3	7.4
ABERDEEN, SD	10.6	11.1	10.9	10.7	11.3
HURON, SD	11.2	11.3	11.7	11.1	11.4
RAPID CITY, SD	11.0	11.2	10.8	10.6	10.9
SIOUX FALLS, SD	10.2	10.7	11.5	10.8	11.1
BRISTOL, TN	4.3	4.7	5.7	5.9	6.5
CHATTANOOGA, TN	4.9	4.9	6.0	6.5	7.0
KNOXVILLE, TN	5.8	5.8	6.9	7.3	7.9
MEMPHIS, TN	7.5	7.7	9.1	9.8	10.1
NASHVILLE, TN	6.4	6.8	8.4	9.0	9.2
OAK RIDGE, TN	3.8	3.6	4.1	4.4	4.8
ABILENE, TX	10.4	11.0	11.6	11.8	11.9
AMARILLO, TX	12.8	12.9	13.1	12.9	13.0
AUSTIN, TX	7.9	8.1	9.0	9.2	9.7
BROWNSVILLE, TX	9.4	9.5	10.7	10.8	11.3
CORPUS CHRISTI, TX	10.4	10.3	11.6	11.5	12.1
DALLAS-FORT WORTH, TX	9.4	9.8	10.8	11.0	11.2
DEL RIO, TX	9.2	9.1	8.5	8.4	8.8
EL PASO, TX	7.6	7.5	8.0	7.9	8.4
GALVESTON, TX	10.1	10.3	11.2	11.3	11.6
HOUSTON, TX	6.9	7.0	7.9	8.0	8.3
LUBBOCK, TX	10.5	11.2	11.6	11.9	12.1

WIND - AVERAGE SPEED (MPH)

DATA THROUGH 1990	SEP	OCT	NOV	DEC	JAN
MIDLAND-ODESSA, TX	10.1	10.1	10.3	10.1	10.3
PORT ARTHUR, TX	8.4	8.8	10.1	10.5	10.9
SAN ANGELO, TX	9.0	9.3	10.0	10.0	10.3
SAN ANTONIO, TX	8.5	8.4	8.8	8.5	9.0
VICTORIA, TX	8.7	8.9	9.8	10.2	10.5
WACO, TX	9.7	10.1	10.9	11.1	11.6
WICHITA FALLS, TX	10.5	10.8	11.4	11.3	11.4
BURLINGTON, VT	8.2	8.7	9.7	9.9	9.7
LYNCHBURG, VA	6.9	7.3	7.9	7.9	8.6
NORFOLK, VA	9.6	10.4	10.7	11.2	11.5
RICHMOND, VA	6.7	7.0	7.5	7.7	8.1
ROANOKE, VA	6.1	6.9	8.3	8.8	9.5
OLYMPIA, WA	5.7	5.9	6.9	7.3	7.1
QUILLAYUTE, WA	5.0	5.5	6.5	6.6	6.7
SEATTLE (SEA-TAC AP), WA	8.1	8.5	9.3	9.6	9.8
SPOKANE, WA	8.3	8.2	8.7	8.6	8.8
WALLA WALLA, WA	4.7	4.5	4.8	5.2	5.1
YAKIMA, WA	7.4	6.6	5.9	5.2	5.7
BECKLEY, WV	7.2	8.5	9.8	10.5	10.6
CHARLESTON, WV	4.7	5.2	6.7	7.1	7.5
ELKINS, WV	4.4	5.0	6.9	6.9	7.3
HUNTINGTON, WV	5.2	5.9	7.1	7.4	7.6
GREEN BAY, WI	9.0	9.9	11.0	10.7	11.0
LA CROSSE, WI	8.1	9.2	9.6	8.8	8.6
MADISON, WI	8.7	9.6	10.8	10.3	10.6
MILWAUKEE, WI	10.5	11.4	12.5	12.3	12.7
CASPER, WY	11.0	12.1	14.4	16.0	16.6
CHEYENNE, WY	11.2	12.3	13.4	14.7	15.4
LANDER, WY	7.0	6.1	5.6	5.7	6.0
SHERIDAN, WY	7.5	7.5	7.7	7.6	7.7

CELSIUS CONVERSION CHART

°C (Celsius)	°F (Fahrenheit)	K(Kelvin)
-40	-40	233
-35	-31	238
-30	-22	243
-25	-13	248
-20	- 4	253
-15	+ 5	258
-10	14	263
- 5	23	268
0	32	273
5	41	278
10	50	283
15	59	288
20	68	293
25	77	298
30	86	303
35	95	308
40	104	313
45	113	318
50	122	323

NORMAL DAILY MEAN TEMPERATURE : DEGREES F

NORMALS 1951-80	SEP	OCT	NOV	DEC	JAN
BIRMINGHAM C.O., AL	74.1	62.1	51.5	45.0	42.4
BIRMINGHAM AP, AL	74.1	62.6	52.1	45.6	42.9
HUNTSVILLE, AL	72.8	61.3	50.5	43.3	40.2
MOBILE, AL	78.2	68.5	58.6	53.1	50.8
MONTGOMERY, AL	76.7	65.3	55.0	48.9	46.7
FORT SMITH, AR	73.9	62.5	49.8	41.2	37.5
LITTLE ROCK, AR	74.3	63.1	51.2	43.2	39.9
NORTH LITTLE ROCK, AR	74.1	63.4	51.5	43.1	39.5
ALAMOSA, CO	54.9	43.8	29.2	18.0	16.0
COLORADO SPRINGS, CO	61.1	50.8	37.7	31.4	28.8
DENVER, CO	62.6	51.9	38.7	32.6	29.5
GRAND JUNCTION, CO	67.1	54.9	39.6	28.3	25.5
PUEBLO, CO	66.0	54.1	40.2	32.8	29.8
BRIDGEPORT, CT	66.2	56.0	45.5	34.2	29.5
HARTFORD, CT	63.3	52.4	41.6	29.1	25.2
WILMINGTON, DE	67.9	56.3	45.6	35.5	31.2
APALACHICOLA, FL	78.9	70.2	61.0	55.0	52.8
DAYTONA BEACH, FL	79.5	73.2	65.2	59.5	57.9
FORT MYERS, FL	81.7	76.5	69.8	64.7	63.4
GAINESVILLE, FL	78.5	70.3	61.9	56.0	54.6
JACKSONVILLE, FL	78.2	69.5	60.8	54.8	53.2
KEY WEST, FL	82.6	80.1	75.5	71.0	68.7
MIAMI, FL	81.8	77.9	72.8	68.5	67.1
ORLANDO, FL	81.1	74.9	67.5	62.0	60.5
PENSACOLA, FL	78.7	69.4	59.7	53.8	51.7
TALLAHASSEE, FL	78.3	68.4	58.8	53.0	51.6
TAMPA, FL	80.9	74.5	66.7	61.3	59.8
VERO BEACH, FL	80.2	75.2	68.9	63.4	61.9
WEST PALM BEACH, FL	81.4	77.3	71.6	67.0	65.2
ATHENS, GA	72.9	62.1	52.1	44.7	42.4
ATLANTA, GA	73.0	62.2	52.0	44.5	41.9
AUGUSTA, GA	74.6	63.5	53.9	46.9	45.0
COLUMBUS, GA	76.0	65.1	54.9	48.4	46.2
MACON, GA	76.0	65.2	55.3	48.7	46.6
SAVANNAH, GA	76.6	66.9	57.5	51.0	49.2
BOISE, ID	63.2	51.9	39.7	32.0	29.9
LEWISTON, ID	63.6	51.8	40.1	34.9	32.1
POCATELLO, ID	59.2	48.1	35.2	26.6	23.8
CAIRO, IL	72.3	61.1	48.5	39.2	34.6
CHICAGO, IL	64.7	53.5	39.8	27.7	21.4

NORMAL DAILY MEAN TEMPERATURE : DEGREES F

NORMALS 1951-80	SEP	OCT	NOV	DEC	JAN
MOLINE, IL	64.7	53.5	39.0	26.4	19.5
PEORIA, IL	65.6	53.9	39.8	27.8	21.5
ROCKFORD, IL	63.3	52.1	37.5	24.8	18.3
SPRINGFIELD, IL	67.6	55.9	42.1	30.7	24.6
EVANSVILLE, IN	69.4	57.3	45.1	35.6	30.6
FORT WAYNE, IN	64.7	53.0	40.1	29.0	23.3
INDIANAPOLIS, IN	66.6	54.8	41.8	31.5	26.0
SOUTH BEND, IN	64.2	53.2	40.3	29.1	23.2
DES MOINES, IA	65.1	54.2	38.6	25.7	18.6
DUBUQUE, IA	61.6	50.9	35.8	22.7	15.6
SIOUX CITY, IA	64.5	52.5	36.4	23.3	16.2
WATERLOO, IA	61.6	50.6	35.2	21.6	14.0
CONCORDIA, KS	67.7	56.7	41.1	30.8	24.9
DODGE CITY, KS	69.1	57.8	42.5	33.7	29.5
GOODLAND, KS	64.3	52.5	38.1	30.3	27.2
TOPEKA, KS	68.5	57.0	42.7	31.8	26.1
WICHITA, KS	70.6	59.1	44.3	34.4	29.6
JACKSON, KY	65.7	54.7	42.5	33.8	31.4
LEXINGTON, KY	68.7	56.8	44.9	36.1	31.5
LOUISVILLE, KY	69.9	57.7	46.1	37.2	32.5
PADUCAH, KY	70.4	58.8	46.7	37.8	33.3
BATON ROUGE, LA	77.9	68.2	58.7	53.1	50.8
LAKE CHARLES, LA	78.2	69.3	59.7	53.9	51.5
NEW ORLEANS, LA	78.5	69.2	60.0	54.6	52.4
SHREVEPORT, LA	77.1	66.7	55.7	48.7	46.0
CARIBOU, ME	53.6	43.1	31.1	15.7	10.6
PORTLAND, ME	58.6	48.4	38.4	25.8	21.5
BALTIMORE, MD	68.9	56.9	46.3	36.5	32.7
BLUE HILL, MA	62.0	52.2	41.8	30.0	25.9
BOSTON, MA	64.6	54.8	45.2	33.7	29.6
WORCESTER, MA	60.3	50.3	39.5	27.4	23.3
ALPENA, MI	56.6	47.1	35.1	23.5	17.4
DETROIT, MI	63.3	51.9	39.5	28.5	23.4
FLINT, MI	61.2	50.6	38.8	27.2	21.3
GRAND RAPIDS, MI	62.1	50.9	38.5	27.3	22.0
HOUGHTON LAKE, MI	57.3	47.1	34.9	22.9	17.0
LANSING, MI	61.7	50.7	38.5	27.0	21.6
MARQUETTE, MI	54.0	44.3	30.1	17.9	12.1
MUSKEGON, MI	61.4	51.0	39.2	28.3	23.1

NORMAL DAILY MEAN TEMPERATURE : DEGREES F

NORMALS 1951-80	SEP	OCT	NOV	DEC	JAN
SAULT STE. MARIE, MI	54.8	45.3	32.8	19.7	13.3
DULUTH, MN	54.0	44.2	28.2	13.8	6.3
INT. FALLS, MN	52.8	42.8	24.9	8.2	0.1
MINN.- ST. PAUL, MN	60.6	49.6	33.2	19.2	11.2
ROCHESTER, MN	59.2	48.7	32.6	18.5	10.8
SAINT CLOUD, MN	57.4	46.8	29.8	15.2	7.0
JACKSON, MS	76.4	65.0	54.9	48.6	45.7
MERIDIAN, MS	75.7	63.9	54.1	48.0	45.5
TUPELO, MS	74.1	62.3	51.1	44.1	41.2
COLUMBIA, MO	68.4	57.1	43.5	32.9	27.5
KANSAS CITY, MO	68.4	57.5	43.1	31.9	25.9
ST. LOUIS, MO	69.7	57.9	44.6	34.2	28.8
SPRINGFIELD, MO	69.5	58.2	45.1	36.2	31.5
BILLINGS, MT	59.4	49.3	35.0	27.1	20.9
GLASGOW, MT	57.4	46.2	29.2	16.9	8.2
GREAT FALLS, MT	57.4	47.9	34.0	25.7	18.7
HELENA, MT	55.6	45.1	31.4	23.5	18.1
KALISPELL, MT	53.9	42.5	30.9	24.2	19.3
MISSOULA, MT	55.7	44.1	31.8	24.9	21.3
GRAND ISLAND, NE	64.3	53.1	37.6	26.7	20.6
LINCOLN, NE	65.5	54.0	38.5	26.6	19.7
NORFOLK, NE	63.3	51.8	36.0	23.9	17.4
NORTH PLATTE, NE	61.9	50.2	35.0	25.9	21.3
OMAHA (EPPLEY AP), NE	65.8	54.5	39.5	27.2	20.2
OMAHA (NORTH), NE	64.4	53.6	38.0	25.7	18.7
SCOTTSBLUFF, NE	61.6	50.2	35.9	27.8	24.2
VALENTINE, NE	61.5	49.5	34.0	24.0	18.7
CONCORD, NH	59.1	48.2	37.3	24.5	19.9
MT. WASHINGTON, NH	40.6	30.5	20.3	9.1	5.1
ATLANTIC CITY AP, NJ	66.6	55.5	45.6	35.8	31.8
NEWARK, NJ	68.2	57.2	46.5	35.5	31.3
ALBANY, NY	61.2	50.5	39.3	26.5	21.1
BINGHAMTON, NY	59.8	49.1	37.9	26.2	21.2
BUFFALO, NY	62.1	51.5	40.3	28.8	23.5
NEW YORK (C. PARK), NY	68.3	57.7	47.2	36.2	31.8
NEW YORK (JFK AP), NY	67.2	56.7	46.4	35.7	31.3
ROCHESTER, NY	62.2	51.7	40.6	29.0	23.6
SYRACUSE, NY	62.1	51.3	40.6	28.3	22.8
ASHEVILLE, NC	66.9	56.0	46.4	39.3	36.8

NORMAL DAILY MEAN TEMPERATURE : DEGREES F

NORMALS 1951-80	SEP	OCT	NOV	DEC	JAN
CAPE HATTERAS, NC	74.2	64.9	56.0	48.7	45.1
CHARLOTTE, NC	72.0	60.7	50.7	42.6	40.5
GREENSBORO, NC	69.9	58.4	48.5	40.2	37.5
RALEIGH, NC	71.0	59.7	50.0	42.0	39.6
WILMINGTON, NC	74.8	64.5	55.4	48.2	45.6
BISMARCK, ND	57.3	46.1	28.6	15.4	6.7
FARGO, ND	57.8	46.3	28.2	12.7	4.3
WILLISTON, ND	56.6	45.1	27.6	14.9	6.6
AKRON, OH	63.8	52.5	41.0	30.3	25.1
CLEVELAND, OH	64.1	53.2	41.8	31.1	25.5
COLUMBUS, OH	65.8	53.9	42.1	32.1	27.1
DAYTON, OH	66.4	54.5	42.1	31.8	26.6
MANSFIELD, OH	64.1	52.9	40.8	29.9	24.8
TOLEDO, OH	63.2	51.7	39.3	28.1	23.1
YOUNGSTOWN, OH	62.4	51.5	40.2	29.4	24.2
OKLAHOMA CITY, OK	73.3	62.3	48.8	39.9	35.9
TULSA, OK	73.8	62.6	49.2	39.8	35.2
ALLENTOWN, PA	64.8	53.4	42.5	31.5	27.2
ERIE, PA	62.1	51.7	40.7	30.0	24.5
HARRISBURG, PA	66.9	55.0	43.9	33.4	29.4
PHILADELPHIA, PA	68.2	56.5	45.8	35.5	31.2
PITTSBURGH, PA	64.1	52.5	41.6	31.4	26.7
AVOCA, PA	62.8	51.7	40.9	29.7	25.2
WILLIAMSPORT, PA	63.9	52.3	41.4	30.7	26.2
BLOCK IS., RI	63.8	54.8	45.9	35.8	31.1
PROVIDENCE, RI	63.5	53.2	43.4	32.3	28.2
CHARLESTON, SC	75.7	65.8	56.7	50.0	47.9
COLUMBIA, SC	74.8	63.4	53.9	46.7	44.7
GREENVILLE, SC	71.7	60.7	50.9	43.4	41.1
ABERDEEN, SD	59.5	47.7	30.2	16.5	8.3
HURON, SD	60.8	48.9	32.2	19.0	11.2
RAPID CITY, SD	60.9	49.7	34.9	26.1	20.8
SIOUX FALLS, SD	61.0	49.4	33.0	19.7	12.4
BRISTOL, TN	68.8	57.1	46.2	38.2	35.0
CHATTANOOGA, TN	72.3	60.0	48.9	41.5	38.7
KNOXVILLE, TN	71.5	59.5	48.8	41.1	38.2
MEMPHIS, TN	74.2	62.9	51.3	43.3	39.6
NASHVILLE, TN	72.3	60.2	48.6	40.9	37.1
OAK RIDGE, TN	70.2	58.3	47.2	39.6	36.7
ABILENE, TX	76.0	65.9	53.4	46.4	43.3

NORMAL DAILY MEAN TEMPERATURE : DEGREES F

NORMALS 1951-80	SEP	OCT	NOV	DEC	JAN
AMARILLO, TX	69.7	59.2	45.4	38.3	35.4
AUSTIN, TX	79.2	69.8	58.7	52.1	49.1
BROWNSVILLE, TX	81.4	75.3	67.7	62.3	60.3
CORPUS CHRISTI, TX	81.5	74.0	65.0	59.1	56.3
DALLAS-FORT WORTH, TX	78.6	67.9	55.6	47.8	44.0
DEL RIO, TX	80.3	70.8	59.4	52.5	50.8
EL PASO, TX	74.1	63.6	51.4	44.4	44.2
GALVESTON, TX	80.0	72.7	63.0	56.8	53.6
HOUSTON, TX	78.4	69.7	60.1	54.0	51.4
LUBBOCK, TX	71.2	61.0	48.5	41.5	38.8
MIDLAND-ODESSA, TX	74.2	64.4	52.3	46.0	43.7
PORT ARTHUR, TX	79.2	70.2	60.6	54.7	51.9
SAN ANGELO, TX	76.5	66.6	54.6	48.0	45.5
SAN ANTONIO, TX	79.4	70.2	59.5	53.0	50.4
VICTORIA, TX	80.1	71.9	62.3	56.1	53.4
WACO, TX	79.2	68.8	57.0	49.5	46.2
WICHITA FALLS, TX	76.2	65.1	52.0	43.9	40.3
BURLINGTON, VT	58.8	47.9	36.6	22.6	16.6
LYNCHBURG, VA	68.4	57.1	47.0	38.3	35.1
NORFOLK, VA	72.2	61.3	51.9	43.5	39.9
RICHMOND, VA	70.2	58.6	48.9	39.9	36.6
ROANOKE, VA	68.2	56.8	46.9	38.3	35.5
WALLOPS ISLAND, VA	70.1	59.1	49.0	39.8	35.8
OLYMPIA, WA	58.1	50.1	42.6	39.0	37.2
QUILLAYUTE, WA	56.8	50.4	43.8	40.8	39.0
SEATTLE, WA	61.1	53.8	46.2	42.6	40.6
SEATTLE (SEA-TAC AP), WA	60.0	52.5	44.8	41.0	39.1
SPOKANE, WA	59.4	47.6	34.9	29.0	25.7
STAMPEDE PASS, WA	51.1	42.1	30.9	26.5	24.1
WALLA WALLA, WA	65.5	54.3	42.5	37.2	34.3
YAKIMA, WA	60.9	49.9	38.2	31.5	28.2
BECKLEY, WV	63.1	52.3	42.2	33.7	30.1
CHARLESTON, WV	67.6	55.9	45.3	36.9	32.9
ELKINS, WV	62.1	50.5	40.6	32.2	28.3
HUNTINGTON, WV	68.0	56.3	45.6	36.9	32.8
GREEN BAY, WI	58.9	48.4	34.2	20.8	14.0
LA CROSSE, WI	61.6	50.9	35.3	21.5	14.0
MADISON, WI	60.1	49.5	35.1	22.4	15.6
MILWAUKEE, WI	61.9	50.9	37.3	25.1	18.7
CASPER, WY	58.4	47.2	32.9	25.7	22.2
CHEYENNE, WY	57.9	47.5	34.8	29.3	26.1
LANDER, WY	58.36	46.8	30.8	23.2	19.6
SHERIDAN, WY	57.6	47.0	32.5	24.6	19.5

NORMAL PRECIPITATION : INCHES

NORMALS 1951-80	SEP	OCT	NOV	DEC	JAN
BIRMINGHAM C.O., AL	4.55	2.77	3.51	4.83	4.97
BIRMINGHAM AP, AL	4.34	2.64	3.64	4.95	5.23
HUNTSVILLE, AL	3.99	2.90	4.24	5.43	5.17
MOBILE, AL	6.56	2.62	3.67	5.44	4.59
MONTGOMERY, AL	4.72	2.27	2.98	4.78	4.20
FORT SMITH, AR	3.22	3.24	3.50	2.85	1.86
LITTLE ROCK, AR	4.26	2.84	4.37	4.23	3.91
NORTH LITTLE ROCK, AR	3.82	2.72	4.08	4.02	3.70
ALAMOSA, CO	0.74	0.68	0.35	0.36	0.27
COLORADO SPRINGS, CO	1.31	0.78	0.54	0.32	0.27
DENVER, CO	1.23	0.98	0.82	0.55	0.51
GRAND JUNCTION, CO	0.70	0.87	0.63	0.58	0.64
PUEBLO, CO	0.81	0.78	0.49	0.31	0.25
BRIDGEPORT, CT	3.29	3.33	3.79	3.75	3.25
HARTFORD, CT	3.94	3.51	4.05	4.16	3.53
WILMINGTON, DE	3.59	2.89	3.33	3.54	3.11
APALACHICOLA, FL	8.66	3.19	2.82	3.50	3.51
DAYTONA BEACH, FL	6.68	4.62	2.59	2.20	2.37
FORT MYERS, FL	8.56	3.86	1.35	1.57	1.89
GAINESVILLE, FL	5.50	2.45	2.04	3.24	3.23
JACKSONVILLE, FL	7.26	3.41	1.94	2.59	3.07
KEY WEST, FL	6.50	4.76	3.23	1.73	1.74
MIAMI, FL	8.07	7.14	2.71	1.86	2.08
ORLANDO, FL	5.62	2.82	1.78	1.83	2.10
PENSACOLA, FL	6.75	3.52	3.42	4.15	4.47
TALLAHASSEE, FL	6.45	3.10	3.31	4.58	4.66
TAMPA, FL	6.23	2.34	1.87	2.14	2.17
VERO BEACH, FL	7.96	5.94	2.55	1.97	2.43
WEST PALM BEACH, FL	9.29	7.77	3.39	2.26	2.71
ATHENS, GA	3.58	2.70	3.32	4.09	4.85
ATLANTA, GA	3.17	2.53	3.43	4.23	4.91
AUGUSTA, GA	3.53	2.02	2.07	3.20	3.99
COLUMBUS, GA	3.59	2.07	3.06	4.75	4.52
MACON, GA	3.29	1.98	2.32	4.04	4.26
SAVANNAH, GA	5.19	2.27	1.89	2.77	3.09
BOISE, ID	0.58	0.75	1.29	1.34	1.64
LEWISTON, ID	0.78	1.01	1.16	1.30	1.37
POCATELLO, ID	0.65	0.92	0.91	0.96	1.13
CAIRO, IL	3.50	2.54	3.97	4.16	3.47
CHICAGO, IL	3.35	2.28	2.06	2.10	1.60

NORMAL PRECIPITATION : INCHES

NORMALS 1951-80	SEP	OCT	NOV	DEC	JAN
MOLINE, IL	3.74	2.70	1.96	1.92	1.64
PEORIA, IL	3.63	2.51	1.96	2.01	1.60
ROCKFORD, IL	3.70	2.92	2.30	1.91	1.42
SPRINGFIELD, IL	3.05	2.52	1.93	2.05	1.56
EVANSVILLE, IN	2.67	2.48	3.36	3.45	2.99
FORT WAYNE, IN	2.53	2.56	2.57	2.44	2.07
INDIANAPOLIS, IN	2.74	2.51	3.04	3.00	2.65
SOUTH BEND, IN	3.22	3.22	2.83	2.95	2.48
DES MOINES, IA	3.09	2.16	1.52	1.05	1.01
DUBUQUE, IA	4.13	2.89	2.47	1.87	1.43
SIOUX CITY, IA	2.51	1.73	0.93	0.74	0.60
WATERLOO, IA	3.43	2.37	1.67	1.15	0.81
CONCORDIA, KS	3.00	1.83	1.05	0.70	0.61
DODGE CITY, KS	1.86	1.27	0.76	0.52	0.45
GOODLAND, KS	1.44	0.91	0.60	0.41	0.38
TOPEKA, KS	3.45	2.82	1.75	1.31	0.88
WICHITA, KS	3.45	2.47	1.47	0.99	0.68
JACKSON, KY	3.10	2.11	3.18	3.53	3.93
LEXINGTON, KY	3.28	2.26	3.30	3.78	3.57
LOUISVILLE, KY	3.35	2.63	3.49	3.48	3.38
PADUCAH, KY	3.49	2.60	4.04	4.16	3.67
BATON ROUGE, LA	4.42	2.63	3.95	4.99	4.58
LAKE CHARLES, LA	5.21	3.47	3.76	5.08	4.25
NEW ORLEANS, LA	5.87	2.66	4.06	5.27	4.97
SHREVEPORT, LA	3.29	2.63	3.77	3.87	4.02
CARIBOU, ME	3.52	3.11	3.22	3.15	2.36
PORTLAND, ME	3.27	3.83	4.70	4.51	3.78
BALTIMORE, MD	3.46	3.11	3.11	3.40	3.00
BLUE HILL, MA	4.03	4.05	4.67	5.02	4.57
BOSTON, MA	3.41	3.36	4.21	4.48	3.99
WORCESTER, MA	4.25	4.21	4.43	4.22	3.82
ALPENA, MI	2.92	1.99	2.21	1.95	1.65
DETROIT, MI	2.25	2.12	2.33	2.52	1.86
FLINT, MI	2.35	2.13	2.29	2.00	1.59
GRAND RAPIDS, MI	3.14	2.89	2.93	2.55	1.91
HOUGHTON LAKE, MI	2.77	2.28	2.26	1.89	1.49
LANSING, MI	2.54	2.13	2.33	2.21	1.74
MARQUETTE, MI	3.92	3.25	2.92	2.44	2.00
MUSKEGON, MI	2.92	2.78	2.87	2.60	2.37

NORMAL PRECIPITATION : INCHES

NORMALS 1951-80	SEP	OCT	NOV	DEC	JAN
SAULT STE. MARIE, MI	3.90	2.89	3.20	2.57	2.20
DULUTH, MN	3.26	2.21	1.69	1.29	1.20
INT. FALLS, MN	3.18	1.78	1.26	0.93	0.89
MINN.- ST. PAUL, MN	2.50	1.85	1.29	0.87	0.82
ROCHESTER, MN	3.07	2.08	1.39	0.84	0.74
SAINT CLOUD, MN	2.78	2.06	1.29	0.87	0.83
JACKSON, MS	3.55	2.62	4.18	5.40	5.00
MERIDIAN, MS	3.57	2.59	3.48	5.66	4.99
TUPELO, MS	3.64	2.99	4.63	5.61	5.65
COLUMBIA, MO	3.64	3.34	2.02	1.95	1.57
KANSAS CITY, MO	4.14	3.10	1.63	1.38	1.08
ST. LOUIS, MO	2.70	2.32	2.53	2.22	1.72
SPRINGFIELD, MO	4.24	3.20	2.89	2.55	1.60
BILLINGS, MT	1.26	1.16	0.85	0.80	0.97
GLASGOW, MT	0.89	0.56	0.31	0.37	0.46
GREAT FALLS, MT	1.03	0.82	0.74	0.80	1.00
HELENA, MT	0.83	0.65	0.54	0.60	0.66
KALISPELL, MT	1.11	0.98	1.29	1.59	1.62
MISSOULA, MT	1.02	0.85	0.88	1.21	1.41
GRAND ISLAND, NE	2.51	1.09	0.80	0.67	0.52
LINCOLN, NE	2.93	1.68	0.96	0.65	0.64
NORFOLK, NE	2.09	1.36	0.72	0.63	0.52
NORTH PLATTE, NE	1.67	0.91	0.56	0.43	0.40
OMAHA (EPPLEY AP), NE	3.50	2.09	1.32	0.77	0.77
OMAHA (NORTH), NE	3.36	2.11	1.16	0.76	0.70
SCOTTSBLUFF, NE	1.08	0.75	0.52	0.51	0.44
VALENTINE, NE	1.42	0.83	0.41	0.33	0.28
CONCORD, NH	3.12	3.10	3.66	3.43	2.78
MT. WASHINGTON, NH	7.15	6.73	8.54	8.94	7.31
ATLANTIC CITY AP, NJ	2.89	3.06	3.73	3.61	3.47
NEWARK, NJ	3.66	3.09	3.59	3.42	3.13
ALBANY, NY	3.23	2.93	3.04	3.00	2.39
BINGHAMTON, NY	3.32	3.00	3.04	2.92	2.54
BUFFALO, NY	3.37	2.93	3.62	3.42	3.02
NEW YORK (C. PARK), NY	3.66	3.41	4.14	3.81	3.21
NEW YORK (JFK AP), NY	3.51	2.98	3.73	3.62	2.93
ROCHESTER, NY	2.66	2.54	2.65	2.59	2.30
SYRACUSE, NY	3.29	3.14	3.45	3.20	2.61
ASHEVILLE, NC	3.96	3.29	3.29	3.51	3.48

NORMAL PRECIPITATION : INCHES

NORMALS 1951-80	SEP	OCT	NOV	DEC	JAN
CAPE HATTERAS, NC	5.78	4.83	4.84	4.48	4.72
CHARLOTTE, NC	3.59	2.72	2.86	3.40	3.80
GREENSBORO, NC	3.64	3.18	2.59	3.38	3.51
RALEIGH, NC	3.29	2.73	2.87	3.14	3.55
WILMINGTON, NC	5.71	2.97	3.19	3.43	3.64
BISMARCK, ND	1.38	0.81	0.51	0.51	0.51
FARGO, ND	1.87	1.29	0.79	0.63	0.55
WILLISTON, ND	1.37	0.74	0.50	0.55	0.55
AKRON, OH	2.96	2.24	2.54	2.65	2.56
CLEVELAND, OH	2.92	2.45	2.76	2.75	2.47
COLUMBUS, OH	2.76	1.91	2.64	2.61	2.75
DAYTON, OH	2.39	2.01	2.64	2.51	2.57
MANSFIELD, OH	3.04	1.94	2.66	2.40	2.25
TOLEDO, OH	2.53	1.94	2.41	2.59	1.99
YOUNGSTOWN, OH	3.10	2.65	2.82	2.76	2.69
OKLAHOMA CITY, OK	3.41	2.71	1.53	1.20	0.96
TULSA, OK	4.37	3.41	2.56	1.82	1.35
ALLENTOWN, PA	4.03	3.05	3.73	3.73	3.35
ERIE, PA	3.89	3.37	3.74	3.25	2.49
HARRISBURG, PA	3.60	2.73	3.24	3.23	2.96
PHILADELPHIA, PA	3.42	2.83	3.32	3.45	3.18
PITTSBURGH, PA	2.80	2.49	2.34	2.57	2.86
AVOCA, PA	3.36	2.78	2.98	2.54	2.27
WILLIAMSPORT, PA	3.57	3.22	3.63	3.24	2.88
BLOCK IS., RI	3.51	3.21	3.99	4.34	3.53
PROVIDENCE, RI	3.54	3.75	4.22	4.47	4.06
CHARLESTON AP, SC	4.94	2.92	2.18	3.11	3.33
CHARLESTON C.O., SC	5.19	2.84	2.04	2.86	3.17
COLUMBIA, SC	4.23	2.55	2.51	3.50	4.38
GREENVILLE, SC	4.35	3.49	3.21	3.93	4.21
ABERDEEN, SD	1.50	1.01	0.60	0.47	0.49
HURON, SD	1.36	1.39	0.69	0.52	0.42
RAPID CITY, SD	1.03	0.81	0.51	0.45	0.42
SIOUX FALLS, SD	2.79	1.57	0.92	0.72	0.50
BRISTOL, TN	3.00	2.50	2.98	3.53	3.56
CHATTANOOGA, TN	4.30	2.92	4.19	5.14	5.20
KNOXVILLE, TN	2.99	2.73	3.78	4.59	4.65
MEMPHIS, TN	3.62	2.37	4.17	4.85	4.61
NASHVILLE, TN	3.71	2.58	3.52	4.63	4.49
OAK RIDGE, TN	3.80	2.89	4.50	5.65	5.25
ABILENE, TX	3.06	2.32	1.32	0.85	0.97

NORMAL PRECIPITATION : INCHES

NORMALS 1951-80	SEP	OCT	NOV	DEC	JAN
AMARILLO, TX	1.72	1.39	0.58	0.49	0.46
AUSTIN, TX	3.60	3.38	2.20	2.06	1.60
BROWNSVILLE, TX	5.24	3.54	1.44	1.16	1.25
CORPUS CHRISTI, TX	6.15	3.19	1.55	1.40	1.63
DALLAS-FORT WORTH, TX	3.31	2.47	1.76	1.67	1.65
DEL RIO, TX	2.73	2.24	0.80	0.55	0.51
EL PASO, TX	1.42	0.73	0.33	0.39	0.38
GALVESTON, TX	5.82	2.60	3.23	3.62	2.96
HOUSTON, TX	4.93	3.67	3.38	3.66	3.21
LUBBOCK, TX	2.06	1.81	0.59	0.43	0.38
MIDLAND-ODESSA, TX	2.08	1.41	0.60	0.45	0.42
PORT ARTHUR, TX	6.13	3.63	4.33	4.55	4.18
SAN ANGELO, TX	3.04	2.05	0.97	0.64	0.64
SAN ANTONIO, TX	3.75	2.88	2.34	1.38	1.55
VICTORIA, TX	6.24	3.31	2.24	2.14	1.87
WACO, TX	3.18	3.06	2.24	1.92	1.69
WICHITA FALLS, TX	3.41	2.61	1.42	1.22	0.93
BURLINGTON, VT	3.20	2.81	2.80	2.43	1.85
LYNCHBURG, VA	3.23	3.36	2.92	3.16	3.06
NORFOLK, VA	4.35	3.41	2.88	3.17	3.72
RICHMOND, VA	3.52	3.74	3.29	3.39	3.23
ROANOKE, VA	3.14	3.48	2.59	2.93	2.83
WALLOPS ISLAND, VA	3.31	3.35	2.81	3.31	3.13
OLYMPIA, WA	2.36	4.68	7.58	8.70	8.50
QUILLAYUTE, WA	5.27	10.51	13.94	16.31	15.07
SEATTLE C.O., WA	2.03	3.40	5.36	6.29	5.94
SEATTLE (SEA-TAC AP), WA	2.02	3.43	5.60	6.33	6.04
SPOKANE, WA	0.71	1.08	2.06	2.49	2.47
STAMPEDE PASS, WA	4.65	7.74	12.14	15.88	14.59
WALLA WALLA, WA	0.83	1.40	1.87	2.19	2.12
YAKIMA, WA	0.33	0.47	0.97	1.30	1.44
BECKLEY, WV	3.38	2.54	2.81	3.23	3.44
CHARLESTON, WV	3.01	2.63	2.90	3.27	3.48
ELKINS, WV	3.21	2.97	2.69	3.33	3.39
HUNTINGTON, WV	3.07	2.40	2.82	3.12	3.24
GREEN BAY, WI	3.17	2.10	1.76	1.42	1.19
LA CROSSE, WI	3.47	2.08	1.50	1.07	0.94
MADISON, WI	3.06	2.24	1.83	1.53	1.11
MILWAUKEE, WI	2.88	2.25	1.98	2.03	1.64
CASPER, WY	0.76	0.88	0.66	0.51	0.50
CHEYENNE, WY	1.06	0.68	0.53	0.37	0.41
LANDER, WY	0.87	1.20	0.76	0.53	0.48
SHERIDAN, WY	1.16	1.16	0.81	0.68	0.74

SNOWFALL (INCLUDING ICE PELLETS)
AVERAGE TOTAL IN INCHES

DATA THROUGH 1990	SEP	OCT	NOV	DEC	JAN
BIRMINGHAM AP, AL	0.0	T	0.0	0.3	0.6
HUNTSVILLE, AL	0.0	T	0.0	0.2	1.7
MOBILE, AL	0.0	0.0	T	0.1	0.1
MONTGOMERY, AL	0.0	0.0	T	0.0	0.2
FORT SMITH, AR	0.0	0.0	0.5	0.9	2.7
LITTLE ROCK, AR	0.0	0.0	0.2	0.7	2.5
NORTH LITTLE ROCK, AR	0.0	0.0	0.3	0.5	3.7
ALAMOSA, CO	0.2	2.9	4.2	5.7	4.6
COLORADO SPRINGS, CO	1.1	3.2	4.9	5.8	5.2
DENVER, CO	1.6	3.7	8.2	7.4	7.9
GRAND JUNCTION, CO	0.1	0.5	2.8	5.3	7.3
PUEBLO, CO	0.5	1.0	4.2	5.3	6.1
BRIDGEPORT, CT	0.0	0.0	0.6	4.6	7.6
HARTFORD, CT	0.0	0.1	2.1	10.6	12.3
WILMINGTON, DE	0.0	0.1	1.0	3.5	6.8
APALACHICOLA, FL	0.0	0.0	0.0	T	0.0
FORT MYERS, FL	0.0	0.0	0.0	0.0	0.0
JACKSONVILLE, FL	0.0	0.0	0.0	0.0	T
MIAMI, FL	0.0	0.0	0.0	0.0	0.0
TALLAHASSEE, FL	T	0.0	0.0	0.0	T
TAMPA, FL	0.0	0.0	0.0	T	0.0
WEST PALM BEACH, FL	0.0	0.0	0.0	0.0	T
ATHENS, GA	0.0	0.0	0.1	0.2	0.9
ATLANTA, GA	0.0	0.0	0.0	0.2	0.9
COLUMBUS, GA	0.0	0.0	T	T	0.1
SAVANNAH, GA	0.0	0.0	0.0	0.1	0.1
BOISE, ID	0.0	0.1	2.2	6.0	6.8
LEWISTON, ID	0.0	0.1	1.7	4.4	6.3
POCATELLO, ID	0.1	1.9	4.9	8.9	9.7
CAIRO, IL	0.0	0.0	0.4	1.4	3.8
CHICAGO, IL	T	0.5	2.0	8.6	10.7
MOLINE, IL	0.0	0.2	2.2	7.2	7.8
PEORIA, IL	0.0	0.1	2.0	6.0	6.5
ROCKFORD, IL	0.0	0.1	2.7	9.3	8.4
SPRINGFIELD, IL	0.0	0.0	1.7	5.1	5.7
EVANSVILLE, IN	T	0.0	0.6	2.4	4.3
FORT WAYNE, IN	0.0	0.3	3.3	7.2	7.9

SNOWFALL (INCLUDING ICE PELLETS)
AVERAGE TOTAL IN INCHES

DATA THROUGH 1990	SEP	OCT	NOV	DEC	JAN
INDIANAPOLIS, IN	0.0	0.2	1.8	5.0	6.1
SOUTH BEND, IN	0.0	0.7	8.1	18.1	19.1
DES MOINES, IA	T	0.2	2.7	6.9	8.1
DUBUQUE, IA	T	0.2	3.5	10.8	9.1
SIOUX CITY, IA	0.0	0.5	3.7	6.1	6.3
WATERLOO, IA	0.0	0.1	3.2	7.4	6.7
CONCORDIA, KS	T	0.2	2.0	4.8	5.2
DODGE CITY, KS	T	0.1	2.0	3.4	4.6
GOODLAND, KS	0.2	1.8	4.6	5.7	6.4
TOPEKA, KS	0.0	0.0	1.2	5.1	5.8
WICHITA, KS	0.0	0.0	1.2	3.4	4.7
JACKSON, KY	0.0	0.1	0.3	3.4	6.2
LEXINGTON, KY	0.0	0.0	0.6	1.8	5.8
LOUISVILLE, KY	0.0	0.0	1.1	2.2	5.4
PADUCAH, KY	0.0	T	T	2.8	3.9
BATON ROUGE, LA	0.0	0.0	T	T	0.0
LAKE CHARLES, LA	0.0	0.0	T	0.0	0.2
NEW ORLEANS, LA	0.0	0.0	T	0.1	0.0
SHREVEPORT, LA	0.0	0.0	0.0	0.2	0.8
CARIBOU, ME	T	1.8	12.3	23.4	23.9
PORTLAND, ME	T	0.2	3.1	14.7	19.4
BALTIMORE, MD	0.0	0.0	1.1	3.6	6.1
BLUE HILL, MA	0.0	0.2	2.8	10.7	15.4
BOSTON, MA	0.0	0.0	1.4	7.4	12.2
WORCESTER, MA	0.0	0.6	3.7	12.7	16.7
ALPENA, MI	T	0.6	8.3	21.2	21.8
DETROIT, MI	T	0.2	3.1	10.6	10.0
FLINT, MI	T	0.2	3.9	9.7	11.4
GRAND RAPIDS, MI	T	0.7	7.4	17.9	20.5
HOUGHTON LAKE, MI	0.0	0.8	9.9	17.1	19.3
LANSING, MI	0.0	0.4	4.5	10.7	11.9
MARQUETTE, MI	0.2	3.8	15.7	26.7	26.7
MUSKEGON, MI	T	0.5	8.8	24.9	31.6
SAULT STE. MARIE, MI	0.1	2.3	15.3	30.0	28.6
DULUTH, MN	0.0	1.3	11.0	15.5	16.9
INT. FALLS, MN	0.1	1.7	11.4	11.4	12.1
MINN. ST. PAUL, MN	0.0	0.4	7.1	9.4	9.9

SNOWFALL (INCLUDING ICE PELLETS)
AVERAGE TOTAL IN INCHES

DATA THROUGH 1990	SEP	OCT	NOV	DEC	JAN
ROCHESTER, MN	0.0	0.6	5.3	10.9	9.9
SAINT CLOUD, MN	0.0	0.5	7.0	8.0	8.8
JACKSON, MS	0.0	0.0	0.0	0.0	0.6
MERIDIAN, MS	0.0	0.0	T	0.4	0.5
TUPELO, MS	0.0	0.0	T	0.5	1.9
COLUMBIA, MO	0.0	0.0	1.8	4.4	5.6
KANSAS CITY, MO	0.0	0.0	1.0	4.5	5.7
ST. LOUIS, MO	0.0	T	1.4	4.0	5.3
SPRINGFIELD, MO	0.0	0.0	1.7	3.1	4.4
BILLINGS, MT	1.2	3.4	6.9	8.7	9.2
GLASGOW, MT	0.2	1.3	3.1	5.6	6.5
GREAT FALLS, MT	1.6	3.1	7.5	8.9	9.9
HELENA, MT	1.6	2.1	6.4	8.4	8.8
KALISPELL, MT	0.1	1.4	8.2	17.1	17.8
MISSOULA, MT	0.0	0.8	6.0	11.0	12.5
GRAND ISLAND, NE	0.1	0.3	3.5	6.4	5.6
LINCOLN, NE	0.0	0.3	2.7	5.5	5.7
NORFOLK, NE	0.0	0.3	3.7	6.1	5.7
NORTH PLATTE, NE	0.1	1.3	4.1	4.8	5.3
OMAHA EPPLEY AP, NE	T	0.3	2.5	5.7	7.3
OMAHA (NORTH), NE	0.0	0.4	3.2	5.5	7.0
SCOTTSBLUFF, NE	0.3	2.3	5.2	6.5	6.4
VALENTINE, NE	0.5	1.0	4.8	4.8	4.6
CONCORD, NH	0.0	0.1	4.0	13.7	18.1
MT. WASHINGTON, NH	1.9	11.9	32.3	43.0	40.3
ATLANTIC CITY AP, NJ	0.0	T	0.4	2.3	5.3
NEWARK, NJ	0.0	0.0	0.6	5.7	7.7
ALBANY, NY	T	0.2	4.3	15.2	16.5
BINGHAMTON, NY	T	0.4	7.6	18.0	20.0
BUFFALO, NY	T	0.2	11.4	22.8	23.8
ISLIP, NY	0.0	0.0	1.2	4.1	7.7
NEW YORK (C. PARK), NY	0.0	0.0	0.9	5.5	7.6
NEW YORK (JFK AP), NY	0.0	0.0	0.3	3.6	7.4
ROCHESTER, NY	T	0.1	6.5	19.4	22.7
SYRACUSE, NY	T	0.6	9.1	26.5	28.7
ASHEVILLE, NC	0.0	T	0.8	1.9	5.2
CAPE HATTERAS, NC	0.0	0.0	T	0.6	0.4
CHARLOTTE, NC	0.0	0.0	0.1	0.5	2.1

SNOWFALL (INCLUDING ICE PELLETS)
AVERAGE TOTAL IN INCHES

DATA THROUGH 1990	SEP	OCT	NOV	DEC	JAN
GREENSBORO, NC	0.0	0.0	0.1	1.3	3.3
RALEIGH, NC	0.0	0.0	0.1	0.8	2.4
WILMINGTON, NC	0.0	0.0	T	0.7	0.4
BISMARCK, ND	0.3	1.3	5.8	6.9	7.2
FARGO, ND	0.0	0.6	5.3	7.0	8.5
WILLISTON, ND	0.4	1.5	4.5	7.4	7.3
AKRON, OH	T	0.5	4.5	10.1	11.4
CLEVELAND, OH,	T	0.6	5.0	11.9	12.3
COLUMBUS, OH	T	0.0	2.3	5.7	8.3
DAYTON, OH	0.0	0.2	2.2	5.7	7.8
MANSFIELD, OH	T	0.1	2.4	8.9	11.0
TOLEDO, OH	T	0.1	3.0	8.8	9.5
YOUNGSTOWN, OH	T	0.4	5.7	12.6	12.9
OKLAHOMA CITY, OK	0.0	T	0.5	1.8	3.1
TULSA, OK	T	T	0.4	1.7	3.4
ALLENTOWN, PA	0.0	0.1	1.3	6.5	8.7
ERIE, PA	T	0.4	10.1	22.8	22.8
HARRISBURG, PA	0.0	0.0	2.0	6.8	9.8
PHILADELPHIA, PA	0.0	0.0	0.7	3.6	6.6
PITTSBURGH, PA	T	0.2	3.4	8.2	11.6
AVOCA, PA	T	0.2	3.6	9.0	11.7
WILLIAMSPORT, PA	0.0	0.0	3.1	8.5	10.8
BLOCK IS., RI	0.0	T	0.2	2.9	5.1
PROVIDENCE, RI	0.0	0.1	1.1	7.1	9.8
CHARLESTON AP, SC	0.0	0.0	T	0.3	0.1
COLUMBIA, SC	0.0	0.0	T	0.2	0.5
GREENVILLE, SC	0.0	0.0	0.1	0.6	2.6
ABERDEEN, SD	0.0	0.7	4.7	6.2	6.6
HURON, SD	T	0.7	5.0	6.4	6.7
RAPID CITY, SD	0.1	1.5	4.9	5.0	4.8
SIOUX FALLS, SD	0.0	0.5	5.2	7.4	6.5
BRISTOL, TN	0.0	0.0	1.0	2.7	5.4
CHATTANOOGA, TN	0.0	T	0.1	0.6	1.9
KNOXVILLE, TN	0.0	T	0.7	1.6	4.2
MEMPHIS, TN	0.0	T	0.1	0.7	2.5
NASHVILLE, TN	0.0	T	0.5	1.6	4.0
OAK RIDGE, TN	0.0	T	0.3	1.8	3.4
ABILENE, TX	0.0	T	0.4	0.7	1.9

SNOWFALL (INCLUDING ICE PELLETS)
AVERAGE TOTAL IN INCHES

DATA THROUGH 1990	SEP	OCT	NOV	DEC	JAN
AMARILLO, TX	0.0	0.2	1.7	2.6	4.0
AUSTIN, TX	0.0	0.0	0.1	T	0.5
BROWNSVILLE, TX	0.0	0.0	T	T	T
CORPUS CHRISTI, TX	0.0	0.0	T	T	0.1
DALLAS-FORT WORTH, TX	0.0	0.0	0.1	0.3	1.3
DEL RIO, TX	0.0	T	T	T	0.7
EL PASO, TX	0.0	0.0	1.0	1.7	1.3
GALVESTON, TX	0.0	0.0	0.0	0.0	0.0
HOUSTON, TX	0.0	0.0	T	0.0	0.2
LUBBOCK, TX	0.0	0.2	1.2	1.8	2.4
MIDLAND-ODESSA, TX	0.0	T	0.5	0.8	1.6
PORT ARTHUR, TX	0.0	0.0	T	0.0	0.1
SAN ANGELO, TX	0.0	0.0	0.5	0.2	1.5
SAN ANTONIO, TX	0.0	0.0	0.0	0.0	0.5
VICTORIA, TX	0.0	0.0	0.0	T	0.1
WACO, TX	0.0	0.0	0.0	0.1	0.8
WICHITA FALLS, TX	0.0	T	0.3	1.0	2.0
BURLINGTON, VT	T	0.2	6.8	18.7	18.8
LYNCHBURG, VA	0.0	0.1	0.8	3.0	5.7
NORFOLK, VA	0.0	0.0	0.0	0.9	2.8
RICHMOND, VA	0.0	T	0.4	2.0	5.1
ROANOKE, VA	T	0.0	1.6	4.0	6.7
WALLOPS ISLAND, VA	0.0	0.0	0.3	1.5	2.9
OLYMPIA, WA	T	T	1.5	3.5	7.5
QUILLAYUTE, WA	T	T	1.1	2.9	5.5
SEATTLE C.O., WA	0.0	T	0.7	2.0	3.2
SEATTLE (SEA-TAC AP), WA	T	0.0	1.3	2.5	5.3
SPOKANE, WA	0.0	0.4	6.2	15.0	16.3
STAMPEDE PASS, WA	1.6	18.1	65.5	77.8	78.4
WALLA WALLA, WA	0.0	0.1	2.0	5.0	7.5
YAKIMA, WA	0.0	0.1	2.2	8.1	8.7
BECKLEY, WV	T	0.3	3.9	10.9	17.8
CHARLESTON, WV	T	0.1	2.2	5.0	10.6
ELKINS, WV	0.0	0.4	6.2	14.0	20.7
HUNTINGTON, WV	0.0	0.0	1.3	3.7	9.0
GREEN BAY, WI	T	0.2	4.5	11.1	10.7
LA CROSSE, WI	T	0.1	3.7	9.3	9.9
MADISON, WI	T	0.2	3.6	11.2	9.7
MILWAUKEE, WI	T	0.2	3.0	10.5	12.9
CASPER, WY	1.2	5.3	10.4	10.9	10.1
CHEYENNE, WY	0.8	3.6	6.8	6.2	6.2
LANDER, WY	2.6	8.9	13.6	10.6	8.9
SHERIDAN, WY	1.4	4.1	9.0	10.8	10.6

❖ AFTER THE SHOT ❖

A. Broken Fore Leg

B. Broken Hind Leg

The tracks left by wounded deer offer clues to the wound's location.

Deer with a broken foreleg (**A**) or a broken hind leg (**B**) will leave drag marks. The lower a leg is broken, the more pronounced the drag mark.

Deer shot through the intestines, liver (**C**) or lungs will often leave tracks that are bunched in twos.

A cross jump track (**D**) results from a bullet through the intestines or liver with the animal standing broadside to the shooter.

C. Bullet through Lungs, Liver or Intestines

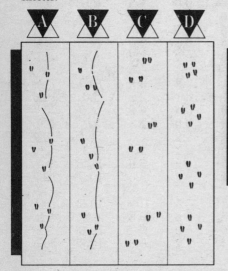

D. Bullet through Intestines or Liver

TRACKING GUIDE

The myth of the waiting game.

REASONS FOR WAITING

1. Deer will lie down and "stiffen up."

2. Hunter needs pipeful of tobacco.

3. Deer will get the "blind staggers."

REASONS FOR NOT WAITING

1. It's snowing.

2. It's raining.

3. You're in an area of high hunter density.

4. Darkness is approaching and you can't hunt in the morning.

5. Tracking takes place freely in warm weather.

6. Deer bleed freely in warm weather.

7. Trailing wounded deer with dogs permitted in the area you hunt.

8. Rigor mortis does not occur until three to six hours after death.

9. A running deer has three times the heart rate of a bedded deer.

10. Movement creates greater and more rapid blood loss, thus inhibiting coagulation.

❖ HOW FAR WILL A DEER TRAVEL ❖ WHEN HIT THROUGH THE HEART?

Every fall around the evening fires in the deer camps the old question has come up as to how it is possible for a deer to run from fifty to 200 yards after his heart had been perforated by a bullet. We all know he does this but to date no answer has really explained how. We usually wound up the evening in agreement on but two points: 1) The deer should drop when circulation ceases and the brain "suffocates." This should happen almost immediately after the heart is perforated, for, of course, it is taken for granted the heart stops instantly. 2) As we know deer have run 200 yards after a heart shot, this explanation cannot be true and there is something phony about it somewhere. So the question has never been logically answered as far as the deer hunters are concerned.

Then, on October 31, 1928, murderer John W. Deering was placed before a stone wall in Utah State Prison with an electro cardiograph attached to his person. He was outwardly calm. The prison doctor placed a target over his heart. Five picked riflemen fired at that target at short range and four bullets simultaneously pierced his heart. Yet Deering's heart did not stop when pierced by four bullets but continued to beat for 15.6 seconds thereafter. The cardiograph record also showed that a few moments before the shots were fired, through fear, Deering's heart beats, normally seventy-two per minute, were increased to 180 per minute.

Now I cannot say that the effect of a heart shot on a deer and a man are in any way similar. But let us see what would happen if we suppose this might have a bearing on the deer question. If the deer is frightened before the shot, his heart beats would increase tremendously, also increasing circulation of blood to the brain and muscles. And how far would he run in the 15.6 seconds before his heart stopped? At Anticosti Island I timed a mature white-tailed deer over a measured course with a stopwatch. It was shot at but purposely missed. Its speed was eighteen miles per hour. The highest speed when another deer was fully extended and had to run, was about thirty miles per hour. At eighteen miles per hour, the deer could travel 137 yards in 15.6 seconds. At twenty-five miles per hour the deer could travel about 152 yards. At thirty miles per hour the deer could travel about 229 yards. Doesn't it sound to you a little bit as if John Deering may have solved the riddle and that the deer's heart does not stop when perforated?

— *William Monypeny Newsom*

Tracking

Responsibilities

Anyone who hunts has a responsibility to the game pursued, to the person or persons who own the land, to other hunters and to him or herself. A good hunter tries to learn all that is possible about the species hunted. Shots should be planned and carefully taken and if a hit is made the game should be trailed until found or until it is reasonable to believe it was not vitality hit. Once the game is found it should be properly handled so it will not be wasted. This ranges from correct field dressing to preparation of the meat and/or the trophy.

Hunters should consider the landowner by treating the landowner as a friend, and the land as if it were their own home. Mutual consideration between hunters and landowners can do much to keep hunting available.

Hunters are conspicuous because of their clothes, hunting devices, and other features. For this reason it is important to realize that the behavior of one hunter will be identified with all hunters. Good field behavior and courtesy will reflect well on the whole sport. Discourteous, illegal and irresponsible behavior of one or a few individuals can prejudice people against all hunters. Realize that hunters are in the minority in this country and that many people who are not hunters are watching. The future laws on hunting and hunting devices may depend on these people. Act accordingly.

There are several procedures recommended when a hit is made on a big game animal.

❖ After a shot, stay put and try to remember where the hit was made on the animal. Wounded deer usually run with their tail down.

❖ Take compass readings on the last sighting and/or sound of the game. If no compass is available, carefully note direction the animal traveled.

❖ With binoculars check the details of the place where the game was last seen. Try to identify some land mark to aid in locating correct trail.

❖ Wait for at least an hour before starting to trail. Wait at least six hours before starting to trail an animal hit in the guts, weather and circumstances permitting. Gut-shot animals almost always die from the wound. Gut-shot animals often "hump" their back when hit.

❖ A string tracking device attached to the bow and arrow is sometimes useful in recovering game. However the string does affect the arrow flight on long shots so practice is required.

When the trailing begins:

❖ Move to the place where the animal was standing at the time of the shot and check for blood, arrow, hair or other signs to verify a hit. Trail very quietly. Avoid talking. Use hand signals or soft whistles if with companion.

❖ Even if there is no blood, mark the beginning of the trail with surveyors tape or other easily visible material, placed high enough to be easily seen from a distance. All tape should be removed once the animal is found or the trail is lost. Some people use colored crepe paper or toilet paper to mark a trail.

❖ Move in the direction the animal travelled checking constantly for blood sign. When first blood is found mark the location with tape. Note location of blood; i.e., in a foot print, on bushes, grasses or other vertical objects, right or left side of trail, etc. See special note on blood sign.

- Look for different or abnormal scuff marks or hoof prints that would identify a wounded animal.

- If trailing alone, mark location of every blood sign until the quantity becomes so great that there is no need for further marking or the sign disappears.

- Be careful not to disturb the trail and sign by staying just to the side.

- If trailing with another person, mark occasional blood sign locations to give direction of travel. The person who locates sign stays put while partner looks for next sign.

- Three people should be the maximum number trailing. Even with this number, trailing should be silent.

- If the blood trail is lost make sure the last blood sign is conspicuously marked. From this point check all main trail lanes or trails for at least half a mile.

- If no more blood sign shows on trails come back to last sign and start walking in concentric circles outward around the last sign. Animals often double back on a trail or stagger off of regular trails shortly before they die.

- Some people have difficulty walking circles, particularly on varying levels of ground. Another method of search is to walk a grid pattern using compass readings: if the grid is tight, 3 to 5 feet in grass and brush, this a good method of searching for more blood signs or a downed animal.

- If no blood or animal can be found but you feel the hit was a lethal one sit down and listen. Often crows, ravens, magpies or jays will be attracted to a downed animal. Listen for their calls.

- Game, after being hit, will often circle back to where it came from. If there is a problem locating a good blood sign, check along the trail on which the animal first appeared.

- Check all major crossing points on human trails, back roads or stream banks for possible sign.

- Vitally hit animals often go down hill rather than climb.

- Be sure to check in streams or swamps for a downed deer if the trail leads in that direction. Gut-shot animals become thirsty and often head towards water.

- Heart-shot animals may travel surprising distances and show little external bleeding.

- Deer, particularly in northern areas, have thick layers of tallow along the back and below the brisket. This can plug wounds preventing a good blood trail. Avoid straight-down shots from tree stands for this reason.

- Do not start to follow big game hit in the gut for six to eight hours if day light permits.

- An exception to the rule about waiting before starting to trail a wounded deer is when the hunter knows the only hit was in the leg. If the animals is kept walking the wound may stay open.

- If there is a threat of rain or snow then it may be necessary to start trailing sooner than preferred. Always trail quietly, even more than when stalking uninjured game.

- In blood trailing sometimes it is necessary to actually rub reddish spots with the fingers to verify that it is not just autumn colors on a leaf. Sometimes getting down to almost ground level will help a hunter spot blood sign that otherwise might be missed.

- When blood trailing, look at specific objects such as stones, twigs and leaves, rather than the whole trail.

Women are often excellent at trailing because they notice detail and fewer are color blind.

❖ Practice blood trailing on a simulated trail with artificial blood.

❖ Near populated areas remove viscera as well as deer from woods. Rotting guts are poor public relations.

H   Hit
BL Blood lost
B   Blood trail found near deer

Types of Blood Sign

❖ Blood that is frothy with bubbles usually indicates a lung hit.

❖ Very dark blood may indicate a liver or kidney hit.

❖ Blood mixed with vegetable material often greenish in color indicates a "gut" or viscera shot.

❖ Blood with bubbles may indicate a neck hit where the arrow has cut the neck arteries and windpipe. The arrow may show almost no sign of blood.

❖ Blood in spattered pattern may indicate a rapidly moving animal or one in which major blood vessels have been cut.

❖ Blood on both sides of the trail usually indicates a pass-through wound. In some instances a one-opening wound may produce this sign if the animal doubles back on trail.

❖ The height of blood sign is an indication of wound location.

❖ Blood spatter drops usually point direction of travel of a rapidly moving animal like the fingers of a hand.

❖ No blood sign doesn't always mean a miss. Bleeding may be internal.

Increasing the "L" Grid

❖ Pick a length unit (e.g. 10 paces)

❖ Walk ahead this distance, looking for sign of deer.

❖ Make a right corner turn and search the same distance. This completes the first "L."

❖ Now make another right angle, turn and search two lengths (20 paces).

❖ Turn again (always to the right) and search two lengths again, completing "L" #2.

❖ Turn again to start "L" #3, which will be three lengths (30 paces) on both sides.

❖ Continue making "L", each one unit longer than the last.

❖ Continue enlarging the grid unit the game is found or the trail is definitely lost.

❖ Another effective search pattern, also using the compass, is the U-shape. However this would miss deer that back-track.

- If a hit is made late in the day, and the weather is cool, wait until morning, unless there are a lot of coyotes, wild dogs, raccoons or bears around that might destroy the game.

- If a late hit is made and there is a threat of rain or snow get good lights, gas or kerosene lantern, leave the bows or guns in camp or vehicle and trail the game. Sometimes it is even easier to trail at night. Be sure to mark trail for two reasons. If the blood trail is lost, there's a better chance of locating it again if tape is tied in conspicuous spots. Also it is very easy to get lost at night while trailing. A well-marked trail will at least get the hunter back to where the trailing started. Reflector tape is a good addition for night trailing.

- If there is no blood, look for compressed or disturbed leaves or vegetation.

- Look for flattened plants with leading edge disturbed. Deer prints are usually narrow and tapered, even in leaves and grass. A running deer tends to scatter leaves to the side of the trail.

Approaching Down Game

When game is found approach cautiously and quietly and, if possible, from the back of the animal. Sometimes a wounded animal will suddenly spring to its feet and run. Try to watch the eyes. If they are glazed or unblinking the animal is safe to approach. If the animal is down but still obviously alive try to get close enough for another shot. Bowhunters should try to place a shot in the rib cage then either quietly back off and wait at a distance or wait silently in place so as not to further "spook" the animal. It's better to have an extra hole in a skin than lose a wounded animal.

Reprinted from **Big Game Recovery Guide.** Courtesy of National Bowhunter Education Foundation.

❖ DRESSING DEER ❖

Field-Dressing Deer

1) With the deer on its back, carefully open the deer's abdomen.

2) Place a small log under the rump to get it off the ground. Cut deeply around the rectum, being careful not to cut off or puncture the intestine. Pull to make sure the rectum is separated from tissue connecting it to the pelvic canal. Do not split the pelvic bone. Lift the animal's back quarters a bit, reach into the front of the pelvic canal, and pull the intestine and connected rectum into the stomach area.

3) If you want to make a full shoulder mount, do not cut open the chest cavity. Reach into the forward chest, find the esophagus, cut it off as far up as possible, and pull it down through the chest. If the buck won't be mounted, split the chest and sever the esophagus at its lower end. Or, simply cut into the deer's throat patch deeply enough to sever the esophagus. After it's cut, reach into the chest cavity, find the lower end of the esophagus and pull it through.

4) Roll the deer onto one side and cut the diaphragm away from the ribs all the way to the backbone area. Roll the deer onto its other side and finish cutting away the diaphragm.

5) Leaving the deer on its side, grab the esophagus with one hand and the rectum/intestine with the other. Pull hard. The deer's innards will come out in one big package with a minimum of mess.

Caping A Trophy

Caping — the process of skinning out a trophy deer's shoulder and head — is best left to the taxidermist. In a remote setting, however, storage problems may require you to cape a deer if you want to preserve it as a full shoulder mount. Follow the illustration above when making your cuts.

1) With a short, sharp knife, slit the skin from the top of the withers, up the back of the neck to the midpoint between the ears. Now, going back to the withers, circle the body with another cut. This should leave plenty of hide for the taxidermist.

2) Peel the skin forward up to the ears and jaws, exposing the point where you want to cut through the neck. The easiest way to separate the head from the neck is to make an encircling cut through the neck to the atlas joint, the first vertebra under the skull. This is the only joint on the neck that has no interlocking bones.

3) After making this cut, simply grasp the antler bases and twist the head off the neck.

4) Remember, when field-dressing a trophy to be mounted, don't cut into the chest or neck area. If blood gets on the area to be mounted, wash it off with snow or water as soon as possible. Also, when taking the deer out of the woods, place it on a sled or rickshaw. All it takes is one sharply broken branch on a deadfall to damage the hide.

Skinning Your Trophy

Skinning deer does not have to be a long, laborious chore that leaves hair all over the meat and a knife-riddled hide. Take a hint from butchers who winch off the hide. A car, truck or come-along works just as well. With practice, this technique requires about five minutes of work.

1) With the deer hanging by its antlers or neck, slice the hide around the neck as close to the head as possible. (Don't cut into the meat. The neck muscles bear much force later as the hide is pulled off.)

2) Cut down the front of the neck to the opening made during field-dressing.

3) Saw off the legs slightly above the knee joints.

4) Pull the neck hide down until about one foot of it is free. Take a golf-ball sized rock or 1.5-inch section of 2-by-2 and wrap it into the hide's end. Make a tight package and cinch it off with high-quality nylon rope of about three-eighths inch thickness. A double half-hitch works well. Pull hard on the rope to make sure everything is secure.

5) Tie the rope's other end to a car, truck or come-along hook. (A rope 10 to 12 feet long is plenty.) Back up the vehicle until the hide is pulled to the brisket and shoulders. It will bind slightly here. If necessary, have someone work the hide around the brisket. With tension on the rope, the hide will slide over fairly easily.

6) Continue backing until the hide is pulled free of the carcass.

WEIGHTS AND HEART GIRTH

To calculate live or hog-dressed weight, first measure heart girth, the circumference of body just behind the front legs. Then consult this chart to convert girth into a close estimate of weight.

Heart girth inches (cm)	Hog-dressed weight Adults pounds (kg)	Live weight Adults pounds (kg)
26 (66.0)	46 (20.9)	60 (27.2)
27 (68.6)	52 (23.6)	68 (30.8)
28 (71.1)	58 (26.3)	75 (34.0)
29 (73.7)	64 (29.0)	83 (37.6)
30 (76.2)	70 (31.8)	90 (40.8)
31 (78.7)	76 (34.5)	98 (44.5)
32 (81.3)	82 (37.2)	106 (48.1)
33 (83.8)	88 (39.9)	113 (51.3)
34 (86.4)	94 (42.6)	121 (54.9)
35 (88.9)	101 (45.8)	128 (58.1)
36 (91.4)	107 (48.5)	136 (61.7)
37 (94.0)	113 (51.3)	144 (65.3)
38 (96.5)	119 (54.0)	151 (68.5)
39 (99.1)	125 (56.7)	159 (72.1)
40 (101.6)	131 (59.2)	166 (75.3)
41 (104.1)	137 (62.1)	174 (78.9)
42 (106.7)	143 (64.9)	182 (82.6)
43 (109.2)	149 (67.6)	190 (86.2)
44 (111.8)	155 (70.3)	197 (89.4)
45 (114.3)	161 (73.0)	205 (93.0)

Virginia Polytechnic Institute & State University

Boone and Crockett Records

The information reproduced in this chapter is taken from the Boone and Crockett Club's *Records of North American Whitetail Deer*, second edition, 1991, with the express written permission of the Boone and Crocket Club. The information that follows is only a partial listing of the top whitetails. For information on the complete record book, write: Boone and Crockett Club, 250 Station Drive, Missoula, MT 59801.

Richard P. Smith

ALABAMA
TYPICAL WHITETAIL DEER

Score	Locality Killed / By Whom Killed	Date Killed
186-3/8	Lee County / Picked Up	1986
182-7/8	Hale County / James C. Bailey	1974
172-1/8	Pickens County / Walter Jaynes	1968
170-2/8	Lee County / George P. Mann	1980
168-2/8	Marengo County / William L. Wright	1979
162-7/8	Perry County / Rodney A. Pilot	1987
161-6/8	Greene County / William H. Fincher	1982
161-4/8	Barbour County / Craig Thompson	1979

NON-TYPICAL WHITETAIL DEER

224-5/8	Perry County / Robert E. Royster	1976
223-1/8	Sumter County / James L. Spidle, Sr.	PR 1942
217-2/8	Dallas County / Robert Tate	1988
199-2/8	Winston County / James W. Huckbay	1973
187	Greene County / William H. Fincher	1976

ARKANSAS
TYPICAL WHITETAIL DEER

189	Crawford County / Tom Sparks, Jr.	1975
186-7/8	Arkansas County / Walter Spears	1952
184-6/8	Desha County / Lee Perry	1961
183	Desha County / R.J. Diekoff	1954
180	Desha County / Turner Neal	1962
179-2/8	Prairie County / Charles Newsom	1962
177-7/8	Chicot County / George Matthews	1923
173-3/8	Arkansas County / Jimmy Hanson	1948
173-2/8	Chicot County / Yan Sturdivant	1951
172	Bearden / Buddy Wise	1962

NON-TYPICAL WHITETAIL DEER

208-5/8	St. Francis County / George W. Hobson	1987
206-1/8	Boydel / Picked Up	1959
201-1/8	Arkansas County / Daniel B. Bullock	1953
196-4/8	Desha County / Turner Neal	1955

COLORADO
TYPICAL WHITETAIL DEER

Score	Locality Killed / By Whom Killed	Date Killed
182-5/8	Yuma County / Ivan W. Rhodes	1978
175-7/8	Logan County / Picked Up	1971
171-2/8	Yuma County / John O. Cletcher	1985

NON-TYPICAL WHITETAIL DEER

204-2/8	Yuma County / Jeff L. Mekelburg	1986

CONNECTICUT
TYPICAL WHITETAIL DEER

177-2/8	Litchfield County / Picked Up	1984
176-2/8	Litchfield County / Frederick H. Clymer	1987

NON-TYPICAL WHITETAIL DEER

195	Windham County / Harold Tanner	1970

FLORIDA
NON-TYPICAL WHITETAIL DEER

186-1/8	Jackson County / Henry Brinson	1959

GEORGIA
TYPICAL WHITETAIL DEER

184-3/8	Paulding County / Floyd Benson	1962
184	Newton County / Gene Almand	1966
184	Hart County / Kenton L. Adams	1986
180-7/8	Jones County / James H.C. Kitchens	1957
180-2/8	Newton County / David Moon	1972
179-2/8	Lamar County / Gary Littlejohn	1968
179-1/8	Twiggs County / Cy Smith	1970
179	Jasper County / Hubert R. Moody	1957
179	Dooley County / Shannon Akin	1981
177-5/8	Macon County / James W. Athon	1976

Score	Locality Killed / By Whom Killed	Date Killed
240-3/8	Monroe County / John L. Hatton, Jr.	1973
215-7/8	Putnam County / Thomas H. Cooper	1974
208-3/8	Decatur County / James L. Darley	1964
199-6/8	Harris County / Kenneth H. Brown	1974
198-4/8	Wheeler County / David Frost	1983
197-4/8	Dooly County / Wayne Griffin	1984
197-3/8	Newton County / R.H. Bumbalough	1969
195-4/8	Worth County / Shane Calhoun	1985
195-3/8	Colquitt County / Olen P. Ross	1976
193-5/8	Henry County / Jason J. Patrick	1986

IDAHO
TYPICAL WHITETAIL DEER

181-7/8	Clearwater County / Richard E. Carver	1985
177-5/8	Idaho County / Donna M. Knight	1986
176-6/8	Idaho County / Edward D. Moore	1986
176-6/8	Idaho County / Frank J. Loughran	1987
175-5/8	Benewah County / Carl Groth	1982
174-2/8	Clearwater County / Douglas B. Crockett	1983
173-6/8	Bonner County / Robert L. Campbell	1967
172	Joseph Plains / Jim Felton	1965
171-4/8	Latah County / Darwin L. Baker	1986
170	Latah County / Lewis L. Turcott	1974

NON-TYPICAL WHITETAIL DEER

267-4/8	Idaho/Jack Brittingham	PR 1923
248-1/8	Nez Perce County / John D. Powers, Jr.	1983
226-3/8	Nez Perce County / Mrs. Ralph Bond	1964
213-5/8	Bonner County / Rodney Thurlow	1968
203-1/8	Kootenai County / William M. Ziegler	1965
201-3/8	Bonner County / Leroy Coleman	1960
200-3/8	Nez Perce County / Tim C. Baldwin	1987
198-1/8	Kootenai County / Frank J. Cheney	1967
197	Kootenai County / D.L. Whatcott & R.C. Carlson	1980

ILLINOIS
TYPICAL WHITETAIL DEER

204-4/8	Peoria County / M.J. Johnson	1965
182-7/8	Rock Island County / Clifton C. Webster	1986
182-2/8	Champaign County / Tom Babb	1985

Score	Locality Killed / By Whom Killed	Date Killed
181-5/8	Wabash County / Mike Drone	1987
181-4/8	Canton / Arnold C. Hegele	1968
181-3/8	Pope County / Jack A. Higgs	1963
180	Pulaski County / Picked Up	1988
179	Perry County / Roy A. Smith	1987
178-4/8	St. Clair County / Emil W. Kromat	1981
178-3/8	Clinton County / Richard V. Spihlmann	1961
178-3/8	Jo Daviess County / Gary J. Flynn	1986

NON-TYPICAL WHITETAIL DEER

Score	Locality Killed / By Whom Killed	Date Killed
267-3/8	Peoria County / Richard A. Pauli	1983
238-1/8	Madison County / Joe Bardill	1985
236-5/8	Pike County / Floyd Pursley	1987
231-4/8	Perry County / Unknown	1968
223-6/8	Greene County / Terry L. Walters	1982
221	Pike County / Frank C. Skelton	1987
220-4/8	Mercer County / Roger D. Hultgren	1970
217-6/8	Macoupin County / Albert Grichnik	1966
215-7/8	Schuyler County / Donald E. Ziegenbein	1981
213-4/8	Pike County / Donald L. Roseberry	1984

INDIANA
TYPICAL WHITETAIL DEER

Score	Locality Killed / By Whom Killed	Date Killed
195-1/8	Parke County / B. Dodd Porter	1985
194-2/8	Vigo County / D. Bates & S. Winkler	1983
185-1/8	Franklin County / Gayle Fritsch	1972
185	Putnam County / Earl G. McCammack	1985
183-6/8	Clinton County / Stuart C. Snodgrass	1977
177	Cass County / Herbert R. Frushour	1974
177	Jasper County / Dan Haskins	1975
175-2/8	Fulton County / Larry A. Croxton	1984
172-7/8	Jefferson County / Chet A. Nolan	1987
171	Pike County / Phil Lemond	1986

NON-TYPICAL WHITETAIL DEER

Score	Locality Killed / By Whom Killed	Date Killed
226-3/8	Clark County / Robert L. Bromm, Sr.	1985
215-4/8	Wayne County / Clyde L. Day	1986
205-7/8	Switzerland County / Paul Graf	1981
198-7/8	Ripley County / William L. Wagner	1982
191-2/8	Delaware County / Robert D. McFarland	1986

IOWA
TYPICAL WHITETAIL DEER

Score	Locality Killed / By Whom Killed	Date Killed
194-4/8	Monroe County / Lloyd Goad	1962
187-6/8	Johnson County / Gregg R. Redlin	1983
187-5/8	Cherokee County / Dennis R. Vaudt	1975
187-2/8	Warren County / Dwight E. Green	1964
185-1/8	Warren County / Joyce McCormick	1968
185-1/8	Harrison County / Marvin E. Tippery	1971
184-7/8	Delaware County / R.E. Stewart	1953
184-2/8	Hardin County / Robert D. Imsland	1985
183-7/8	Taylor County / Wayne Swartz	1947
182-5/8	Jefferson County / William J. Waugh	1985

NON-TYPICAL WHITETAIL DEER

282	Clay County / Larry Raveling	1973
256-2/8	Monona County / Carroll E. Johnson	1968
229-6/8	Decatur County / Edgar Shields	1986
229-3/8	Wapello County / Robert D. Harding	1985
222-4/8	Davis County / James L. Fine	1987
222-1/8	Hancock County / Jerry M. Monson	1977
221-7/8	Tama County / Charles Upah	1959
221-4/8	Humboldt County / Donald Crossley	1971
220-2/8	Union County / George Foster	1968
220	Wayne County / Dallas Patterson	1975

KANSAS
TYPICAL WHITETAIL DEER

198-2/8	Nemaha County / Dennis P. Finger	1974
194-7/8	Leavenworth County / William R. Mikijanis	1985
191-4/8	Chautauqua County / Michael A. Young	1973
186-3/8	Morris County / Garold D. Miller	1969
185	Seward County / Michael D. Gatlin	1987
184-4/8	Chase County / Thomas D. Mosher	1984
184	Saline County / James R. Bell	1985
182-3/8	Waubausee County / Norman Anderson	1966
181-6/8	Lyon County / Kenneth C. Haynes	1969
180	Edwards County / David R. Cross	1985

NON-TYPICAL WHITETAIL DEER

Score	Locality Killed / By Whom Killed	Date Killed
258-6/8	Republic County / John O. Band	1965
251-1/8	Mitchell County / Theron E. Wilson	1974
248-7/8	Greenwood County / Clifford G. Pickell	1968
239	Lyon County / Don E. Roberts	1987
229-2/8	Linn County / Merle C. Beckman	1984
227	Miami County / Gary A. Smith	1970
216-6/8	Barber County / Robert L. Rose	1972
209-6/8	Edwards County / Tim C. Schaller	1984
206/5-8	Chase County / Jay A. Talkington	1983
205-6/8	Cloud County / Gary G. Pingel	1982

KENTUCKY
TYPICAL WHITETAIL DEER

187-1/8	Pulaski County / Scott Abbott	1982
186	Warren County / Arnold M. Bush	1986
185-2/8	Todd County / C.W. Shelton	1964
184	Grayson County / Floyd Stone	1987
181-2/8	Hardin County / Thomas L. House	1963
181	Gallatin County / Kenneth D. Hoffman	1979
178-2/8	Ohio County / Earl R. Trogden	1986
178	Union County / Gary L. Gibson	1983
177-4/8	Grayson County / David W. Mercer	1986
175-3/8	Todd County / Gary W. Crafton	1981

NON-TYPICAL WHITETAIL DEER

236-3/8	Union County / Wilbur E. Buchanan	1970
226-5/8	Pulaski County / H.C. Sumpter	1984
221-7/8	Trigg County / Bill McWhirter	1982
218-4/8	Logan County / Robert L. Schrader, Jr.	1987
215	Hardin County / Michael F. Meredith	1980
210-3/8	Lyon County / Roy D. Lee	1975
209-5/8	Butler County / Dean A. Hannold	1979
208-6/8	Daniel Boone Natl. For. / Richard G. Lohre	1968
204	Webster County / Jeff Robinson	1982
202	Powell County / Hershel Ingram	1980

LOUISIANA
TYPICAL WHITETAIL DEER

Score	Locality Killed / By Whom Killed	Date Killed
189-5/8	St. Landry Parish / Leonce Mallet	1965
184-6/8	Madison Parish / John Lee	1943
184-4/8	Bossier County / Earnest O. McCoy	1961
184-2/8	Franklin Parish / H.B. Womble	1914
180-5/8	St. Landry Parish / Shawn P. Ortego	1975
180-4/8	Madison Parish / Buford Perry	1961
180-3/8	Union Parish / Picked Up	1963
177-3/8	Claiborne Parish / Steven L. Morton	1986
176-5/8	Tensas Parish / Sam Barber	1974
176-2/8	Richland Parish / Willard Roberson	1968

NON-TYPICAL WHITETAIL DEER

Score	Locality Killed / By Whom Killed	Date Killed
218-4/8	St. Martin Parish / Drew Ware	1941
206-7/8	Claiborne Parish / J.H. Thurmon	1970
206-6/8	Grant Parish / Richard D. Ellison, Jr.	1969
201-3/8	Concordia Parish / G.O. McGuffee	1963
198-5/8	Concordia Parish / Raymond Cowan	1961
190-2/8	Concordia Parish / John T. Lincecum	1986

MAINE
TYPICAL WHITETAIL DEER

Score	Locality Killed / By Whom Killed	Date Killed
192-7/8	York County / Alphonse Chase	1920
186-2/8	Hancock County / Gerald C. Murray	1984
184-5/8	Washington County / Unknown	1944
184-1/8	Waldo County / Christopher Ramsey	1983
181-4/8	Oxford County / Dean W. Peaco	1953
181-1/8	Waldo County / Clarendon Pomeroy	1946
180-6/8	Hancock County / Cyrus H. Whitaker	1912
179-7/8	Hancock County / Butler B. Dunn	1930
179-6/8	Penobscot County / Dale Rustin	1984
178-6/8	Aroostook County / John R. Hardy	1983

NON-TYPICAL WHITETAIL DEER

Score	Locality Killed / By Whom Killed	Date Killed
248-1/8	Penobscot County / Unknown	1945
228-7/8	Cherryfield / Flora Campbell	1953
228-1/8	Maine / Henry A. Caesar	PR 1911
224	Hancock County / Picked Up	PR 1975
223-3/8	Maine / Frank Maxwell	1900
219-2/8	Aroostook County / Harold C. Kitchin	1973
218-7/8	Waldo County / Roy C. Guse	1957

208-7/8	Washington County / Robert E. Cooke	1972
208-1/8	Hancock County / Hollis Staples	1922
207-6/8	Aroostook County / Alfred Wardwell	1945

MARYLAND
TYPICAL WHITETAIL DEER

183-3/8	Dorchester County / John R. Seifert, Jr.	1973
181-6/8	Montgomery County / Gary F. Menso	1985
172-1/8	Queen Annes County / James R. Spies, Jr.	1976
172	Caroline County / Garey N. Brown	1986
170-6/8	Carroll County / Wes McKenzie	1971
170-5/8	St. Marys County / Brian M. Boteler	1980
170-1/8	Harford County / Edward C. Garrison	1987

NON-TYPICAL WHITETAIL DEER

228-4/8	Montgomery County / John W. Poole	1987
217-2/8	Talbot County / Vincent L. Jordan, Sr.	1974
210	Calvert County / Robert E. Barnett	1984
208-7/8	Charles County / Robert A. Boarman	1984
201-3/8	Queen Annes County / Franklin E. Jewell	1978
196-2/8	Dorchester County / Kevin R. Coulbourne	1979
185-7/8	Charles County / Robert Sparks	1980

MICHIGAN
TYPICAL WHITETAIL DEER

193-2/8	Jackson County / Craig Calderone	1986
186-3/8	Ontonagon County / Unknown	1980
184-7/8	Baraga County / Louis J. Roy	1987
181-5/8	Ionia County / Lester Bowen	1947
180-4/8	Iron County / John Schmidt	1927
180-3/8	Huron County / Picked Up	1985
178	Hillsdale County / Dudley N. Spade	1972
177-7/8	Iron County / Felix Brzoznowski	1939
176-6/8	Clinton County / Ray Sadler	1963
176-3/8	Baraga County / Paul Korhonen	1945

NON-TYPICAL WHITETAIL DEER

238-2/8	Bay County / Paul M. Mickey	1976
218-3/8	Keweenaw County / Bernard J. Murn	1980
215-5/8	Iron County / C. & R. Lester	1970
212	Iron County / Ben Komblevicz	1942

Score	Locality Killed / By Whom Killed	Date Killed
209-1/8	Keweenaw County / Nathan E. Ruonavaara	1946
201-5/8	Charlevoix County / Robert V. Doerr 1973	
201-5/8	Baraga County / Dennis D. Bess	1981
201	Delta County / Ernest B. Fosterling	1953
198-5/8	Iron County / Eino Macki	1930
197-5/8	Luce County / Sid Jones	1917

MINNESOTA
TYPICAL WHITETAIL DEER

202	Beltrami County / John A. Breen	1918
195-5/8	Marshall County / Robert Sands	1960
193-2/8	Itasca County / Picked Up	1935
192	Pine County / Frank Worlickey	1952
192	Clay County / Mark L. Peterson	1984
191-5/8	Goodhue County / David C. Klatt	1985
189-3/8	Fillmore County / Tom Norby	1975
187-6/8	Houston County / Donald M. Grant	1978
187-5/8	Winona County / Ken W. Koenig	1976
187-4/8	Winona County / Dan Groebner	1974

NON-TYPICAL WHITETAIL DEER

268-5/8	Norman County / Mitchell A. Vakoch	1974
258-2/8	Becker County / J.J. Matter	1973
249-2/8	Fillmore County / Dallas R. Henn	1961
245-5/8	Itasca County / Peter Rutkowski	1942
245-3/8	Itasca County / Mike Hammer	1956
240-6/8	St. Louis County / John Cesarek	1964
236	Winona County / Francis A. Pries	1964
232-5/8	Wabasha County / Robert F. Friese	1948
231-1/8	Winona County / Robert E. Bains	1973
230-1/8	Pope County / Harvey J. Erickson	1974

MISSISSIPPI

182-7/8	Noxubee County / Glen D. Jourdon	1986
182-7/8	Claiborne County / R.L. Bobo	1955
181-5/8	Wilkinson County / Ronnie P. Whitaker	1981
180-4/8	Leflore County / W.F. Smith	1968
178-5/8	Bolivar County / Grady Robertson	1951
176-5/8	Bolivar County / Sidney D. Sessions	1952
175-2/8	Wilkinson County / Johnnie J. Leake, Jr.	1978
174-7/8	Coahoma County / O.P. Gilbert	1960
173-5/8	Lowndes County / Geraline Holliman	1982

Score	Locality Killed / By Whom Killed	Date Killed
172-5/8	Adams County / Adrian L. Stallone	1983

NON-TYPICAL WHITETAIL DEER

217-5/8	Carroll County / Mark T. Hathcock	1978
209-6/8	Franklin County / Ronnie Strickland	1981
205-6/8	Lowndes County / Joe W. Shurden	1976
202-5/8	Carroll County / George Galey	1960
202-1/8	Oktibbeha County / Oliver H. Lindig	1983
201-6/8	Wilkinson County / Jimmy Ashley	1985
196-5/8	Wilkinson County / Robert D. Sullivan	1982
195-7/8	Monroe County / Kenneth A. Dye	1986
195-5/8	Adams County / Kathleen McGehee	1981

MISSOURI
TYPICAL WHITETAIL DEER

205	Randolph County / Larry W. Gibson	1971
199-4/8	Clark County / Jeffrey A. Brunk	1969
187-2/8	Scotland County / Robin Berhorst	1971
187-2/8	Atchison County / Unknown	1984
187.1	Cooper County / Joe Ditto	1974
187.1	Mercer County / Picked Up	1986
186-7/8	Atchison County / Mike Moody	1968
186-2/8	Laclede County / Larry Ogle	1972
185-5/8	Dallas County / James E. Headings	1986
183-4/8	Sumner / Marvin F. Lentz	1968

NON-TYPICAL WHITETAIL DEER

333-7/8	St. Louis County / Picked Up	1981
259-5/8	Chariton County / Duane R. Linscott	1985
225-1/8	Nodaway County / Ken Barcus	1982
219-5/8	Warren County / James E. Williams	1959
218-5/8	Chariton County / Stanley McSparren	1979
217-7/8	Maries County / Gerald R. Dake	1974
215-5/8	Worth County / B.M. & R. Nonneman	1974
214	Atchison County / Warren E. Davis	1983
208-7/8	Atchison County / Kenneth W. Lee	1964
207-3/8	Lincoln County / Melvin Zumwalt	1955

MONTANA
TYPICAL WHITETAIL DEER

Score	Locality Killed / By Whom Killed	Date Killed
199-3/8	Missoula County / Thomas H. Dellwo	1974
191-5/8	Flathead County / Earl T. McMaster	1963
189-1/8	Blaine County / Kenneth Morehouse	1959
187-5/8	Montana / Unknown	PR 1984
186-3/8	Flathead County / Unknown	1973
186	Flathead County / Douglas G. Mefford	1966
184-7/8	Yellowstone County / Picked Up	1984
184-7/8	Missoula County / Jack Greenwood	1985
183-3/8	Flathead County / Unknown	1957
182-7/8	Montana / Unknown	PR 1983

NON-TYPICAL WHITETAIL DEER

Score	Locality Killed / By Whom Killed	Date Killed
252-1/8	Hill County / Frank A. Pleskac	1968
248-5/8	Snowy Mts. / Unknown	PR 1980
241-7/8	Flathead County / George Woldstad	1960
234-1/8	Glacier County / Unknown	1968
224	Lincoln County / Ray Baenen	1935
223-4/8	Richland County / Verner King	1960
219-1/8	Flathead County / R.C. Garrett	1962
216-2/8	Richland County / Joseph P. Culbertson	1972
215	Fergus County / Robert D. Fleherty	1958
214-3/8	Missoula County / Lyle Pettit	1962

NEBRASKA
TYPICAL WHITETAIL DEER

Score	Locality Killed / By Whom Killed	Date Killed
194-1/8	Dakota County / E. Keith Fahrenholz	1966
189-1/8	Nuckolls County / Van Shotzman	1968
185-5/8	Nenzel / Richard Kehr	1965
184-5/8	Polk County / Keith Houdersheldt	1985
182-1/8	Frontier County / Robert G. Bortner	1985
180-7/8	Keya Paha County / Steve R. Pecsenye	1966
179-4/8	Pawnee County / Kenneth C. Mort	1975
178-5/8	Harlan County / Don Tripe	1961
178-2/8	Pawnee County / Picked Up	1960
178-1/8	Dismal River / Gift Of. G.B. Grinnell	PR 1909

NON-TYPICAL WHITETAIL DEER

Score	Locality Killed / By Whom Killed	Date Killed
277-3/8	Hall County / Del Austin	1962
242-5/8	Nance County / Robert E. Snyder	1961
238	Keya Paha County / Donald B. Phipps	1969

Score	Locality Killed / By Whom Killed	Date Killed
233-6/8	Custer County / Lonnie E. Poland	1986
215-7/8	Long Pine / Picked Up	1964
214-6/8	Hitchcock County / David W. Oates	1985
212-3/8	Hershey / Ray Liles	1959
211-5/8	Alda / Donald Knuth	1964
208-4/8	Dixon County / Dan Greeny	1969
208-1/8	Antelope County / Leon McCoy	1965
208-1/8	Atkinson Highway / Russell Angus	1966

NEW YORK
TYPICAL WHITETAIL DEER

198-3/8	Allegany County / Roosevelt Luckey	1939
181-3/8	Orange County / Roy Vail	1960
180-3/8	Livingstone County / Edward Beare	1943
179-3/8	Essex County / Herbert Jaquish	1953
176-2/8	Erie County / Wesley H. Iulg	1944
176-2/8	Warren County / Frank Dagles	1961
175-7/8	Lewis County / Andrew Lustyik	1942
175-5/8	Allegany County / William L. Damon	1981
174-2/8	Livingston County / Kenneth Bowen	1941
174-1/8	Essex County / Denny Mitchell	1933

NON-TYPICAL WHITETAIL DEER

244-2/8	Allegany County / Homer Boylan	1939
224	New York / Unknown	PR 1983
219-7/8	Genesee County / Robert Wood	1944
207-7/8	Suffolk County / George Hackal	1950
207-4/8	Portageville / Howard W. Smith	1959
206-2/8	Cortland County / Hank Hayes	1947
205-7/8	Steuben County / Fred J. Kelley	1938
199-1/8	Clinton County / Unknown	PR 1971
196-1/8	Wyoming County / Eric D. Baney	1985

NORTH CAROLINA
TYPICAL WHITETAIL DEER

181-7/8	Guilford County / Terry E. Daffron	1987
178	Caswell County / Picked Up	1988
172-1/8	Granville County / Dudley Barnes	1985

NORTH DAKOTA
TYPICAL WHITETAIL DEER

Score	Locality Killed / By Whom Killed	Date Killed
189-3/8	McKenzie County / Gene Veeder	1972
187-5/8	Emmons County / Joseph F. Bosch	1959
187-2/8	McLean County / Frank O. Bauman	1986
182	Zap / Wally Duckwitz	1962
178-1/8	Concrete / Lawrence E. Vandal	1947
177-7/8	Cass County / Joe D. Chesley	1987
177-2/8	Golden Valley County / Allen Goltz	1964
175-6/8	Burleigh County / Earl Haakenson	1963
175	New Salem / John T. Cartwright	1957
174-4/8	McKenzie County / Ben Dekker	1976

NON-TYPICAL WHITETAIL DEER

254-6/8	Stanley / Roger Ritchie	1968
232-1/8	McLean County / Olaf P. Anderson	1886
220-7/8	Pembina County / Gary F. Bourbanis	1985
216-6/8	Kathryn / Gerald R. Elsner	1963
210-5/8	Renville County / Glen Southam	1978
206-1/8	Dunn County / Kenneth E. DeLap	1982
203-5/8	Grand Forks County / Thomas G. Bernotas	1975
203-2/8	McHenry County / Garry L. Heizelman	1987
202-6/8	Garrison / Clarence Hummel	1961
201-1/8	Slope County / Arthur Hegge	1961

OHIO
TYPICAL WHITETAIL DEER

184-6/8	Muskingum County / Dale Hartberger	1981
184-1/8	Vinton County / Dan F. Allison	1965
183	Piedmont Lake / J. Rumbaugh & J. Ruyan	1958
182-7/8	Wayne County / Gary E. Landry	1975
181-4/8	Licking County / Arle McCullough	1962
181-3/8	Portage County / Robert M. Smith	1953
179	Logan County / Gregory K. Snyder	1982
178-7/8	Monroe County / Roger E. Schumacher	1958
178-2/8	Tuscarawas County / Ray D. Gerber, Jr.	1983
177-5/8	Harrison County / Mark Dulkoski	1984

NON-TYPICAL WHITETAIL DEER

328-2/8	Portage County / Picked Up	1940
256-5/8	Holmes County / Picked Up	1975
250-6/8	Richland County / David D. Dull	1987

Score	Locality Killed / By Whom Killed	Date Killed
235-4/8	Ashtabula County / James L. Clark	1957
231-3/8	Licking County / Norman L. Myers	1964
226-4/8	Muskingum County / Rex A. Thompson	1981
226-1/8	Trumbull County / Paul E. Lehman	1948
211-5/8	Adams County / William J. DeCamp	1987
210-2/8	Columbiana County / Harold L. Hawkins	1981
207	Stark County / Tad E. Crawford	1987

OKLAHOMA
TYPICAL WHITETAIL DEER

177-6/8	Atoka County / Skip Rowell	1972
173-5/8	Woods County / Jack Clover	1983
170-3/8	Haskell County / Loyd Long	1985
160	Le Flore County / Carl E. Hale	1978

NON-TYPICAL WHITETAIL DEER

247-2/8	Johnston County / Bill M. Foster	1970
234-2/8	Alfalfa County / Loren Tarrant	1984
299-4/8	Dewey County / Ricky C. Watt	1987
216-3/8	Comanche County / Dwight O. Allen	1962
209	Hughes County / Lane Grimes	1987
206-1/8	Osage County / Wesley D. Coldren	1986
204-4/8	Love County / William B. Heller	1970
203-6/8	McCurtain County / Gary L. Birge	1981
201-3/8	Pushmataha County / Maurice Jackson	1975
197-4/8	Garfield County / Derald D. Crissup	1980

OREGON
TYPICAL WHITETAIL DEER

178-2/8	Wallowa County / Sterling K. Shaver	1982

PENNSYLVANIA
TYPICAL WHITETAIL DEER

184-6/8	Greene County / Ivan Parry	1974
182-2/8	Sullivan County / Floyd Reibson	1930
177-4/8	Bedford County / Raymond Miller	1957
176-5/8	Mifflin County / John Zerba	1936
176	Bradford County / Clyde H. Rinehuls	1944
175-4/8	McKean County / Arthur Young	1830
174-2/8	Butler County / Ralph Stoltenberg, Jr.	1986

Score	Locality Killed / By Whom Killed	Date Killed
173-3/8	Clarion County / Mead Kiefer	1947
173-3/8	Clarion County / Picked Up	1954
172-6/8	Somerset County / Edward B. Stutzman	1945

NON-TYPICAL WHITETAIL DEER

207-7/8	Port Royal / C. Ralph Landis	1951
207	Lycoming County / Al Prouty	1949
201-1/8	Westmoreland County / Richard K. Mellon	1966
196-6/8	Perry County / Kenneth Reisinger	1949
196	Westmoreland County / Edward G. Ligus	1956

SOUTH CAROLINA
NON-TYPICAL WHITETAIL DEER

208-5/8	Beaufort County / John M. Wood	1971

SOUTH DAKOTA
TYPICAL WHITETAIL DEER

193	South Dakota / Unknown	1964
192	Lyman County / Bob Weidner	1957
189-5/8	Tabor/Duane Graber	1954
184-3/8	Kingsbury County / Rudy F. Weigel	1960
181-3/8	Harding County / Gregg Else	1985
180-4/8	Clay County / James E. Olson	1975
180-3/8	Hand County / Vernon Winter	1965
177-1/8	Gregory County / Harold Deering	1969
176-7/8	Day County / William B. Davis	1959
176-5/8	Roberts County / Fred Kuehl	1964

NON-TYPICAL WHITETAIL DEER

256-1/8	Marshall County / Francis Fink	1948
250-6/8	South Dakota / Howard Eaton	1870
249-1/8	Lily / Jerry Roitsch	1965
216-7/8	Brown County / Francis Shattuck	1960
210	Gregory County / Richard C. Berte	1982
208-4/8	Day County / Unknown	PR 1950
207-7/8	Perkins County / W.E. Brown	1957
207-3/8	Roberts County / Delbert Lackey	1975
206-4/8	Yankton County / William Sees	1973
203-4/8	Lawrence County / Ernest C. Larive	1957

TENNESSEE
TYPICAL WHITETAIL DEER

Score	Locality Killed / By Whom Killed	Date Killed
186-1/8	Roane County / W.A. Foster	1959
184-4/8	Fayette County / Benny M. Johnson	1979
178-5/8	Scott County / Charles H. Smith	1978
173-4/8	Shelby County / John J. Heirigs	1962
173-2/8	Decatur County / Glen D. Odle	1972
173-1/8	White County / Same H. Langford	1980
173	Sullivan County / C. Alan Altizer	1984
172-3/8	Decatur County / Danny Pope	1982
172-2/8	Stewart County / Joe K. Sanders	1984

NON-TYPICAL WHITETAIL DEER

223-4/8	Hawkins County / Luther E. Fuller	1984
209-7/8	Hawkins County / Johnny W. Byington	1982
198-3/8	Montgomery County / Clarence McElhaney	1978
196-6/8	Unicoi County / Elmer Payne	1972

TEXAS
TYPICAL WHITETAIL DEER

196-4/8	Maverick County / Tom McCulloch	1963
196-1/8	McMullen County / Milton P. George	1906
192-2/8	Frio County / Basil Dailey	1903
190	Dimmitt County / C.P. Howard	1950
187-7/8	Zavala County / Donald Rutledge	1946
187-5/8	Starr County / Picked Up	1945
187-4/8	Frio County / Kenneth Campbell	1987
186-2/8	La Salle County / Herman C. Schliesing	1967
186-2/8	Kenedy County / Jack Van Cleve III	1972
186-1/8	Zavala County / Picked Up	1965

NON-TYPICAL WHITETAIL DEER

286	Brady / Jeff Benson	1892
272	Junction / Picked Up	1925
247-7/8	Frio County / Raul Rodriguez II	1966
240	Kerr County / Walter F. Schreiner	1905
235-1/8	Frio County / C.J. Stolle	1919
226-7/8	Dimmit County / Lake Webb	1937
226-4/8	La Salle County / A.L. Lipscomb, Sr.	1909
220-2/8	Zavala County / J.D. Jarratt	1930
219-3/8	Webb County / Richard O. Rivera	1972
215-2/8	Parker County / Pleasant Mitchell	1982

VERMONT
TYPICAL WHITETAIL DEER

Score	Locality Killed / By Whom Killed	Date Killed
170-1/8	Essex County / Kevin A. Brockney	1986

VIRGINIA
TYPICAL WHITETAIL DEER

188-6/8	Shenandoah County / Gene Wilson	1985
178-3/8	Goochland County / Edward W. Fielder	1981
177-2/8	Augusta County / Donald W. Houser	1963
176-7/8	Prince George County / Fred W. Collins	1949
176-2/8	Rappahannock County / George W. Beahm	1959
174-4/8	Charlotte County / Jerry C. Claybrook	1977
173-4/8	Augusta County / David H. Wolfe	1957
172-6/8	Surry County / Edward B. Jones	1984
172-5/8	Surry County / Picked Up	1987
170-7/8	Bath County / Maurice Smith	1953

NON-TYPICAL WHITETAIL DEER

232-4/8	Buckingham County / James R. Shumaker	1986
221-3/8	Louisa County / Picked Up	1981
217	Isle Of Wight County / Peter F. Crocker, Jr.	1963
216-4/8	Surry County / Stanley M. Hall	1986
216-3/8	Powhatan County / William E. Schaefer	1970
215-5/8	Wise County / Edison Holcomb	1987
211-7/8	Rockingham County / Dorsey O. Breeden	1966

WASHINGTON
TYPICAL WHITETAIL DEER

181-7/8	Whitman County / George A. Cook III	1985
180-4/8	Okanogan County / Joe Peone	1983
179-4/8	Spokane County / Bert E. Smith	1972
178-4/8	Addy / Irving Naff	1957
176-5/8	Washington / Unknown	PR 1953
173-3/8	Pend Oreille County / Tom R. Lentz	1987
172-6/8	Spokane County / Maurice Robinette	1968
171-3/8	Metaline Falls County / Scott Hicks	1970
170-2/8	Spokane County / Edward A. Floch, Jr.	1970
170	Stevens County / Clair Kelso	1966

NON-TYPICAL WHITETAIL DEER

Score	Locality Killed / By Whom Killed	Date Killed
234-4/8	Stevens County / Larry G. Gardner	1953
233-6/8	Thompson Creek / George Sly, Jr.	1964
231	Stevens County / Joe Bussano	1946
227-4/8	Pullman / Glenn C. Paulson	1965
210-7/8	Stevens County / Charles Tucker	1966
209	Chesaw / Charles Eder	1967
207-2/8	Oroville / Victor E. Moss	1967
206-1/8	Loon Lake / Bill Quirt	1955
204-3/8	Newport / David R. Buchite	1960
203-3/8	Okanogan County / Michael A. Anderson	1962

WEST VIRGINIA
TYPICAL WHITETAIL DEER

182-3/8	Braxton County / William D. Given	1976
180-5/8	Cheat Mt. / Joseph V. Volitis	1969
175-1/8	Wetzel County / Matthew Scheibelhood	1984
171	Hampshire County / Conda L. Shanholz	1958

NON-TYPICAL WHITETAIL DEER

205-6/8	Ritchie County / Charles E. Bailey, Jr.	1979
204-6/8	Gilmer County / Brooks Reed	1960
203-1/8	Wetzel County / Tom Kirkhart	1981

WISCONSIN
TYPICAL WHITETAIL DEER

206-1/8	Burnett County / James Jordan	1914
197-5/8	Wood County / Joe Haske	1945
191-3/8	Vilas County / Robert Hunter	1910
189-7/8	Trempealeau County / Emil Stelmach	1959
186-1/8	Waupaca County / Fred Penny	1963
185	Vernon County / Harold Christianson	1968
184	Menominee County / Keith Miller	1969
183-7/8	Forest County / James M. Thayer	1980
183-6/8	Pepin County / LaVerne Anibas	1965
183-5/8	Buffalo County / Lee F. Spittler	1953

NON-TYPICAL WHITETAIL DEER

245	Buffalo County / Elmer F. Gotz	1973
241-3/8	Wisconsin / Unknown	1940
233-7/8	Loraine / Homer Pearson	1937

Score	Locality Killed / By Whom Killed	Date Killed
233	Burnett County / Victor Rammer	1949
232	Waukesha County / John Herr, Sr.	1955
231-5/8	Dane County / Dennis D. Shanks	1979
231-2/8	Forest County / Robert Jacobson	1958
228-2/8	Cable / Charles Berg	1910
227-4/8	Bayfield County / Earl Holt	1934
226-6/8	Rusk County / Joe Michalets	1911

WYOMING
TYPICAL WHITETAIL DEER

Score	Locality Killed / By Whom Killed	Date Killed
191-5/8	Albany County / Robert D. Ross	1986
177-1/8	Newcastle / H.W. Julien	1954
174-3/8	Goshen County / Casey L. Hunter	1984
170-3/8	Niobrara County / Joseph A. Perry III	1985

NON-TYPICAL WHITETAIL DEER

Score	Locality Killed / By Whom Killed	Date Killed
238-7/8	Crook County / Picked Up	1962
224-1/8	Crook County / John S. Mahoney	1947
214-2/8	Crook County / Clinton Berry	1953
211-7/8	Crook County / Curtis U. Nelson	1971
204-2/8	Crook County / David Sipe	1956
202-3/8	Crook County / Marshall Miller	1968
200-3/8	Crook County / Paul L. Wolz	1967
198-7/8	Weston County / G. Huls & B.L. Arfmann	1973
198-4/8	Cow Creek / Thelma Martens	1951

ALBERTA
TYPICAL WHITETAIL DEER

Score	Locality Killed / By Whom Killed	Date Killed
204-2/8	Beaverdam Creek / Stephen Jansen	1967
190-5/8	Buffalo Lake / Eugene L. Boll	1969
188-4/8	Metiskow / Norman T. Salminen	1977
184-7/8	Vermilion / C. Letawsky & B. Myshak	1986
183	Red Deer River / Picked Up	1966
181-7/8	Hotchkiss / Andy G. Petkus	1984
181-7/8	Lesser Slave Lake / Picked Up	1985
181-4/8	Pine Lake / Robert Crosby	1977
181	Stettler / Archie Smith	1962
180-7/8	Castor / Norman D. Stienwand	1981

NON-TYPICAL DEER

Score	Locality Killed / By Whom Killed	Date Killed
277-5/8	Hardisty / Doug Klinger	1976
267-7/8	Shoal Lake / Jerry Froma	1984
255-4/8	Pigeon Lake / Leo Eklund	1973
241-1/8	Bighill Creek / Donald D. Dwernychuk	1984
233-2/8	Acadia Valley / James J. Niwa	1973
232-5/8	Winfield / Harry O. Hueppelshevser	1986
233-2/8	Thursby / Robert G. MacRae	1987
231-6/8	Peace River / Terry Doll	1978
230-6/8	Red Deer / Delmer E. Johnson	1973
222-5/8	Edgerton / Nick Leskow	1964

BRITISH COLUMIBA
TYPICAL WHITETAIL DEER

177-7/8	Ymir / Frank Gowing	1961
175-7/8	Pouce Coupe River / Dale Callahan	1986
174-5/8	Baldonnel / D. Ian Williams	1978
174-4/8	Fort Steele / John Lum	1958
174-1/8	Anarchist Mt. / George Urban	1980
173-6/8	Hartr Creek / Greg Lamontange	1984
171-6/8	Gray Creek / Ross Oliver	1982
171-3/8	Whatshan Lake / Ernest Roberts	1957
171	Okanagan Range / Picked Up	1984

NON-TYPICAL WHITETAIL DEER

245-7/8	Elk River / James I. Brewster	1905
218	West Kootenay / Karl H. Kast	1940
205-5/8	Midway / Gordon Kamigochi	1980
202-2/8	East Kooteney / Andrew W. Rosicky	1956
198-1/8	Nelway / Edward John	1935

MANITOBA
TYPICAL WHITETAIL DEER

197-7/8	Assiniboine River / Larry H. MacDonald	1980
189	Red Deer Lake / Will Bigelow	1986
188-4/8	Souris River / Wes Todoruk	1986
188-3/8	Sanford / Picked Up	1982
187-6/8	Mantagao Lake / Picked Up	1988
183	Lorne / Alain G. Comte	1987
182-5/8	Virden / Darryl Gray	1957
179-7/8	Hamiota / Alan J. Sheridan	1984
179-4/8	Whitemud River / L. Greg Fehr	1985

Score	Locality Killed / By Whom Killed	Date Killed
179-3/8	Oberon / Arnold W. Poole	1968

NON-TYPICAL WHITETAIL DEER

Score	Locality Killed / By Whom Killed	Date Killed
257-3/8	Elkhorn / Harvey Olsen	1973
241-5/8	Manitoba / Unknown	1984
238-3/8	Assiniboine River / Doug Hawkins	1981
237-3/8	Whiteshell / Angus McVicar	1925
231-3/8	Holland / W. Ireland	1968
214-7/8	Aweme / Criddle Bros.	1954
212-1/8	Minnedosa / Albert Pfau	1966
208-1/8	Griswold / J.V. Parker	1946
207-7/8	Assiniboine River / Terry L. Simcox	1987
206-7/8	Whitemouth River/ Tom Clark, Jr.	1987

NEW BRUNSWICK
TYPICAL WHITETAIL DEER

Score	Locality Killed / By Whom Killed	Date Killed
180-6/8	New Brunswick / Unknown	1937
178-3/8	Queens County / Bert Bourque	1970
176-4/8	Charlotte County / Albert E. Dewar	1960
175-6/8	Nine Mile Brook / Leopold Leblanc	1973
175-4/8	Canaan / Marcel Poirier	1985
171-1/8	Kings County / Wayne F. Anderson	1987
173-1/8	St. George / Gilbert Leavitt	1962
172-3/8	Snider Mt. / Jack W. Brown	1975
172	Westmoreland County / Edgar Cormier	1983
171-5/8	Bonnell Brook / Steve R. McCutcheon	1984

NON-TYPICAL WHITETAIL DEER

Score	Locality Killed / By Whom Killed	Date Killed
249-7/8	Kings County / Ronald Martin	1946
243-7/8	Wirral / H. Glenn Johnston	1962
242-2/8	Auburnville / John L. MacKenzie	1958
224-2/8	Salmon River / Ford Fulton	1966
214-7/8	St. John County / T. Emery	1968
204-1/8	Charlotte County / Gary L. Lister	1984
204-6/8	George Lake / Henry Kirk	1903
199-7/8	Queens Lake / George Lacey	1915
198-3/8	Clark's Brook / Bernard V. Sharp	1985
196-4/8	Charlotte County / Clayton Tatton	1959

NOVA SCOTIA
TYPICAL WHITETAIL DEER

Score	Locality Killed / By Whom Killed	Date Killed
170-6/8	Guysborough County / Roy B. Simpson	1968

NON-TYPICAL WHITETAIL DEER

264-5/8	West Afton River / Alexander C. MacDonald	1960
253	Goldenville / Neil MacDonald	1945
233-1/8	Condon Lakes / Don McDonnell	1987
222-4/8	Ostrea Lake / Verden M. Baker	1949
218-7/8	Bay of Fundy / Basil St. Lewis	1983
200-1/8	Parrsboro / Allison Smith	1960
196	Annapolis Valley / David Cabral	1984

ONTARIO
TYPICAL WHITETAIL DEER

174-1/8	Amherstview / Tony H. Stranak	1987

SASKATCHEWAN
TYPICAL WHITETAIL DEER

200-2/8	Whitkow / Peter J. Swistun	1983
195-4/8	Porcupine Plain / Philip Philipowich	1985
193-6/8	Christopher Lake / Jerry Thorson	1959
191-6/8	Hudson Bay / George Chalus	1973
188-4/8	Burstall / W.P. Rolick	1957
185-3/8	Canwood / Clark Heimbechner	1984
184-6/8	Dore Lake / Garvis C. Coker	1971
184-5/8	Hudson Bay / Picked Up	1986
182-4/8	Carrot River / Lori Lonson	1960
182-1/8	Round Lake / Jesse Bates	1984

NON-TYPICAL WHITETAIL DEER

265-3/8	White Fox / Elburn Kohler	1957
248-4/8	Moose Mtn. Park / Walter Barkto	1964
245-4/8	Carrot River / Picked Up	1962
243-5/8	Govan / A.W. Davis	1951
238-1/8	Whitewood / Jack Davidge	1967
236-4/8	Reserve / Harry Nightingale	1959
235-4/8	Pipestone Valley / E.J. Marshall	1958
233-7/8	Tompkins / Don Stueck	1961
233	Punnichy / Steve Kapay	1968

Score	Locality Killed / By Whom Killed	Date Killed
231-7/8	Harris / Herman Cox	1954

MEXICO
TYPICAL WHITETAIL DEER

Score	Locality Killed / By Whom Killed	Date Killed
181-7/8	Coahuila / German Lopez Flores	1986
181-6/8	Nuevo Leon / J.P. Davis	1985
180-5/8	Nuevo Leon / Charles H. Priess	1985
174-2/8	Cerralvo / Unknown	1900
173-4/8	Tamaulipas / John F. Sontage, Jr.	1987
172	Coahuila / Picked Up	1986
170-1/8	Coahuila / Rodolfo F. Barrera	1988
160-2/8	Coahuila / Jesus H.G. Villarreal	1988

NON-TYPICAL WHITETAIL DEER

Score	Locality Killed / By Whom Killed	Date Killed
233-6/8	Nuevo Leon / Ron Kolpin	1983
210-6/8	Coahuila / Picked Up	1981
208-1/8	Mexico / Unknown	1959

ARIZONA
TYPICAL COUES' WHITETAIL DEER

Score	Locality Killed / By Whom Killed	Date Killed
143	Pima County / Ed Stockwell	1953
131-7/8	Cochise County / George W. Kouts	1935
130-4/8	Pima County / Kim J. Poulin	1981
126-5/8	Cochise County / Mike Kasun	1959
126-5/8	Pima County / DeWayne M. Hanna	1977
126-1/8	Pima County / Robert G. McDonald	1986
125-4/8	Arivaca / Gerald Harris	1953
125	Ft. Apache Res. / Picked Up	PR 1969
124-5/8	Rincon Mts. / James Pfersdorf	1936
123-7/8	Gila County / Stephen P. Hayes	1965

NON-TYPICAL COUES' WHITETAIL DEER

Score	Locality Killed / By Whom Killed	Date Killed
158-4/8	Santa Cruz County / Picked Up By Walter H. Pollock	1988
151-4/8	Cochise County / Charles C. Mabry	1929
150-5/8	Sasabe / Robert Rabb	1954
149-7/8	Chiricaua Range / Marvin R. Hardin	1950
143-6/8	Pima County / Oscar C. Truex	1983
142-7/8	Apache Indian Res. / Indian	1950
142-6/8	Pinal Mts. / Phil Rothengatter	1967
139-7/8	Patagonia Mts. / Howard W. Drake	1968

Score	Locality Killed / By Whom Killed	Date Killed
137-6/8	Patagonia Mts. / Ivan J. Buttram	1969
134-2/8	Yavapai County / William B. Bullock	1986

NEW MEXICO
TYPICAL COUES' WHITETAIL DEER

119	Hidalgo County / Jesse E. Williams	1971
114	Animas Mts. / F.C. Hibben	1955
113-1/8	Grant County / Andrew A. Musacchio	1985
111-6/8	Catron County / Charles Tapia	1959
110/38	Hidalgo County / Ronald M. Gerdes	1979
110-2/8	Hidalgo County / Jay M. Gates III	1981
110-1/8	Hidalgo County / Neuman Sanford	1981

NON-TYPICAL COUES' WHITETAIL DEER

122-6/8	Hidalgo County / Jack Samson	1984
127-6/8	Hidalgo County / Michael C. Finley	1983

MEXICO
TYPICAL COUES' WHITETAIL DEER

130-5/8	Chihuahua / Wayne Kleinman	1958
124-5/8	Sonora / Enrique Lares	1959
122-4/8	Sonora / Lloyd L. Ward, Jr.	1945
121	Sierra Madre Mts. / Herb Klein	1965
120-6/8	Sonora / Manual A. Caravantez	1960
120-5/8	Sonora / George W. Parker	1969
120-4/8	Sonora / Diego G. Sada	1969
119-7/8	Sonora / Picked Up	1960
117-5/8	Libertad / Abe R. Hughes	1967
117-3/8	Sonora / Charles B. Leonard	1974

NON-TYPICAL COUES' WHITETAIL DEER

134-2/8	Sonora / Unknown	PR 1986
132	Sonora / Picked Up	PR 1988
125-3/8	Sonora / Enrique C. Cicero	1967
144-4/8	Sonora / Arturo R. Campoy	1979

"Venison Recipes"

BARBECUE/RIBS — HEART/LIVERS

Venison and Barbecue Sauce

4-6 pound roast
1/4 cup brown sugar
1/2 cup vinegar
Salt and pepper to taste
1/2 cup melted butter
1 cup catsup

5 tablespoons chopped onions
2 tablespoons Worcestershire
  sauce
1 cup water
1 clove garlic, mashed
Flour

Rub meat with combined sugar and vinegar, marinate 3-4 hours. Rub meat with salt and pepper and dust with flour. Brown roast. Combine all remaining ingredients for sauce.

Place roast in pan and add small amount of water, baste with sauce. Roast at 350 degrees for 30 minutes per pound. Baste occasionally, remove roast and thicken sauce for gravy.

Michael Ramach
Jacksonville, NC

Stuffed Hearts

2 to 3 deer hearts
2 cups boiling water
1 cup fresh bread crumbs
1 cup minced ham
1 egg, slightly beaten
1/4 cup chopped parsley
1 sprig marjoram, chopped or
  1/4 teaspoon dried

1 sprig rosemary, chopped, or
  1/4 tsp. dried
1 teaspoon grated lemon peel
Salt and freshly ground pepper
3 strips bacon
2 tablespoons flour
2 teaspoons tomato paste

Soak hearts in cold water 1 hour. Remove the veins and arteries with a sharp knife, then wash out and dry hearts.

Prepare the stuffing by mixing the bread crumbs, ham, egg, herbs and lemon peel together. Salt and pepper as desired.

Make a 2- to 3-inch slash on one side of each heart and fill with the stuffing. Wrap each stuffed heart with a strip of bacon and secure it with a skewer.

Place hearts upright in an earthenware casserole and bake in a 350 degree oven for 2 to 3 hours, until meat is tender.

Remove the hearts to a heater platter. Add the flour to the pan drippings, stir and cook a minute or so. Remove from heat and pour in the boiling water and tomato paste, then return to the heat and stir as the sauce thickens. Simmer a few minutes, then place in a sauceboat along with the hearts.

Venison Heart

Deer heart
1 onion sliced
1 teaspoon whole black pepper
1 teaspoon ground cloves

1 teaspoon salt to a quart of
  water
2 bay leaves

Cover heart with water. Add salt, onion and spices. Cover and simmer until tender. Small heart-3 hours. Large heart-4 hours. Can be eaten hot or cold.

Eunice Clausing
Neenah, WI

Venison Liver

1 pound venison liver,
  sliced 1/2-inch thick
Bacon or onions to your taste,
  fry in advance

6 tablespoons butter
2 tablespoons lemon juice
Salt and pepper

Dip the liver in flour, salt and pepper and saute over fairly high heat in the hot butter, turning once. 4 minutes to a side. Stir in the lemon juice, pour the lemon butter over liver. Serve with fried bacon or fried onions. Serves 6.

MAIN DISHES

Stir-Fry Venison and Mushrooms

1 cup rice
1 pound venison steaks
1 tablespoon soy sauce
2 tablespoons sweet red wine
2 teaspoon cornstarch
1/4 teaspoon ginger powder

1/4 teaspoon garlic powder
1/8 teaspoon salt
1 pound mushrooms
1 large onion
1 cup peas

About 30 minutes before serving, prepare rice as directed; keep warm. Cut venison into 1/2-inch cubes. In medium bowls mix venison, soy sauce, wine, cornstarch, ginger, salt and garlic powder. Set aside.

Thinly sliced mushrooms and onions. Cook mushrooms and onions in a large skillet over medium to high heat, stirring quickly and frequently until mushrooms are tender. Remove the mixture to a bowl.

In same skillet, over high heat, cook venison in 3 more tablespoons of butter. Stir quickly and frequently until tender. Return mushroom mixture to skillet, add peas, heat through. Serve with rice. Makes 4 servings.

Venison Meatballs

1 pound ground venison
1/2 cup rice, uncooked
1 tablespoon onion, minced
1 teaspoon salt

1/4 teaspoon pepper
1 can tomato soup
1/4 cup water

Combine meat, rice, onion and pepper. Shape into meatballs. Mix soup and water in cooker. Gently place meatballs in soup. Cover pressure cooker and cook for 10 minutes. Cool cooker normally for five minutes, then hold under water. Serves 4.

Venison Cheese Bake

8 ounces egg noodles
2 pounds venison, ground
1 teaspoon salt
1/4 teaspoon pepper
1 medium onion, chopped
1 green pepper, chopped
1-1/2 cups cottage cheese

1 clove garlic, minced
1 large (16-ounce) can tomato
 sauce
1 teaspoon oregano
1 large package cream cheese
1/2 cup sour cream

Cook noodles and drain. In a large skillet brown venison in butter, add salt, onion, green pepper and garlic. Stir in tomato sauce and oregano. Set aside. Soften cream cheese at room temperature, blend with sour cream and cottage cheese. In a 13x9x2-inch baking dish, place half of the cooked noodles. Cover noodles with cheese mixture; spread remaining noodles and top with meat mixture. Bake in 350 degree oven for 2 minutes. Serves 8.

Easy Venison Porcupines

1 cup uncooked rice
1-1/2 pounds ground venison
Garlic to taste

1 small onion, diced
2 cans tomato soup
1/2 cup mushrooms, chopped

Combine all the ingredients except soup and form into meatballs. Place in crockpot and add two cans tomato soup but only one can of water. Cover and cook on low about 6 hours.

Thomas K. Squier
Aberdeen, NC

Venison Cheese Meat Loaf

2 pounds ground deer burger
1 onion, chopped
4 crackers, crushed
3 eggs, slightly beaten

1 teaspoon garlic salt
1/8 teaspoon pepper
Mild cheese slices

Mix all ingredients except cheese slices. Place half of the mixture in baking dish, place thin slices of cheese on first half. Cover cheese with rest of meat mixture. Bake in 350 degree oven for one hour.

Eunice Clausing
Neenah, WI

Venison Lasagna

1 pound ground venison	1 16-ounce can tomatoes
1 tablespoon oil	1 8-ounce can tomato paste
1/3 cup onion, diced	1 tablespoon vinegar
Salt & pepper	1 teaspoon sugar
1 garlic clove, diced	1 package lasagna noodles
1/2 teaspoon thyme	1-1/2 cups cottage cheese
1 pound sliced Mozzarella cheese	1 cup Romano or Parmesan cheese

Saute onions in oil, add garlic and meat, brown. Add vinegar, sugar, thyme, tomato paste, tomato, salt and pepper. Simmer 20 minutes.

Cook lasagna noodles until done. Rinse and cover with cold water. In shallow pan layer meat sauce, lasagna noodles, layer of cottage cheese, meat sauce, Parmesan cheese and last Mozzarella cheese. Repeat layers, with last layer meat sauce and cover with remaining cheese.

Bake in 350 degree oven for 45 minutes. Let cool 10 minutes.

Oliver Bugelli
Westville, IL

Italian Venison Steak

4 venison cubed steaks, or round steaks, tenderized (about 2 pounds)

1/4 cup cooking oil

1/2 cup flour or crushed Ritz crackers

1 egg

1 26-ounce bottle of your favorite Italian sauce

1 cup grated Parmesan cheese

Preheat oven to 350 degrees. Slowly heat oil in large cast iron skillet. Dip steaks in egg, then in flour or crackers, and brown in hot oil. Drain oil from skillet and add Italian sauce to steaks. Bake covered (use foil if you don't have a lid) for 45 minutes. Sprinkle liberally with Parmesan cheese. Serves 4.

Camille W. Sewell
West Palm Beach, FL

Venison Sauerbraten

4 pound venison roast

2 onions, sliced

1 bay leaf

10 black whole peppercorns

10 juniper berries

6 cloves

2 teaspoons salt

6 cups boiling water

1/2 cup red wine vinegar

2 tablespoons oil

1 medium-sized red cabbage cut into 8 wedges

Caraway Sauce:

15 gingersnaps, crushed

2 teaspoons sugar

Caraway Dumplings:

1-1/2 cups sifted flour

1 cup milk or water

7 cups boiling water

Place meat in bowl with onions, bay leaves, cloves, juniper berries, salt, water, and vinegar. Cover and marinate 6 to 8 hours. Drain the venison and reserve the marinade. In a heavy Dutch oven heat the oil over medium-high heat and brown the venison on all sides. Add the reserve marinade; then cover, lower heat and simmer 2 hours or until tender. Drain the venison and keep warm.

Strain and measure the marinade (add water if needed) to equal 4 cups and return to the Dutch oven.

Combine the dumpling ingredients with a fork. Mold 2 tablespoons of dumpling mixture into balls and drop them into boiling water. Cook 10 minutes, remove and rinse with hot water and drain. Bring the marinade to a boil; then add the cabbage wedges and place the dumplings on top. Cover to steam and cook over medium heat for 10 minutes or until the cabbage is tender. Mix the crushed gingersnaps and sugar and stir into the cabbage liquid and simmer 3 minutes more. Serve on a platter topped with gingersnap sauce.

This authentic dish makes a superbly filling after-hunt meal, often served during duck season or after skiing. As always, follow the recipe exactly the first time you make the dish (don't leave out the gingersnaps or use green cabbage instead of red!) to taste the real version of a dish too often toned down by food writers. It needs no side dish.

Venison Goulash

3 pounds venison cut into 1-inch squares	1/4 teaspoon paprika
2 medium onions	1 tablespoon sifted flour
1/4 pound bacon, cut into small pieces	1 can tomatoes
2 cloves garlic, mashed	Salt and pepper
	1/4 teaspoon marjoram

Fry bacon until brown. Add onions and venison and cook until brown. Add water to cover, add garlic, marjoram and paprika. Add tomatoes. Salt and pepper to taste. Cover tightly and bring to a boil. Reduce heat and simmer until meat is tender (about 1 hour). Drain off liquid. Mix flour in a little water until smooth and add to the liquid. Heat to boiling and boil for 2 minutes, stirring constantly. Pour gravy back over meat and serve.

Venison Chop Suey

1-1/2 pounds venison steak,
  cut into 1/2-inch pieces
2 cups diagonally cut celery
1/3 cup chopped onion
3 tablespoons cooking oil
1 tablespoon soy sauce

1-1/2 cups water
1 28-ounce can bean sprouts,
  drained
1 8-ounce can water chestnuts,
  drained and sliced
4 teaspoons instant beef broth

In a large Dutch oven, brown venison well in oil. Add soy sauce, water, instant beef broth, celery and onions. Bring to a boil, reduce to simmer, cover, cook 10 minutes. Add bean sprouts and water chestnuts, cover, simmer another 3 minutes. If desired thicken with cornstarch paste or beef gravy mix. Serve over cooked rice.

H.F. Coleman
Norwich, NY

Deeros (Venison Gyros)

2 pounds venison round steak
2 tablespoons olive oil

3 garlic cloves, pressed or
  minced
3 garlic cloves, pressed or
  minced
2 sprigs fresh parsley, chopped
  fine
1 teaspoon salt
6 pieces of pita pocket bread
1 sweet Spanish onion, sliced

Sauce:1/4 teaspoon salt
1 garlic clove, pressed or
  minced
1 16-ounce container plain
yogurt
2 tablespoons cucumber,
  chopped fine

Stir Fried Stew Meat

1 pound of stew meat cup up
  into small chunks
1/3 cup soy sauce
1 cup of Italian dressing
1 cup Teriyaki sauce

1/2 can of beer
1 teaspoon of Tabasco sauce
1 tablespoon of garlic, crushed
  (or garlic powder)
1 teaspoon pepper or to taste

Combine all ingredients together and marinate meat overnight. Put meat in frying pan and saute on medium heat until browned. Drain and serve.

Ed Thompson
Windsor Locks, CT

New Meat Loaf Pie

2 pounds ground venison
1/2 cups packaged, dry season
  bread crumbs
1 cup fresh mushrooms,
  chopped
1 large onion, chopped

2 carrots, shredded
1 large egg, lightly beaten
1 tablespoon prepared mustard
Ground pepper

In a large bowl, combine all ingredients; mix well. Pat mixture into a deep 9" pie plate. Bake in a preheated 350 degree oven for 30 minutes. Removed from oven, let pie set five minutes before slicing. Makes 6 services.

Wild Rice and Venison

2 pounds ground venison
1-1/2 cups cooked wild rice
1 can cream of mushroom soup
1 can chicken soup
1 cup sliced celery

1 cup sliced mushrooms
1 cup water
1 chopped onion
3 teaspoons soy sauce

Brown venison in skillet. Add rest of ingredients and mix well. Pour into 2 quart casserole dish, cover and bake in 350 degree oven for 30 minutes. Uncover and bake for 30 more minutes.

Microwave Venison Stroganoff

2 pounds venison round steak, cut into strips 2-inches long

1/2 pound mushrooms, sliced

1/2 cup butter

1 large onion, chopped

2 large cans cream of mushroom soup

8 ounces sour cream

Noodles or rice

Microwave 1/4 cup butter in small saucepan for 1 minute until melted. Add onions and mushrooms (do not mix); microwave on high for 3 minutes. Set aside.

Microwave another 1/4 cup butter in large saucepan or casserole dish until melted. Add meat and heat thoroughly. Cover. Microwave on high for 9 minutes, stirring thoroughly every 3 minutes. Stir in onions and cream of mushroom soup. Microwave on 50 percent (simmer) for 12 to 15 minutes. Meat should still be pink.

Stir in mushrooms and sour cream. Microwave on high for 3 to 4 minutes. Serve over noodles or rice. Serves 8 to 10.

Venison Stroganoff

1-1/2 pounds round steak, cut 3/4-inch thick

Flour seasoned with salt and pepper

3 tablespoons butter

2 onions, chopped

1/4 teaspoon basil

1/4 teaspoon thyme

Salt and pepper

1-1/2 cup beef bouillon

1 cup sliced mushrooms

1 tablespoon butter

2 tablespoons flour

1-1/2 teaspoons prepared mustard

1 cup sour cream

Cut the meat into strips 1-1/2 inches long. Roll the meat in the seasoned flour. Brown the meat in the 3 tablespoons of butter in a skillet. Transfer the browned meat into a casserole. Place the onion, thyme, basil, salt and pepper in the skillet with the bouillon and heat the mixture until it boils. Scrape the skillet bottom to loosen any meat particles, then pour the mixture until it boils. Cover the casserole and bake in a 350 degree oven for 1 hour, turning once during that period.

In a skillet, fry the mushrooms over medium heat in the 2 tablespoons of butter for 5 minutes. Stir in the 2 tablespoons of flour, then add liquid from the casserole (add a little water if most of the liquid has cooked away). Stir constantly until the mixture thickens. Add the mustard and sour cream and bring to the boiling point. Pour atop meat and serve over cooked rice. Serves 4.

TNT Pepper Steak over Noodles

2 pounds cubed venison	6 diced cayenne peppers
2 cups barbecue sauce	6 diced jalapeno peppers
1 cup of honey	1 large onion (diced)
1 teaspoon garlic powder	1 small can mushrooms (sliced)
1 tablespoon butter or shortening	3 to 4 cups egg noodles

Cut 2 pounds of venison into 1-inch cubes. Brown in 10-to 12-inch skillet with butter or shortening. Add mushrooms, diced onion and garlic powder to venison in skillet. Mix barbecue sauce, honey, cayenne and jalapeno peppers in a large bowl. Mix well. Pour sauce mix in skillet and cook until meat is thoroughly cooked, stirring occasionally.

Boil about 6 cups of water in a large pot. Add noodles and cook as directed on package. Drain noodles. Serve Pepper Steak over noodles.

Lonny R. Robertson
McDonald, PA

Venison Parmesan

2 15-ounce cans tomato sauce
2 tablespoons butter
1 tablespoon Worcestershire
  sauce
2 tablespoons brown sugar
1/2 teaspoon white pepper
1 teaspoon season all

2 eggs
1/2 teaspoon season all
1 teaspoon dried whole
  oregano
1 teaspoon dried whole basil
1/2 teaspoon garlic powder
1/2 teaspoon white pepper

2 pounds venison
(cube steak cut or flank,
  pounded) cut into serving
  size pieces
1/4 cup freshly grated
  Parmesan cheese

4 cups Italian style bread
  crumbs
1/2 cup olive oil
1 8-ounce package Mozzarella
  cheese

To make sauce combine the first 9 ingredients in saucepan over
medium heat for 5 to 10 minutes, stirring occasionally - set aside.
  Beat eggs and add 1 teaspoon season all, 1/2 teaspoon white
pepper, dredge venison in bread crumbs. Saute venison in the olive
oil 4 to 5 minutes (until brown). Place venison in lightly greased
baking dish - pour sauce over and sprinkle with Parmesan cheese.
Bake for 30 minutes covered. Uncover and top with the Mozzarella
cheese slices, bake an additional 5-10 minutes until cheese melts.
  Bake 350 degree oven. Serves 4 to 6.

Janeann Dailey
Duluth, GA

Venison Spanish Rice

1 pound ground venison
2 large onions, chopped
2 large green bell peppers,
  chopped

1 32-ounce jar spaghetti sauce
3 bags boil-in-bag rice, cooked
4 tablespoons butter

Saute venison, onions, peppers in large Dutch oven. Add cooked rice and spaghetti sauce, mix well. Pour into 10x10x2 casserole dish. Dot top with butter. Bake, uncovered in a 350 degree oven for 45 minutes. If you prefer it a little moister, add another 1/2 jar of spaghetti sauce or an 8-ounce can of tomato sauce.

H.F. Coleman
Norwich, NY

Venison Stroganoff

2 pounds venison round steak	Salt & pepper
3 tablespoons flour	1 can cream of mushroom soup
1 large onion, sliced	1 cup sour cream

Cut steak into thin strips. Dip in the flour and brown in small amount of fat. Add onions, salt, pepper, and soup, cook on low till tender. Add sour cream and heat. Serve over noodles.

Wanda Woosley
Madison, TN

Venison Goulash

2 pounds venison, cut into 1-inch cubes	1 tablespoon dark brown sugar
1/4 cup shortening	2 teaspoons salt
1 cup onions, sliced	2 teaspoons paprika
1 garlic clove, minced	1/2 teaspoon dry mustard
3/4 cup ketchup	1-1/2 cups water
2 tablespoons soy sauce	For thickening: 1/4 cup water, 2 tablespoons flour

Melt shortening. Add meat, onion and garlic. Brown until onion is tender. Stir in remaining ingredients. Cover and simmer for 2-1/2 to 3 hours.

Blend 1/4 cup water and 2 tablespoons flour; stir gradually into meat mixture. Heat to boiling, stirring constantly. Boil and stir 1 minute or until thickened. Serve over hot rice or noodles. Serves 4-5.

Barbara J. Stang
St. Michaels, MD

Baked Venison Spaghetti

3 pounds of ground venison   7 slices of Velveeta cheese
1-3/4 pounds spaghetti noodles   1 dash of salt
6-1/2 cups tomato sauce   1 dash of pepper
5 slices of American cheese

Brown your ground venison in a skillet and break it up into small pieces using medium heat. Since most ground venison is mixed with fat, drain the grease off after browning. On low heat, add tomato, sauce, salt and pepper and mix with ground meat. Cover and let simmer.

Boil noodles until soft. Drain noodles and rinse in cold water for five minutes and drain again.

Break American cheese slices into small pieces and add to the simmering meat and sauce. Cook for 15 minutes on low heat and stir occasionally.

Put noodles in large buttered stainless bowl. Pour in meat and sauce and blend thoroughly.

Preheat oven to 350 degrees. Top with seven slices of Velveeta cheese and bake for one hour. Serve with French bread. Serves 6 to 8.

Vikki Trout
Boonville, IN

*D*eer Browse

Anyone who spends much time in the woods knows deer are unpredictable. Whether it's their behavior, travel patterns or physical traits, no two deer are exactly alike. As soon as you create labels such as "typical behavior" or "normal pattern," the next deer that comes along will shatter your notions.

Years ago, the editors of *Deer & Deer Hunting* decided the magazine needed a special section devoted to short articles that discuss unusual occurrences. The unique stories contained in "Deer Browse" come from all corners of the United States. Sometimes they're about the deer themselves, and other times they're about newsworthy local events that involve deer. The response to this special section has been phenomenal. Readers stuff the *Deer & Deer Hunting* mailbox with letters, newspaper clips, unique photographs and personal observations that are entertaining and informative. Many of these end up as items in "Deer Browse."

We hope you will enjoy the selections that follow.

New Colorado Record Non-typical

It appears the versatile whitetail, comfortable from steamy Southern swamps to frigid Canadian prairies, also wears a cowboy hat.

In November 1992, a hunter shot a state-record Colorado whitetail that was packing 258-2/8 Boone & Crockett inches of non-typical antlers on his head. Besides being Colorado's record, the rack ranks about 13th in the world.

This is all the more remarkable when considering the deer was taken in mule deer and pronghorn antelope habitat, which contained no whitetails less than 40 years ago. The "Eastern woodland" deer gained a hoof-hold in Colorado when ranchers and farmers began controlling range fires and planting crops like milo, sorghum and wheat. Trees began to survive around homesteads, creeks and rivers. As wooded habitat grew along the Republican, Platte and Arkansas rivers, whitetails migrated up those valleys from Nebraska and Kansas. Then they spread cross-country to isolated woods and crop fields, places where no one thought to look for them.

Thus protected, sometimes even completely undiscovered, the deer thrived and grew old. With plenty of protein-rich grains to eat, bucks maximized antler growth. And now the whitetail's aficionados have discovered them.

Mike Okray

Mike Okray shot this record buck in Colorado in October 1992. The deer's antlers scored 258-2/8 on the Boone & Crockett scale. The deer is Colorado's No. 1 non-typical buck.

One of the first men to capitalize on Colorado's big whitetails was Greg Pink of Beaver Canyon Outfitters. After bow hunting a few eastern Colorado ranches, he leased the hunting rights and began guiding six to eight trophy hunters a year. They enjoyed about a 50 percent success on bucks in the 140 to 160 class, but none ever tagged one of the Boone & Crockett bucks Pink saw during the bow seasons.

Then Mike Okray of Stevens Point, Wis., hunted with Pink in late October 1992. Temperatures hit 85 during the sunny afternoons and dropped only to 50 at night. Bucks were moving at night from dense thickets along the river to irrigated corn fields to feed.

Because Okray could only hunt four days instead of the usual six, he was especially worried. Nevertheless, one evening he passed up a 10-pointer that might have scored 160 or better.

On the morning Okray was due to fly out, Pink took him to an area they hadn't yet hunted. It was a rutting grounds where Pink had seen a huge non-typical the previous two seasons, but only in late November.

At the crack of dawn, Pink placed Okray on stand overlooking a field. Then he circled wide with the idea of driving the tall cover toward his hunter. Before Pink could make the circle, he spotted the big non-typical standing in the field.

It took Okray some time to detect the buck through the heavy cover, but, at his second shot, it went down.

The buck weighed over 300 pounds and its unusual antlers feature six drop tines, 6-4/8 inch circumference bases, and a total of 29 points. As the 13th largest nontypical whitetail ever recorded, Okray's buck proves emphatically that Colorado cowboy country is now white-tailed deer country, too.

— *Ron Spomer*

■ Sportsmanship Pays

Too often, the only hunting stories that make news are about poachers, accidents and unsafe hunters. We seldom hear much about the vast majority of men and women who hunt, those who are safe, considerate and believe in sportsmanship.

For a change of pace there's. the unusual story that came out of northern Minnesota during the 1991 deer season. While sitting on his favorite stand on opening day, Glen Bergland, of Warroad, Minn., heard several distant shots and then several more close by. Suddenly a nice-sized buck bounded out of the woods and onto Bergland's land. Bergland dropped it with one shot at about 50 yards.

As he climbed out of his tree stand, Bergland saw a hunter had been following the buck's trail. The stranger approached and asked Bergland if he'd killed the buck. Bergland confirmed that he had. "Darn," the stranger said.

As they examined the 10-point buck, the other hunter introduced himself as Loren Olson, and said he owned land nearby. Olson had wounded the buck and had been following it for some time.

As Bergland told a newspaper later, "I'm not sure what the protocol is in such situations. I've heard many hunters claim that the deer belongs to the person making the killing shot. But I've always taken the opposite approach."

Bergland soon told Olson, "Sure is a nice deer you got here." Olson appreciated Bergland's sportsmanlike approach to the situation and, as the two men dragged the buck out, he told Bergland, "Maybe someday I can return the favor." Although Bergland admitted that he thought that was indeed a nice thought, he didn't think it would happen any time soon.

However, later in the afternoon that day, Bergland got a chance at another buck. He missed on the first shot, but thought the second shot had hit. Further examination showed he had wounded the deer. As Bergland trailed the deer, he suddenly realized he was now on Olson's land. In a while he met Olson, who was still afield, hoping to help other members of his party fill their tags, which is legal in Minnesota. Olson told him he had not seen the buck, but knew where it was probably going.

Bergland stayed on the trail while Olson circled ahead. In a little while Bergland heard a rifle shot. "I struggled to the edge of the woods," he said, "and there was Loren Olson, proudly pointing to the buck he'd gotten for me!"

— *Tom R. Kovach*

that the buck suffered a head injury early in his life. As you can see in the photograph the antler bases, or pedicels, are tipped to the side. Biologists who studied the photograph said the buck probably suffered a serious skull injury while growing the antlers. Another theory was that the buck suffered a blow to his head at birth or shortly after when the skull is still soft and flexible.

At this stage, everyone who has seen the buck agrees on at least one point: The actual cause of the deformation is anyone's best guess.

— *Patrick Durkin*
Editor

■ Cow-Horned Deer

Wayne E. Thomas

A Pennsylvania bow hunter killed this "cow-horned" buck in 1992. Although it's not certain how the buck's antlers came to grow at these angles, it was likely the result of an injury.

A Pennsylvania bow hunter killed the "cow-horned" buck in the accompanying photograph during 1992.

Although it's not certain how the buck's antlers came to grow at these angles, one possibility is

■ Bow Hunter Bags Unique Trophy

Bow hunter Ken Stewart bagged a tremendous, yet unusual, whitetail during Wisconsin's late archery season in 1992. The Bloomer, Wis., man was hunting near his home in Chippewa County when he shot the trophy.

Stewart originally saw the big buck on the last day of early archery season in mid-November. Although he and members of his family hunted that area hard during the nine-day firearms season, they never saw the deer.

Stewart returned and hunted the area periodically throughout the first week of the December archery season. Late on the afternoon of Dec. 14, Stewart saw a deer moving his way. He knew it was a buck, but because of the underbrush, Stewart couldn't see its rack clearly.

Eventually, the deer walked through a small opening at 15 yards and Stewart released an arrow. The buck died after going 50 yards. Upon recovering the buck, Stewart noticed the rack's right side was severely stunted and deformed. Closer inspection showed the deer had suffered a broken left hind leg at least a year earlier. Other than a large calcium deposit on the knee-joint, the leg seemed to have healed well. Still, the injury caused the rack's right side to "stub-out."

The deformed right antler grew normally until just past the brow tine. At this point, the main beam curves back and slightly downward. The total length of the main beam is about 16 inches. The deformed antler carries four points, with two others broken off.

Measurements from the left antler indicate that, had normal growth occurred, the rack would have been a candidate for the Boone & Crockett record book. Its inside spread, for example, would have been close to 24 inches. Stewart is confident this buck was the same big deer he had seen in November.

— *Greg Miller*

■ Bow Hunter Kills Unusual Buck

When southern Indiana bow hunter Mark Williams released an arrow at a small buck a few yards from his tree stand, he assumed it carried an almost ordinary rack. The right antler looked normal, and the left antler appeared to be only slightly out of place. However, after tracking the wounded deer a short distance, Williams discovered its unusual head gear.

The right antler, which carried a fork, was positioned properly and attached securely to the skull. But the 3-point left antler was loose and protruded toward the deer's nose. As Williams inspected the antler's base, he found a hole in the buck's skull.

"I could see a hole about the size of a nickel," Williams said. "There was a scab covering the hole, but when you looked down inside it, you could see it was all the way through."

Williams also found a 1-inch portion of skull bone was at the base of the loose antler. Williams said it probably would have fallen off soon after.

Williams believes the deer suffered a severe blow, or fell very hard on its head. Either that or it clashed with an aggressive sparring partner. The 5-pointer appeared healthy and acted normally, but its estimated field-dressed weight was only 80 to 85 pounds. That's far less than most 1.5-year-old Hoosier bucks.

— *John Trout*

■ Deer Sale Results in Fines

Deer farm operators near Chippewa Falls, Wis., and Foley, Mo., pleaded guilty to federal Lacy Act charges of illegally transporting 30 deer.

The Lacy Act forbids unauthorized transportation of animals across state lines. Missouri law requires that imported animals have a health certificate and be tested for disease, particularly tuberculosis.

The charges were filed after a Wisconsin conservation warden and a United States Fish & Wildlife Service special agent examined the records of O'Neil Creek Campground and Deer Farm, operated by Irene and Albert Prybylsi of Chippewa Falls.

The DNR charged that white-tailed, fallow and Sika deer were illegally shipped from Wisconsin without proper records to Jeff Mennemeier, Foley, Mo.

The operators of the Chippewa County deer farm also pleaded guilty to two Wisconsin charges of records violations in Chippewa County Circuit Court, and paid penalties of $456 under plea agreements. Under the agreement, they also paid $1,650 for Lacy Act violations.

In Missouri, Mennemeier was charged by F&WS special agents in St. Louis, and paid $500 in penalties under a plea agreement.

The deer are under quarantine in Missouri. None of the animals had been tested for tuberculosis.

■ Buck Survives Fall into Canal

An 8-point Canadian buck struggled for 40 minutes against powerful currents before escaping a canal that leads to the Ontario Hydro turbines off the Niagara Gorge.

The deer had tumbled off a cliff into the intake canal not far from Devil's Hole, and was carried toward water turbines, which generate electricity at Ontario Hydro's Martin Beck plant.

"The odds of anything surviving that current are phenomenal," said Joseph Mombrea, a public relations photographer with the New York Power Authority. "The current in the canal is stronger than in the gorge. People from Ontario Hydro were trying to scare him away from the gates that cover the mouth of the turbine. If anything gets beyond the gates, they go into this huge rotor blade that's like a huge meat grinder."

As much as the buck tried to fight upstream, the current forced him back into the gates two or three times, Mombrea said. After crashing into the gate a final time, the buck managed to wrestle himself away and swim about 50 yards to the canal wall.

— *Anthony Cardinale*
Buffalo Evening News, N.Y

■ Bear Pulls Young Archer From Tree

An Altoona, Wis., youth was pulled from his tree stand in September 1992 by a black bear and chased more than 100 yards while bow hunting in northwestern Wisconsin.

Joshua "Bucky" Gore, 14, was about 18 feet up when he first saw the bear.

"It was just about dark, and here comes a big bear. I kind of waved my hands and tried to scare her away without making any noise," Gore said. "She just kind of growled and walked away and laid down."

Soon four cubs came by. About 30 minutes later one of them began climbing the boy's tree. Gore, a freshman at Altoona High School, said his stand was surrounded by several trunks that sprang from the same base. All of the cubs were now climbing up the trunks.

When one cub reached Gore's stand, he kicked it, causing it to fall from the tree. The sow, apparently angered, then came up the tree.

"I kicked her a few times, and she got a hold of my foot," Gore said. "She basically threw me right out of the tree with her mouth."

"I landed on both my feet. I looked to my right and the mother bear was coming at me. She came down the tree so fast it was unbelievable. I started running and the bear chased me."

Gore thinks the sow could have easily caught him if she had wanted.

Gore was treated for a gash to the foot. He limped a couple days but was soon walking normally.

→ Joe Knight
Eau Claire Leader-Telegram

■ Hunter Bags Two Back-Yard Bucks

Tim DeVought of rural Marquette, Mich., never made it to deer camp on the second day of the gun season in 1992. On the morning of Nov. 16, he was distracted by a pair of bucks fighting in a field next to the home he rents.

As he prepared for a day at his deer camp, he spotted the two deer in a large field adjacent to his home. When DeVought emerged from the house with his scoped rifle, he heard clashing antlers. A look through the scope confirmed the deer were a pair of fighting bucks.

DeVought waited until it was light enough to make a good shot, and then aimed carefully with his .222-caliber rifle. The bucks were 250 yards away, and the 4-pointer dropped instantly when DeVought fired. The remaining buck, a 6-pointer, stood over the dead buck, allowing DeVought to take a second shot. It then ran off.

"I think the 6-pointer thought it won the fight because it didn't go far," DeVought said. He followed the 6-pointer's tracks to determine if he had hit it. He spotted the buck ahead in the brush, enabling him to take a second shot. A careful search indicated both shots had missed.

DeVought then returned to look for the 4-pointer's body. Because of high grass in the field, the buck was hard to locate. DeVought then climbed a hill at the field's edge for a better view. While doing so, he spotted the 6-pointer again. His third shot brought it down.

The lucky hunter filled both of his buck tags within view of his house. He said those were the first bucks he had seen in the area.

— *Richard Smith*

■ Pennsylvania Bow Season Extended

The Pennsylvania bow deer season has been extended by two weeks for the fall of 1993, giving participants their first opportunity to hunt whitetails during the rut.

The season will open Oct. 2 and run through Nov. 13, according to Joe Maddock, president of the United Bowhunters of Pennsylvania.

Maddock said bow season normally opens on the first Saturday in October and ends the last Saturday of the month. Gun season doesn't begin until late November or early December, so there has been no deer hunting at all in the state during the rut, until now.

"Hunters in other states take hunting during the rut for granted," Maddock said. 'This will be our first chance to be hunting when bucks are most active.'

"Bow season was extended by a week last year, on an experimental basis for bucks only, and it went well. There wasn't a significant increase in the buck kill like opponents of the extension claimed. Bow hunters simply don't have a high rate of success regardless of when they hunt. Deer of either sex will be legal during this year's extension."

Rock star Ted Nugent was one of the bow hunters who spoke on behalf of extending the archery season during the April 6 Game Commission meeting, at which time the extension was approved.

"Ted was a big part of our game plan," Maddock said. "Getting the season extension was a total team effort and he was a part of the team."

— *Richard P. Smith*

■ Exchange Student Bags Buck

Included among the mementos Miho Isono of Japan hopes to bring home this summer is a head mount of a 9-point buck she bagged in Michigan's Upper Peninsula last fall.

Isono, 17, an exchange student from Narashino, was staying with the James Wetton family of Negaunee, Mich. Deer hunting was one of the high points of her stay with the Wettons. She lived with them while enrolled in the senior class of the local high school.

"In Japan we're not allowed to have a gun," Isono said, "so when I came here I had never shot a gun before. I was interested in hunting and shooting a gun."

Richard P. Smith

Japanese exchange student Miho Isono 17, killed this buck last fall in Michigan's Upper Peninsula.

The first rifle she shot was a .22-caliber rimfire. After becoming proficient, she fired a round from a .30-06 to prepare for the gun season. The bullet hit close to the bullseye. She later switched to a 7mm Remington Express, or .280 Remington.

On the third day of the season, a big buck appeared during the morning about 150 yards away. The deer ran when Isono shot, but it didn't go far before falling.

The purpose of the Youth For Understanding International Exchange is for youngsters to "experience life as we live it," and those staying with the Wettons certainly have done that.

— *Richard P. Smith*

■ Maned Deer: How Common Are They?

Deer & Deer Hunting magazine published a short article of mine in August 1984 about deer with manes. Soon after, I received 15 letters or reports from hunters who have shot or observed maned deer.

I put together a map showing where the deer were shot or seen. It's obvious that maned deer are not confined to one region. Nor are manes specific to one age or sex of deer. Manes occur on fawns and does as well as bucks. The manes come in different lengths, colors and textures.

Now that we know this type of abnormal hair growth is not a freak occurrence in one or two deer, the question remains, "What causes manes?" Before all the reports came in, I thought these thick, bristle-like hair growths may have resulted from an injury to the deer. Deer are known to go under, rather than over, barbedwire fences. Therefore, it's possible that a discolored hair growth could grow over scar tissue on the back of the neck.

But the chances of this type of accident and subsequent healing process were too slim to account for so many manes. A little time in the library proved manes are not a new phenomenon. In an article in the February 1963 issue of the Journal of Mammalogy, researcher L.A. Ryel reports two deer with short manes. One was a yearling buck taken during the 1953 hunting season in Michigan's Cheboygan County. The other was a 4.5-year-old buck killed on Drummond Island in November 1960.

Manes on white-tailed deer are likely the result of genetic anomalies, much like those that cause albino deer.

We must conclude that manes are simply anomalies, meaning a deviation from the natural order. The late Terry Amundson, a Wisconsin wildlife disease specialist,

believed deer manes are likely a genetic anomaly similar to albinism or melanism in the case of hair-coat color. In other words, as Amundson put it, "Deer manes are probably caused by a recessive gene being expressed in a certain (very small) percentage of the population."

These recessive genes would be genetic "leftovers" from some long-ago ancestor of the whitetailed deer that was normally maned. They exist in the gene pool of a deer population, much like the recessive gene(s) for albinism exist in a fraction of the population. They only surface when paired with the same recessive gene(s) from another deer of the same genetic makeup.

Hunters will continue to observe or shoot maned deer in very small numbers. The manes should remind us of the long process of evolution that has led to today's whitetail.

— William E. Ishmael
Wisconsin Department of
Natural Resources

■ Being in the Right Spot Pays Off

During a hunt in Michigan, Indiana archer Kevin Witbart learned that it pays to be in the right spot, even if it's many hours after the hunt ends.

While bow hunting near Vestaburg, Mich., Witbart made a liver shot on a medium-sized buck. He and his hunting partner, Tom Stamper, decided to wait before trailing the deer, and so they drove into town to eat supper. As they ate, a pouring rain moved in. Realizing they would now be unable to find any blood, they waited until morning to look for the buck.

After searching for 30 minutes the next day, Witbart heard Stamper exclaim, "Oh no!" At Stamper's feet was a gut pile with an arrow hole through the liver.

The bow hunters returned to town to eat breakfast, still wearing their camouflage clothes. One of the diners asked if they had been bow hunting and whether they had any luck. Before long they had told him their story. A little while later the diner's friend asked how many points the buck had. "He was a 7- or 8-pointer," Witbart said.

"I'll tell you what he was," the man said. "He was a 7-pointer and he's hanging in my garage. Do you want to see him?"

As it turns out, the two locals were raccoon hunters, and their dogs had found the buck the night before. The men figured whoever shot the buck had probably given up the trail. They didn't want the buck to spoil, so they dressed it out and took it home.

The chance meeting ended up making four hunters very happy, and they went on to become good friends.

— *Kevin Witbart*

■ Deer/Car Crash Kills Man

An Illinois man died in November 1991 after his car struck a deer near Thorntown, Ind.

James Payne Jr., 62, of Bridgeview died on Interstate 65 about two miles north of Indiana Highway 47. The deer crashed through the windshield, causing head and chest injuries to Payne.

The deer also was killed.

— *Indianapolis Star*
Nov. 11, 1991

■ Two Plead Guilty To Killing 20-Point Buck

Two Wisconsin men were fined $1,950 each in Iowa County Circuit Court in January 1992 for illegally shining and shooting a 20-point buck and removing its antlers.

Leroy Parmer Sr., 42, and John (Randy) Pitman, 33, both from Arena, pleaded guilty and no contest, respectively. The two men also had their hunting, fishing and trapping privileges revoked for three years.

A third man, Ricky R. Roll, 33, Arena, was cited for being party to the crime of shining deer after 10 p.m. He faces a $111 fine.

Informants helped Wisconsin conservation wardens make the arrests. The men shot the buck in late October 1991. The deer's antlers were cut off, and its carcass was left to rot. A search of Parmer's home turned up the antlers. The carcass was found lying off Blue Ridge Road.

— *Wisconsin Department of Natural Resources*

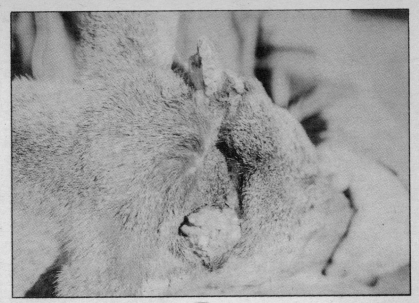
This buck apparently lost both of his antlers to the same bullet.

■ Buck's Antlers Shot Off

While hunting in 1974, I saw a deer that appeared to be a doe. When it got to within 10 yards of me, I realized it was a buck and shot. Upon examination, I found that both antlers had been broken off at the base, and a healing scar devoid of all hair - ran from one pedicle to the other atop the deer's skull.

I believe the antlers were both shot off by the same bullet. Nothing else could explain the physical evidence. The odds of this happening must be astronomical, considering that the two antlers had to be in perfect alignment with the rifle, both vertically and horizontally. In addition, the slug could not have ricocheted after it hit the hard, rounded surface of the first antler. Not only that, but the deer had to survive a heavy blow to the cranial area. Perhaps it was momentarily knocked unconscious, but it's amazing it didn't die from the concussion.

I suspect the unlucky hunter had the shock of his life when both antlers flew into the air. Additionally, he had an amazing but unbelievable story to tell when he returned to camp.

— *Dinny Slaughter*

■ Deer Suffers Possible Snakebite

Paul Bone of Sebree, Ky., has raised deer for several years with no problems. However, Bone suspects a copperhead snake bit one of his deer, a 2.5-year-old buck that carries a 9-point rack.

In September 1991, Bone went out to feed his deer and noticed the buck lying down. As Bone approached, he saw a swollen mass on the deer's chin. Bone concluded the buck was bitten by a copperhead, probably while feeding or when it attempted to smell the snake out of curiosity. Bone had seen several copperheads around the 2-acre pen in the past.

The buck didn't have much energy in the days that followed, and it had problems eating and drinking. After a week, the swelling began to subside and the buck showed signs of a partial recovery. Unlike smaller bucks in the pen, the injured deer refused to rub his antlers as the rut approached. Nor did he chase does when the rut began to peak. The buck still carried a few strands of shredded velvet on his antlers by late November. Several weeks after the peak of the rut, the buck began to act aggressive toward the does.

— *John Trout Jr.*

■ Sometimes Wishes Come True

After arriving at his Alabama deer camp in November 1990,

Bob Rutherford of Muscle Shoals read a newspaper article about a Macon hunter who had killed a 10-point doe.

Alabama's Bob Rutherford with his 8-point doe.

Rutherford told his friends that he had always wanted to get a doe with antlers, but he realized his chances were slim because the creatures are rare. In fact, few hunters ever see such an oddity.

On the fourth day of the hunt, Nov. 20, Rutherford decided to watch a greenfield in the evening. After sitting a couple hours, he saw a 'buck' in velvet leap a fence and begin eating in the field. Rutherford fired when the deer gave him a broadside shot. He didn't realize he had a unique trophy until a friend began to help him clean the deer.

The friend said, "Bob, he ain't no he. You better look at your deer." A conservation warden later looked at the 138-pound doe, and aged her at 2.5 years old.

— *Patrick Durkin*
Editor

■ Tough Choice for Bow Hunter

Most archers dream of getting a chance at a Pope and Young buck. Others hope to some day take a rare white buck.

Dean Stallion, an avid bow hunter and taxidermist from Newburgh, Ind., had one of each approach his tree stand at the same time during the fourth week of Indiana's season. He had set up the stand on a line of several large rubs a short distance from a corn field. Just before dark he spotted a huge 8-pointer approaching.

At the same moment, Stallion heard another deer from the opposite direction. Although he tried to ignore it while waiting for an opening to shoot the big buck, he finally gave in and sneaked a peak. Standing only a few yards away was a white buck that carried about a 6-point rack.

Stallion admits the decision was tough, but he finally tried for the bigger buck. The light of day was nearly gone when Stal-

lion drew his bow. Unfortunately, his shot deflected off a branch and into the ground. The big buck ran off, snorting all the way. The white buck ran the opposite direction.

All Stallion could do was climb down to retrieve his broken arrow.

— *John Trout Jr.*

■ Wisconsin's Late-Season Monster

Wisconsin archer Greg Miller arrowed the state's largest non-typical buck of 1990 while hunting last December in Eau Claire Co. The buck also ranks as the state's fourth largest non-typical bow-kill of all time.

Wisconsin's late archery season is not the best time for a bow hunter to single out, hunt and arrow a record-book whitetail. But that didn't deter Miller as he stubbornly hunted for the big buck, which lived about a half-hour from his home in Bloomer.

Miller had a couple factors in his favor, however: He was hunting privately owned land, and it had been closed to firearms hunting since 1985. Miller and his brother, Jeff, had been hunting the buck on the farm for more than two years.

Greg Miller

Greg Miller and Wisconsin's fourth largest non-typical bow kill of all time.

"Until the night of December 13th, we had never actually seen the buck," Miller said. "We kept track of him by periodically checking preferred travel routes for huge antler rubs. The stand where I eventually shot him is along the edge of an alfalfa field at the confluence of two rub lines."

The buck walked into Miller's view a little after 4 p.m. on Dec. 13. "Six does had walked into the field about a half-hour earlier," Miller said. "When I heard this seventh deer coming, I thought it was probably another antlerless deer. When I turned my head and saw that big rack heading toward me, I nearly lost my breath."

The buck walked to within 15 yards of Miller's stand before stopping to feed. Unfortunately, the angle was wrong.

"He was directly head-on," Miller said. "There was nothing I could do except wait and hope the buck would give me the shot I wanted before he figured out something was wrong."

Nearly three minutes later, the buck finally turned and gave a broadside target. Miller's Zwickey-tipped arrow took the animal through both lungs. After a 200 yard sprint, the trophy deer was down for good.

The buck's dressed weight was a "skinny" 190 pounds. The 18-point, non-typical rack has an inside spread of 21-1/8 inches and an outside spread of 23-3/8 inches. The bases circumference measurements are 5-3/8 and 6-2/8 inches, while the main beam lengths are 27-6/8 and 26-3/8 inches. The brow tine lengths are 10 and 9-1/8 inches. The rack's gross score is 202-5/8, and the net score is 193-7/8.

■ Whitetails and Chestnuts

As every deer hunter knows, one of the whitetail's most important foods over much of its range is oak mast. Acorns are rich in nutrients and an ideal focal point for hunters. However, a century ago the American chestnut was the whitetail's key foodstuff across much of its range.

From Alabama and Mississippi to Maine and parts of Michigan, the chestnut was the dominant tree in mature hardwood forests. Old chestnut trees consistently provided bushels of tasty, nutritious nuts. Man ate them raw or roasted, and pounded them to make bread or dressing. Deer, squirrels, chipmunks, wild hogs and wild turkeys ate almost nothing else when the nut fall was at its peak.

Then, early in this century, a deadly fungus from Asia doomed this giant of the Eastern forests.

By the mid-1920s the blight had spread widely. By 1950 the American chestnut was, for all practical purposes, no more. A few isolated stands in Michigan, Minnesota and other locales outside the tree's original range escaped. But in hardwood forests, where about 60 percent of all trees had been chestnuts, the monarch had fallen. Chestnut trees, which once reached heights of 60 to 100 feet, now seldom grow past 15 feet because the blight usually girdles them near the base.

While few people remember a time when chestnut trees dominated the landscape, they do know deer love this nut. With that in mind, hunters who plant and manage land for deer will be glad to know there is a glimmer of hope for chestnuts. A resistant variety, the so-called Chinese chestnut, has been grown selectively in backyards and occasionally in woodlots. Its nuts are inferior in taste, and the species does not approach the size or productivity of the American chestnut.

Promising work to restore the tree through breeding and genetic research is being done by the American Chestnut Foundation. Selective breeding that seeks to transfer the blight resistance of the Asiatic species to the American chestnut also continues. In addition, seedlings from a grove in Michigan are shipped elsewhere each year for planting. While a breakthrough has yet to occur, there seems to be hope that science will soon revive this part of the natural world.

Should this occur, whitetails will benefit. Possibly no woodland browse has as much nutrition as chestnuts, and the trees also grow rapidly. If the blight can be overcome, chestnuts can become productive food producers once again.

— *Jim Casada*

◼ One Morning, Two Trophy Bucks

Bow hunter Jim Hunsaker of Hidalgo, Ill., filled his antlerless permit Nov. 14, the day before firearms season opened. Five days later, after the three-day firearms season ended, he was back in his stand, hoping to fill his two buck archery tags.

Just after the sun peeked over the horizon, Hunsaker spotted a good buck walking slowly toward him from a nearby slough. The big buck stopped short of bow range and stood behind a bush.

It then began working a scrape. Hunsaker used the time to get himself calmed down. Suddenly the buck raised his head and stared to the north. He laid back his ears, and the hair on his back began to flair. Hunsaker then spotted another buck of equal size approaching.

The bucks began circling each other aggressively. Finally, the first buck gave Hunsaker a chance for a shot, but Hunsaker's arrow hit the buck farther back than he had aimed. Surprisingly, the buck merely walked a few steps and began making another scrape. Hunsaker wasted no time in nocking another arrow. His second shot passed through the chest. The buck made a small loop and piled up 15 yards from Hunsaker's stand.

The other buck walked toward the downed buck with his ears laid back, still showing aggression. When the deer passed through an opening, Hunsaker drew and shot it through the lungs. The deer ran about 35 yards and stopped. It then started to slowly walk back to the buck on the ground. After a few yards, the buck began weaving and then dropped.

Hunsaker said the incident lasted no more than two minutes. The first buck was an 8-pointer with an inside spread of 17-7/8 inches. Its Pope & Young green score was 134-6/8 points. The other buck, also an 8-pointer, grossed 127 points but broken points reduced the score to 120. Both deer had a field-dressed weight of 200 pounds.

— *John Trout Jr.*

■ Top Hoosier Buck

On opening day of the 1990 firearms deer season, Shawn Sears had no idea the foggy, cool morning would produce a life-long memory that would also make the record books.

Shawn Sears and his 28-point buck from Indiana.

Sears hunts a logged-out woods that has a good undergrowth of briars and rose bushes. At about 8 a.m., he heard a noise in some brush to his right. A doe was coming toward him, and a large buck was following a short distance behind.

Sears sat tight, trying hard to control his tension and shaking. At 10 yards, the doe stopped in front of his tree stand, with the buck just behind her. Sears aimed his father's 12-gauge shotgun just below the buck's chin and fired. The buck crashed to the ground.

The non-typical rack later scored 248-4/8, which gave Sears a tie for second place in the Indiana record book. The deer was No. 3 in the Boone and Crockett non-typical records in 1990. The rack had 28 points, it measured 20-1/8 inches from tip to tip and 23-5/8 inches between the beams.

— *Ted Rose*

■ Poachers Nabbed

Two men from Fort Pierce, Fla., Murl Williams and Charles Norvell, were charged with illegal hunting after an overnight stakeout at Cades Cove, Tenn., on Jan. 9, 1991.

Cades Cove is on the Tennessee side of the Great Smoky Mountains National Park, which straddles the Tennessee-North Carolina line. The park is a favorite site for photographers and naturalists because of its abundant wildlife.

According to authorities, the two Florida men used an unregistered, silencer-equipped rifle to kill two huge bucks, one an 11-pointer and the other a 12-pointer. One park ranger said the deer were shot "for the sole purpose of possessing their trophy-sized racks."

A federal magistrate sentenced the men to two months in jail, 200 hours of community service, and four years of probation. In addition, Williams paid a $500 fine, $1,000 in restitution costs to the Park Service, and forfeited his 1985 Ford Bronco and hunting equipment valued at $500. Norvell paid a $1,500 fine and $1,000 for restitution.

The men still may face felony charges for using the illegal silencer on the rifle. They have filed an appeal in U.S. District Court.

Park officials in the Smokies say they have been plagued by poaching, and hope the convictions and penalties will deter poachers. This would be a major breakthrough. In the Smokies and other national parks, poaching-related incidents have increased the past three years.

— *Jim Casada*

■ Pet Deer Gores Woman

Buck, a family's pet deer since he was a fawn, never caused any trouble, so Janice Sullivan had no reason to fear the animal when she went into her back yard in Jemison, Ala.

But Buck turned on her, goring and seriously injuring her.

A friend had found Buck 'abandoned' in the woods five years ago and gave him to Janice Sullivan and her husband, Terry. Mrs. Sullivan raised him on a bottle.

Buck followed them and their daughters like a puppy.

Terry Sullivan said the family always kept an eye on Buck during the mating season, but the deer had never been a problem.

"I've been in that pen with him nearly every day and he's never been rough in the five years we've had him," he said.

But then Buck escaped from his pen, which had never happened before. The Sullivans left the gate open in case he returned during the night.

"I got up that morning and went to work," Sullivan said. "While our four daughters were getting ready for school, my wife walked down to see if he had come back. He was standing in the back yard. She said, "Come on Buck, and started toward the pen. She said he just went crazy and attacked her. He gored her in the abdomen and shook her like a rag doll. She was skinned and scraped from her head to her feet."

One of the daughters, Amy, 15, went on the back porch to call Mrs. Sullivan, heard her mother crying for help and found her in the yard.

"She lost a lot of blood and nearly bled to death," Sullivan said. "Her kidneys had quit functioning and he punctured her colon. It was just touch-and-go for I don't know how many hours."

After the attack, Sullivan tracked down Buck and killed him.

"I hated to do it, but I just couldn't take a chance on somebody else getting hurt," he said.

Alabama conservation officials say the goring of Mrs. Sullivan by the pet deer illustrates the danger of trying to make pets out of wild animals.

"They're wild animals, and they never completely lose that," said Keith Guyse, assistant chief of Alabama Department of Conservation's wildlife section.

Enforcement officer Bill Fuller said the department probably receives 75 inquiries a year about keeping wild animals as pets.

"We try to tell everybody to take it back where you got it. It's a lot better for it to be raised in the wild," Guyse said.

— Rollin Moseley

■ Handgun Hunter Kills Record Buck

Bill E. Smith shot a record-breaking 18-point non-typical buck with his handgun during the 1991 firearms season in Michigan.

The buck's antlers scored 210-2/8, setting a Michigan record for nontypical handgun kills. The buck's teeth were worn to the gum line, so biologists estimate he was at least 10 years old, and that likely wouldn't have survived the winter if Smith hadn't shot him.

Another unusual thing about the buck was that it had lost one eye, apparently in a fight with another buck. A taxidermist who mounted the buck, Skip Van-Buren of Marquette, speculates that the eye was probably punctured by another buck's antler tine.

The 18-point non-typical must have been in a fierce battle with another buck before it was shot. Van Buren said that when he skinned the buck he found puncture marks from tines in the hide, and the buck's ribs on both sides were badly bruised.

Strangely enough, this was just one of three bucks Van Buren mounted in 1991 that had lost eyes. He said it appeared all three had lost an eye, while fighting with another buck.

In fact, Van Buren said he saw a buck lose an eye in a fight while he was bow hunting last fall. These two bucks had small racks with a similar number of points, but one deer was bigger than the other. Van Buren guessed the smaller buck weighed less than 100 pounds and had at least four points.

At one point, an antler tine from the bigger buck flipped one of the 5 pointer's eyeballs out of its socket, Van Buren said. He said there was no visible bleeding. The tine must have entered the socket in such a way to simply pop the eye out of place.

Three days later, another bow hunter bagged the one-eyed 5-pointer. Van Buren said the archer sneaked up on the buck's blind side while it was feeding. The bow hunter didn't know the whitetail was missing an eye until after he shot it.

— *Richard P. Smith*

■ Deer Jumps Through Car Window

A white-tailed deer jumped into the driver's side window of a Ford Granada near the northwestern Wisconsin town of Ladysmith, injuring the car's two occupants.

Mark R. Stewart, 38, Sheldon, was southbound on County I near Prairie Road shortly before 9 a.m. on May 12, 1992, when a deer came from the east and went through his side window, according to a Rusk County sheriff's deputy report. The deer thrashed around inside the car before escaping. Stewart suffered injuries to his head, chest and arm. His passenger, Brent A. Stewart suffered chest injuries. Neither required an ambulance.

The deer was not located.

— *Ladysmith News*

■ Locked Buck Oddities

Most hunters go their entire lives and never see two bucks locked together by their antlers.

However, within the space of three weeks, I came across two pairs of locked bucks. The first pair was discovered by Tim and Tyler Wischmeier of Brownstown, Ind. They were scouting on Nov. 9, 1991, when they noticed a deer carcass in the woods. Upon closer examination, they were shocked to see two dead 8-point bucks locked together. An area the size of a large living room was torn up, indicating a vicious battle had occurred.

Although the Wischmeiers were surprised to find the bucks, they were even more amazed to see the bucks were locked back to back. This apparently means that in the heat of the battle, one buck flipped the other over its head.

The small buck apparently died

Brad Herndon

Believe it or not, these dead bucks are locked together. The left main beam on the smaller buck had penetrated the larger buck's neck. This, combined with the slight entanglement of their right main beams, held the bucks tight.

first, its broken neck turned almost 180 degrees. The bigger buck apparently lived for some time after. Its carcass was cleaned of meat, but the smaller buck's was virtually untouched. I assume the smaller buck was already rotting when discovered by coyotes, so they ate the fresher meat of the 8-pointer.

I was unable to get a photograph of the Wischmeiers' bucks. However, I was more fortunate with the next pair of locked whitetails. Ronnie Gray found the dead bucks on Thanksgiving Day near his home in Washington County.

My first reaction to seeing the bucks was that they were not locked. They couldn't be. The bigger buck's left main beam was not touching the smaller buck in any manner, but their right main beams were only slightly entwined. Yet, when I grabbed the buck's antlers, they were locked tightly.

The left main beam on the smaller buck had penetrated the larger buck's neck. The tip of the beam reached the larger buck's esophagus, severely bruising it. This, combined with the slight entanglement of their right main beams, had the bucks locked tightly

Gray donated the bucks to the Indiana DNR. They will be mounted as they were locked, and they'll be displayed at the Starve Hollow State Recreation Area Nature Center near Vallonia, Ind.

— *Brad Herndon*

■ Wisconsin Archer Takes B&C Buck

Wisconsin's 1991 archery season certainly didn't start out on a good note for Menomonie native Jim Belmore. First, just before the season opened, a limb on Belmore's compound bow broke. He immediately secured a bow to use until his own bow could be fixed. But even though he practiced diligently, the slight unfamiliarity with the borrowed bow cost him. In a span of two weeks during mid-October, he missed relatively easy shots at two fine bucks and a doe.

Just when the rut was kicking in, Belmore received the repaired bow from the dealer. After a little practice and some last-minute fine-tuning, he thought he had regained the form he had lost while using the borrowed bow. With a slight bit more confidence, Belmore headed out before daylight on the morning of Nov. 7 to spend some time in his tree stand.

A short time after getting settled, Belmore noticed a deer walking down a steep hill toward his position. Immediately, he identified the deer as a buck, and a huge one at that. At 25 yards, the monster animal turned broadside and gave the excited bow hunter a perfect opportunity. Belmore's arrow found its mark and the buck ran only a short distance before dropping.

The rack of the Dunn county giant had an inside spread of 20-3/4 inches. The four longest tines on the symmetrical 10-pointer range from 10-4/8 to 13-4/8 Boone and Crockett inches. The base circumference measurements are both 4-6/8, while beam lengths are 24-6/8 and 23-4/8. The final net typical score was 171-6/8 inches. The buck was the largest typical taken with archery gear in Wisconsin for 1991. The deer also ranks in the top 10 all-time in the state.

— *Greg Miller*
Bloomer, Wis.

Greg Miller

Jim Belmore with his buck that scored 171-6/8. The deer ranks in the state's top 10 bucks of all time.

■ Souvenir Beer Mugs Sport Joke Buck

The world's largest brewer doesn't lose many bar fights, but Anheuser-Busch suffered a black eye recently after marketing souvenir beer steins with an unsubstantiated claim about a record white-tailed deer.

The steins, selling for $100 apiece in at least one Wisconsin liquor store, show a picture of a huge buck above a short history of what is purported to be a world record rack from a deer killed in that state. The stein states: "The King of Bucks was taken at Webster, Wis., in 1874. His world record rack had an amazing 162 points."

The problem is that the deer never existed. Anheuser-Busch spokesman Scott Patterson said the brewer had been led to believe the buck was part of Wisconsin legend. Patterson said the St. Louis-based company learned about the mysterious buck from a wholesaler in Menomonie, Wis.

The brewer took a partial photo of a deer with a giant rack and had an artist do a complete drawing, which wasn't intended to look exactly like the "real" Webster buck, Patterson said.

"Anheuser-Busch thought it was good information, though it wasn't officially verifiable, like many things in the 1800s," said

"Anheuser-Busch did not attempt to trivialize this record or manipulate it for product sales," he said.

The tall tale gets even larger because the picture of the deer on the stein is a duplicate of a photo of a fake rack used for a humorous circulation promotion by *Deer & Deer Hunting* magazine in the mid-1980s. That rack, which involved gluing dozens of fake points onto a real deer head, was created for the promotion by Appleton, Wis., taxidermist Dennis Rinehart, said Al Hofacker, the magazine's editor at large.

"There was never any intention to try to deceive anybody," Hofacker said. "It was made as a novelty thing, an attention grabber. I believe we called it a dream buck."

Contacted at his Woodruff, Wis., home, Rinehart, who now teaches for the American Institute of Taxidermy in Janesville, Wis., said the promotional head included the only fake rack he ever created.

Rinehart, stressing that the magazine never tried to pass off the head as real, said he used an authentic deer head as a base and then glued on many chunks of deer antlers. About 20 percent of the points were created with sculpturing compound, he said. The project took at least six weeks.

Patterson, who likened it to a fish story passed down through the generations.

Craig Cousins, a past president of the Wisconsin Buck and Bear Club and an official measurer for the Boone and Crockett Club, said the story of a 102-point deer from Webster is false.

"Someone either told a fictitious story or it was misunderstood," said Cousins, an active deer historian from Milltown, Wis. "I've measured the second most deer of anyone in Wisconsin. As far as stories about a giant buck, I think I would have heard them."

Patterson said the brewer did not attempt to mislead people.

Oddly enough, an image of a deer head with an identically shaped rack also has appeared on promotional products for Keystone beer, produced by Adolph Coors Co. of Golden, Colo. The picture is accompanied by Keystone's slogan, "Wouldn't It Be

Great?"

When its promotion ended, the magazine sold the head to a Black River Falls, Wis., man. The huge rack now hangs in collector Norm Jurjen's dining room south of Eau Claire, Wis.

By official standards, which only recognize points at least an inch long, the fake rack has about 68 points. Including every little bump, the non-typical rack has about 90 points. No deer in the Wisconsin record books has ever had more than 47 points.

Anheuser-Busch produced 1,872 of the limited-edition steins, which were distributed in Wisconsin as part of a Budweiser series recognizing the state's wildlife. The company sold all of the steins to distributors last year, and no more will ever be produced, Patterson said.

Duke Thompson, owner of Sting Ray Liquor in Altoona, Wis., said he originally sold the steins for $35, then raised the price to $75 and later to $100 as demand soared. He has sold about a dozen, the last four for $100.

— *Eric A. Lundquist*
Eau Claire Leader-Telegram

■ Flying Whitetail Triggers Crash

As a hunter, Maureen Sorum knows deer. But a brush with a deer in June was much too close for her comfort. In a freak accident near Hokah, Minn., a deer that was struck by an oncoming car flew into the windshield of a car in which Sorum was riding. The deer crashed through the windshield and ended up in the back seat, injuring Sorum, her mother and her son.

"It was really weird, let me put it that way," Sorum, 39, of Mabel, Minn., said. "But it could have been a lot worse."

Sorum and her mother, Madonna Mathison, 63, of Mabel, and Sorum's son, Dean Sorum, 15, were treated at Lutheran Hospital for cuts and bruises. Maureen Sorum and her mother were treated and released while Dean Sorum underwent surgery for a broken left arm.

Mathison was driving west on Highway 16 about one mile west of Hokah at 8:30 p.m. when a deer was struck by an oncoming car. In an instant the deer was airborne and coming toward Mathison's car, Maureen Sorum said. The deer was decapitated in the collision with the other car.

The collision was the second serious accident caused by a deer in southeastern Minnesota in two days. Earlier that week, a Wyeville, Wis., boy was killed and four others injured after a rearend collision with a truck on Interstate 90 near Dakota. In that accident, a collision with a deer broke and shorted out the lights of the car, causing the truck, which was following the car, to lose sight of it in the dark.

— *La Crosse Tribune*

Rescued Deer Hit and Killed by Car

A deer assisted out of Lake Michigan by a Coast Guard boat was frightened by a guardsman's pet dog. When it ran away, it was struck and killed by a car driven by an off-duty Coast Guard fireman.

The unhappy ending in early July came about 15 minutes after the deer was guided to shore by a recovery boat from the Coast Guard station near downtown Kenosha, Wis., according to Petty Officer Kipp Bachman. The station received calls about 10 a.m. from citizens concerned about a panicky deer in the lake.

"We got alongside it, although you can't get too close because you might get kicked." Bachman said.

The boat stayed with the deer until it reached Simmons Island beach. The deer then trotted toward the Coast Guard station, where it was frightened by the barking of the dog. The deer reversed course on the beach and plunged back into the water.

After the deer eluded the Labrador retriever, it returned to shore, sprinted through a motel parking lot and was killed about 15 minutes later when it collided with a car driven by Eric Nelson, and offduty Coast Guardsman.

— *Milwaukee Journal*

Deer Claims Third Victim

A white-tailed deer on a rampage attacked its third victim in two days in late June in the New Jersey town of Great Meadows.

Police said Werner Weibel, 70, of Townsbury Road in Great Meadows, was hunting crows on land behind his home when a buck attacked him. Officials said he got off a shot, and slightly wounded the deer.

Weibel suffered several cuts on his arms, legs and head, and was admitted to the Hackettstown Community Hospital.

Earlier, the 6-point buck rammed and treed two dairy farmers who were working in a field. The men, Seth Harris and Mitchell Cortwright, had seen the buck and had tried to catch him, police said.

— *The Express, Independence, N.J.*

U.S. Congress Upholds Deer Hunt

In a vote described as "the first pure hunting vote in the U.S. Congress in years," the National Rifle Association claimed victory after successfully lobbying the Congress on the 1993 Department of Interior Appropriations Bill.

The House of Representatives voted 255-160 to strike a provision in the bill that would have ended hunting in the Mason Neck Wildlife Refuge Area in Virginia.

"Hunting is an American heritage and an essential element of wildlife conservation," said David Gibbons, director of federal affairs for the NRA's institute for legislative action. "Safeguarding hunting is a primary and long standing NRA goal."

The NRA shared with congressmen a letter from Mike Haydon - assistant secretary for Fish, Wildlife and Parks - who cited "extensive overgrazing" at Mason Neck "which threatened the vegetative cover of the refuge a classic precursor to widespread die-offs among the deer population, either by disease or starvation."

Hayden stated: "Hunting is a legitimate, recreational experience and, in this instance, the only means of controlling excess deer populations. The hunt has occurred for two years without causing any problems for nearby residents. Congress should not allow the views of a few individuals to override the professional decisions of our managers."

Gibbons said: "This was the first, pure vote on the issue of hunting in the U.S. House of Representatives in years ... and the first vote that pitted hunters and wildlife managers against animal-rights radicals. NRA's next step will be to share with our members the names of congressmen who cast their vote against hunting, scientific wildlife conservation and hunters."

— *NRA News release*

■ Man who was Gored by Deer Can't Sue

A man gored by a captive deer in Rock County Sportsman's Park can't sue the county because the deer was a wild animal under state law, the Wisconsin Supreme Court decided in May.

The court said the Legislature meant to include domesticated deer in a law that bans lawsuits against landowners by people injured by wild animals on their land.

Justice William Bablitch, who dissented with Justice Shirley Abrahamson, said the 5-2 decision was absurd and ignored the purpose of the law "to encourage landowners to open up their lands for recreational use by the public."

Tom Hudson, of Kenosha, had sued the county after a buck in rut charged him in December 1987 and used its antlers to rip a hole in his left thigh. Hudson had been feeding the deer near Janesville.

Justice Louis Ceci wrote a detailed account of the attack in three pages copied almost word-for-word from the brief of Hudson's lawyer, Robert DuMez.

"Mr. Bambrough explained that the buck ... had been acting strangely of late but that it was fearful of a particular shovel," Ceci (and DuMez) wrote. "Accordingly, Mr. Bambrough asked his nephew to enter the pen, armed with the shovel. Unfortunately, Mr. Bambrough misgauged the buck's respect for the implement. After Mr. Bambrough had unloaded one bucket of feed ... the buck dropped its head and, without provocation or warning, charged the plaintiff. ... The buck's wild flailing struck the plaintiff and ripped open a gaping wound in his leg...

Unable to escape and powerless to do more, the plaintiff seized the deer's head in a manner similar to a rodeo contestant and simply hung on."

Such an attack certainly indicated the buck was wild and its behavior wasn't even unusual, Ceci said. Quoting Mammals of Wisconsin, he added: "An old buck ... often develops an ugly disposition, particularly in the rutting season, and may fight anything."

Bablitch said the decision, which reversed a 4th District Court of appeals ruling, misinterpreted a law that is meant to shield landowners from liability "for random attacks by wild animals over which they had no control."

— *Wisconsin State Journal*

■ Kansas Produces Huge Non-typical

Time was running out once again for 20-year-old Chris Theis. On the next to last day of the 1992 Kansas firearms season, Dec. 12, Theis was still looking for a deer.

This was Theis' fifth year of deer hunting, and he had yet to shoot one. But he had his chances. Earlier that morning, he had seen a forkhorn buck on his uncle's farm north of Leavenworth, but he let it pass.

That proved to be a wise move.

"About 10 a.m., I heard my dad shoot," Theis said. "I started walking along the creek in that direction, and saw a doe and a buck coming my way. The buck looked like it had a bunch of brush in its antlers. That was the impression I had."

The buck parted ways with the doe and crossed the creek. Theis waited until the buck came out of the creek bed.

"I took a couple steps toward it and raised my rifle and fired," Theis said. "I saw blood ... and shot again but missed."

After waiting five minutes, Theis started into the woods. He found the buck 30 yards from where he'd last seen it.

Jim Ramberg

Chris Theis of Kansas holds that state's record non-typical white tailed deer rack. The rack had 40 points and received a Boone & Crockett score of 279.

"When I saw him on the ground, I thought it was pretty weird," Theis said. "I couldn't believe it."

Official scorers later counted 50 points on the rack. Forty of the points - 20 on each side - were large enough to score. The spread was more than 29 inches.

Two Boone & Crockett scorers on Feb. 10 scored the non-typical whitetail at 279 points. The buck is a Kansas record and will score high on the all-time Boone & Crockett list.

The buck was unusual in other regards. It was extremely secretive. No one in the area recalled seeing it before. It also had no testicles. It likely lost them in an accident. As a result, the antlers still carried some velvet.

The deer was not particularly heavy-bodied. Its estimated field-dressed weight was 175 pounds.

— *Jim Ramberg*

■ Hunter Bags Two White Deer

Many hunters dream of taking a white deer, much as 20-year-old Indiana bow hunter Tim Hunt did in autumn 1991. But one year later, Hunt repeated the feat.

During summer 1991, Hunt spotted two young white deer in a field near his home in Indiana's Warrick County. After seeing the deer several times, he vowed to hunt for one of them. In October he spotted both white deer approaching his bow stand.

Moments later, a well-placed arrow killed the white button buck. Before the 1992 season, Hunt spotted the other white deer, a 1.5-year-old doe, traveling alone.

Hunt's chance for the second

ghostly deer arrived on a cold October morning shortly after the bow season opened. He made the most of the opportunity.

Both deer were taken from the same tree stand.

— *John Trout*

Paul J. Drobny

This heavily rubbed post was on a tree line in Minnesota. The post was broken two years after this photo was taken.

■ Well-Worked Rub

The accompanying photograph shows an amazing buck rub found in 1984 in Minnesota's Lac Qui Parle County. My group noticed the first marks on this cedar fence in 1981. In 1986, two years after we took this photograph, the post Matt Usitalo of

Houghton, Mich., bagged this 10-point buck in 1992. Its green score was 176-3/8, which was likely the largest rack taken in the Upper Peninsula last year.

■ Big Michigan Buck

Matt Usitalo of Houghton bagged a buck with the largest set of typical antlers known taken in Michigan's Upper Peninsula in 1992. The buck may have also been the heaviest. The massive 10-point antlers had a green score of 176-3/8, and the carcass had a dressed weight of 245 pounds. After the 60-day drying period, the antlers were expected to surpass the 170 minimum required for national records maintained by the Boone and Crockett Club.

Usitalo bagged the buck on the evening of Nov. 17 behind his house. He said he decided to hunt for a while after dinner, hoping to see one of the 6-pointers he had observed in a nearby field earlier in the fall. He had been posted for only about 20 minutes when he heard some noise, and then saw the big buck approaching. One shot from his Marlin .30-30 at 40 yards dropped the deer. Usitalo said he knew the antlers were large when he shot the deer, but he didn't realize how large until he reached the fallen buck,

He's sure the buck is the same one he twice saw crossing a nearby road after dark last fall. In addition, his brother had missed the buck on the fifth day of the 1991 gun season. All seven of his bullets were deflected by brush as the buck remained in one spot.

Richard P. Smith

Matt Usitalo of Houghton, Mich., bagged this 10-point buck in 1992. Its green score was 176-3/8, which was likely the largest rack taken in the Upper Peninsula last year.

The record-book buck is only Usitalo's second deer during 13 years of hunting. He got his first buck in 1991, a small 8-pointer.

— *Richard P. Smith*

■ Velvet Found

James Arthurs from Manistee, Mich. doesn't normally pay much attention to antler rubs in early fall because they don't often mean much about where the buck might be when deer season opens later. However, a rub he found Sept. 29 while grouse hunting in Marquette County caught his eye and he's glad he investigated.

Arthurs saw something hanging from the sapling that had been rubbed by a buck. When he reached the object he realized it was a piece of antler velvet. He had heard that bucks rub trees when shedding their velvet, but had never seen it for himself.

Velvet shed by bucks when their antlers harden apparently dries up and disappears or is eaten so fast that hunters seldom find any.

Upon closer inspection, a larger piece of velvet was spotted in vegetation at the base of the rubbed sapling. The fact that the shreds of tissue were still recognizable and intact indicates the velvet had not been there long.

Richard P. Smith

This velvet was found shortly after being shed.

A number of other rubbed saplings were visible near the one where the velvet was found. A check of those rubs failed to turn up any more velvet. In the future, Arthurs will probably pay more attention to rubs he sees during early fall on the chance he can pick up more mementos.

— *Richard P. Smith*

■ Pet Deer Killer Convicted

A man who killed a pet deer in its pen on Christmas Eve 1991 - a deer described as being so tame strangers could pet it - was convicted of cruelty charges by a

Lauderdale County, Ala., jury.

Roger Pitts, 22, of Waterloo, was accused of posting a picture of himself and "Bucky" the deer on a bulletin board in a store frequented by hunters.

George Taylor of Florence, whose family owned the deer, identified Pitts as the man in the picture. "That was my deer," Taylor said. "That fellow right there was in the picture," he said, pointing at Pitts.

Taylor said his family had owned the 4-year-old deer since it was 3 weeks old.

Pitts was sentenced to six months in jail on a cruelty to animals charge, suspended on payment of a $1,000 fine; and three months in jail on a criminal trespassing charge, suspended on payment of a $500 fine. Pitts must also perform 240 hours of community service with the Department of Conservation or an animal control service.

Defense attorney Don Holt said he plans to appeal the case.

— *Rollin Moseley*

Dinny Slaughter

This fawn died after losing its lower hind legs to a hay cutter. The fawn was hiding in waist-high grass and didn't move until it was too late.

■ Large Mower Kills Fawn

In 1979 I lived and worked on a government installation. About half of the 4,000 acres was open land used primarily for hay production.

In May each year, as the farm tractors with their sickle-bar mowers cut the grass, the installation's large population of white-tailed deer was also dropping fawns.

The mowers, which resemble 10-foot hedge clippers, are attached to the right side of a tractor where they can be watched by the operator. This allows the operator to avoid hitting rocks or other objects that might damage the bar's 3-inch teeth.

Unfortunately, the white-tailed doe hides its newborn fawns in the same waist-high hay grasses. The fawns' ability to hug the ground and remain motionless places them in a precarious position because the tractor operator cannot always see them in time to stop.

On one occasion, despite the clatter of the mower blades and the noise of the tractor, one unnoticed fawn refused to move. The sickle bar, which glides only inches above the ground, somehow passed over the animal. I examined the fawn, which still refused to move, took some pictures and left it in place to await the return of its mother.

The next day I noticed a flock of crows in another area feeding on a carcass in a cut-over field. Their victim, another white-tailed fawn, had decided too late to make a run for it. Unlike the other fawn, however, this one had lost its hind legs to the mower blades.

— *Dinny Slaughter*
Marshall, Va.

■ Minnesota Archer Drops 20-Point Non-Typical

Bow hunter Matt Stone of Bemidji, Minn., wasted little time last fall in getting a 20-point Pope & Young non-typical whitetail that scored 205-3/8 points and weighed 218 pounds field-dressed.

Stone was hunting in the Bemidji area on Sept. 17, the third day of Minnesota's 1990 archery season. He decided to hunt a staging area in the woods between a field and a ridge, even though this location usually produced better results later in the season. After setting up, Stone thought he heard a deer 60 to 70 yards away. Even though he concentrated on pinpointing the source of the noise, he didn't hear another sound. Suddenly, a huge buck appeared 20 to 30 yards away. The deer was quietly browsing and took almost five minutes to move 30 feet.

Stone drew on the deer once but had to relax the bow when he couldn't get a clear shot. A short while later he saw his chance when the buck was about 32 yards away. His arrow caught the deer a bit high and farther back than Stone wished, but he and his friends recovered the buck about 1:15 a.m. with the aid of lanterns.

This was Stone's second P&Y buck. His first, taken only the year before, was a 10-pointer that scored 137-7/8 and weighed 235 pounds field dressed.

Stone, 27, has bow hunted seriously since about 1986. What are some of his secrets?

"I don't scout a lot during the season, but I do a lot of scouting during the pre-season and post-season," he said. "I always try to hunt fresh spots. I jump around

Matt Stone and his 20-point non-typical buck from Minnesota.

quite a bit. I don't let the deer pattern me. I haven't found a spot yet that gets better with use. Two to three evenings is the most I'll sit in one spot. If something is going to happen, it usually happens quickly, during the first couple of hunts."

Stone's 1990 buck is listed in about fourth place in the Minnesota P&Y record book for non-typicals.

— Patrick Durkin
Editor

■ What Alarmed This Fawn?

While on a small pond, I nearly fell from my rowboat when the spring silence was shattered by the bleating cry of a white-tailed fawn.

It took a moment to collect my thoughts. Glancing about, I saw no sign nor heard any sound from a predator, but suddenly a little white-tailed fawn flushed from the brush and stood at the edge of the pond. The fawn looked at me, stamped, snorted twice and leaped into the water. The fawn - probably not more than a couple weeks old began swimming across the deep end of the pond. I could see only its head and ears as it swam to within 10 feet of the boat. It then looked at me and snorted.

It kept going and soon crawled out of the water, soaking wet from the ears down. It almost bellycrawled into the high grass in the adjacent uncut hay field. The fawn disappeared into the tall hay, never making another sound.

— *David A. Manch*

■ Seeing Double?

Taxidermists never know what will come through their door next, but Doug Bolyard of Arthurdale, W. Va., must have thought he was seeing double last winter when a hunter showed him a set of antlers to score.

The antlers were brought in by Tom Ridenour of nearby Fellowsville. Ridenour had shot the big non-typical white-tailed buck in 1980, and decided after 10 years to have its antlers scored. The buck's rack carried two drop tines on its right antler. Bolyard immediately saw a similarity between the rack and a shed antler his brother Frank had found in 1979.

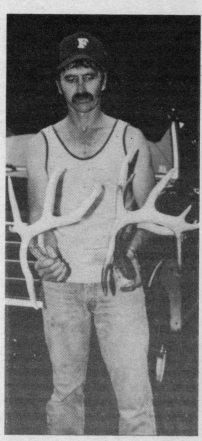

Tom Ridenour with his non-typical rack and a shed dropped one year before by the same buck.

"The moment I saw the right antler I recognized that it matched the one at my brother's house," Doug Bolyard said. The only difference was that the shed didn't have the forward drop tine.

"It was just a coincidence," Bolyard continued. Tom just happened to come into my shop. He said he got the deer about 30 miles away, and that's the same area where my brother found the shed. They almost had to be from the same deer."

After exchanging stories, Bolyard measured Ridenour's 12-point rack, and gave it a gross score of 140. Ridenour said the buck had weighed 200 pounds.

— Patrick Durkin
Editor

■ Deer Near Downtown in Indianapolis

The morning rush-hour rat race in Indianapolis became a deer race one morning in April as authorities tracked three deer spotted by commuters near the downtown.

Animal control officers in nine trucks finally caught one of the deer. Another was hit by a car, and the other escaped.

Animal Control Center dispatcher Louis J. Galardo said the center began getting calls about 7 a.m. that day about three deer seen first in the 1200, 1300 and 1400 blocks of north Delaware Street.

A car struck one deer in the 900 block of north East Street. The badly injured animal was taken to the animal control center and put to death.

After a morning-long chase involving as many as nine animal control trucks, the other two deer were cornered in the 1400 block of north Park Avenue. Both bolted again, but one was immobilized by animal control officers in the 2400 block of Park. It was taken to Eagle Creek Park and released unharmed. The other was still at large at 11 a.m. Officers in four trucks were looking for it near the 2300 block of north Greenbriar Lane.

— Indianapolis News
April 1991

■ Partner Payoff

Timothy Page of Milan, Mich., shot his first and second bucks during that state's 1989 gun season. Both had trophy racks. But if it weren't for Page's hunting partner, Darryl Murray, he might not have gotten either buck.

Neither hunter had scored by the season's third day, Nov. 17, and Page was discouraged. He didn't want to hunt that day, but Murray talked him into it.

"I kept telling him you have to pay your dues," Murray said. "You can't get them if you're not there."

Murray finally motivated Page to go by threatening to hunt from his partner's blind. Page wasn't hunting long when a buck with a massive eight-point rack showed up. He dropped it at 15 yards with a 12-gauge slug. The antlers scored 155.

The next day, Murray sat in Page's blind to change his luck. All he had seen from his spot was does. Page, meanwhile, was in Murray's blind about 30 minutes when a doe showed up. She was followed by a huge buck. Page dropped the 19-pointer at 12 paces. Its antlers scored 166-3/8.

Murray hunted alone the rest of gun season and into black-powder season without getting a buck. His persistence paid off the final evening of the muzzle-loader hunt, though. He made a 65-yard shot on a 14-pointer that scored 156-3/8.

— *Richard P. Smith*

■ Unusual Discovery

When southern Indiana deer hunter Steve Peters climbed into his tree stand on the morning of Nov. 25, 1990, he hoped to fill his "bonus" doe tag. And, as luck had it, a doe passed within range shortly after daylight. The slug gun roared and the doe ran, showing signs of being hit.

After a wait, Peters climbed down and began following the blood trail. He had covered nearly 200 yards and was beginning to get that uneasy feeling hunters sometimes know when he spotted a fallen deer. He first assumed it was the doe. How-

ever, as he approached he saw an antler. As he glanced back, he could see the blood trail continuing east, opposite to where the buck was lying.

After following the trail a short distance, a shot rang out. Peters knew his hunting companion was ahead. He marked the blood trail and walked ahead to talk with his partner. He soon discovered his friend had shot the wounded doe.

After tagging and field-dressing the doe, they walked back to the buck. He was lying in a bedded position with his front legs tucked underneath. It was obvious the buck had not been dead long, and it had no wounds anywhere.

Peters looked closer and discovered the buck's left eye was missing. Only a trace of blood was visible. The hunters concluded that the wound was not caused by another hunter. The bone and tissue around the eye were fine.

After checking the area, they found leaves and other debris were out of place, indicating a possible buck fight. The only explanation was that the buck was gored through its eye socket from the antler of another buck.

The buck was not record-book material, but its nine-point rack was respectable. Peters had seen the buck twice before during the early Indiana archery season but had never had it within range.

— *John Trout Jr.*

■ Surprise Dinner Guest

Robert Kuenzli of Boonville, Ind., had just sat down to the dinner table with his family in their rural home. It was near dusk, and the second day of the Hoosier firearms season. Ordinarily he would have been in his tree stand at this time, but things went well that morning and Kuenzli had filled one of his tags.

"We were just sitting there when all of a sudden we heard glass shattering in our recreation room at the other end of the house," Kuenzli said.

He and the rest of his family immediately headed for the room and heard a great deal more disturbance. Upon arriving, they saw a panicked doe running through the room, knocking lamps to the floor, and jumping over the furniture.

The bottom portion of the bay window was knocked out. Kuenzli and his wife tried to get their two children out of the way. The doe then ran into a pair of glass doors leading to the patio and became tangled in the screens. Excited and unsure of what he should do, Kuenzli ran and grabbed his slug gun. After it seemed hopeless that the deer could be freed, he shot the doe and called the local sheriffs office to report the incident.

Considerable damage was done to the house and furniture. Four mounted deer heads were on display on the walls in the recreation room. Maybe the deer saw the mounted heads and leaped through the glass in an attempt to get to them.

The game warden arrived later and issued a special permit for the young doe, and the Kuenzli family took the deer to be processed.

— *John Trout Jr.*

■ Angler Catches Fawn

Jay Isley from Adrian, Michigan has been fishing Marquette County's Lake Michigamme for forty years, but Friday, June 22, was the first time he had the opportunity to catch a fawn. The day became foggy as he boated toward his summer home. At one point he noticed something in the water ahead of him, and as he got closer he realized it was a doe and fawn swimming across the large lake.

Disturbed by the approaching boat, Isley said the doe turned back toward shore, leaving the fawn behind. He moved away from the deer, giving the young whitetail the opportunity to follow its mother, but the animal became disoriented in the fog and began swimming in circles.

Isley said the fawn lifted its head above the water and called periodically, but the doe didn't return.

After watching the fawn swim in circles for fifteen minutes, Isley figured it would continue until it drowned. He then motored toward the fawn and was surprised when it swam toward his boat. When alongside, he lifted the fawn on board and brought it to shore where the doe left the water, which was a distance of about 200 yards.

Obviously tired from swimming, the fawn laid down for a few minutes after leaving the water. Then it walked into the brush in the direction its mother had gone, and the two were probably reunited soon afterward.

— *Richard P. Smith*

■ Our Most Respected Buck

For three years I saw large deer tracks revealing a hole in the ground where the right, rear foot print should be. A mature whitetail had survived serious wounding and was living in the northeast quadrant of my hunt club.

A local farmer regularly saw a large-bodied buck in one of his soybean fields. The deer would limp out to nibble at the field's edge just at dusk.

These sightings by the farmer proved to be of great assistance to me. In my scouting I documented, mapped, and studied this animal's behavior. The buck never left a dense, 200-acre parcel. Other members eventually found the tracks and the word of this wounding spread to adjacent clubs. The area buzzed with this story of survival.

We enjoy a four and one-half-month-long season in South Carolina. In three years of hunting and scouting, neither myself nor any other member laid eyes on this elusive animal. Numerous man drives, constant relocation of tree-climbing portables, and hours spent in mid-day in the permanent stands proved to be just games to this buck.

Respect mounted for this deer and we named him "Pegleg." We eventually abandoned his area of residence, as an unspoken code grew among the club to not hunt him.

The inevitable happened. I found "Pegleg" on the skinning rack when getting into camp in the wee hours one weekend. A youngster had made a shot he couldn't duplicate in twenty years... and with a borrowed rifle unshot in three years.

Even at 2:00 A.M., the clubhouse was a beehive with hunters still up, the campfire blazing, and people standing around gazing at this legend hanging there. This was a touching story of courage hanging there, and there were a lot of wet eyes.

I kept the head for mounting with much time spent in amazement looking at that right, rear leg. The foot was destroyed except for a partial hoof pointed downward, the size of a nickel, that took full weight! The right knee was locked in 90 degrees of flexion and the size of a softball. The joint was hot, swollen, and draining purulent fluids emitting a stench that was offensive.

The knee and foot were severely arthritic. The entire leg was atrophied and deformed. The back was crooked with the left hip musculature massive for the compensation indicated for

Old Pegleg managed to elude members of Big Jim's Hunt Club for more than three years. When this 7.5-year-old buck died his right knee was locked in 90 degrees of flexion and the size of a softball as a result of a previous wound. The joint was hot, swollen, and draining purulent fluids that emitted an offensive stench.

his gait needs.

Yet, even with this devastating situation the animal was a powerful specimen, well over 180 pounds. The rack was symmetrical on the right with four points, with three on the left that were irregular. Shoulder scars revealed breeding activities remained prevalent.

Even in the harvesting of "Pegleg," our respect for him grew not only in my club, but in the entire town. After seeing "Pegleg" on the rack, one member went home early the next day. While gassing up at the local station, the attendant told him the story of the harvesting of this buck ... the scenario of the story was already alive in this quiet, southern town by dawn the following day!

We often speak about this powerful buck around camp to this day. The word "courage" is the common denominator in these discussions. The stamina and will to live this buck revealed, created his legend.

The wounding percentages in my club dropped to 2.2 percent. We lost two out of eighty-nine deer harvested over a four-year span, as documented on the harvest log.

The members wait for a clear shot to make a sure harvest. Ballistic charts hang on the clubhouse wall. The practice range has been rebuilt and is active at mid-day.

Hunter integrity is impressive in this club. Peer pressure for individual responsibility to be a premiere predator package is strived for. The effect "Pegleg" had on the lives of the members of this club for hunter responsibility, is indelible, and lives on ...

— *James I. McKee*

■ Cactus Buck Shot in Texas

Dianne Arringdale of Corpus Christi, Texas, wasn't sure what to make of the large deer that was following a doe about 80 yards away from her blind.

Arringdale could see something between the big deer's ears, but it almost looked like a tangled clump of flowers. She continued to sit tight, unsure what to do. Soon, the two deer moved out of sight. When they returned about 7:30 a.m., Arringdale could see

antler tips above the big deer's "flowers." She aimed her .25-06 and took the oddlooking buck.

The day was Jan. 13, 1991. When Arringdale stood over the buck, she knew she had a unique trophy. The mass on the buck's head wasn't flowers. Rather, each antler was piled in thick, shapeless, tumor-like growths covered in velvet. Because of the appearance, such deer are called 'cactus bucks.'

Arringdale and her husband, John, didn't realize how extremely rare the buck was until they tried to find information about its head gear. Few people have seen such growths, and even scientists aren't sure what produces them. About the only thing certain is that the oddity is linked to damaged or severed testicles. In this case, the buck was estimated to be at least 8 years old, and its testicles appeared to be wasting away. Perhaps the antlers hadn't received the proper flow of testosterone to guide their growth. This would also explain why the antlers were still in velvet.

Still, most white-tailed bucks that damage or lose their testicles don't produce cactus growths. Usually, the result is normal-appearing antlers that remain covered in velvet indefinitely. Also, the condition is seen more often in mule deer and blacktails. In the United States, cactus bucks are seen in the Southwest more than the North. This may be related to cold weather, which would freeze the velvet-covered masses and cause them to fall off.

Professor Anthony Bubenik of

John Arringdale

Ontario, Canada, said he has seen only four white-tailed deer with cactus antlers. Bubenik is an expert on antler development. He said some cactus bucks might have their testes inside their body. Another possibility is that they're hermaphrodites, meaning they have male and female sex organs.

Bubenik's son, George, is an associate zoology professor at the University of Guelph in Ontario. He said the cactus growth might be related to a species' control of its antler development. Europe's roe deer, for example, have almost no control after castration. At times, the shapeless antler mass becomes so large that it covers the roe buck's head like a wig, eventually killing it. These bucks are referred to as "perukes," the name for Frenchstyle wigs of the 17th and 18th centuries.

Whitetails, however, still have some control over the antlers after damaging or losing their testicles. George Bubenik said it's possible some deer species, like caribou and reindeer, carry enough male hormones to produce and control antlers, with or without testicles. Or, some species may have highly sensitive receptors, which require few male hormones to produce and control antler development.

"There has been no real study of cactus bucks so far," George Bubenik said. "Until someone does the research, it's hard to say why it occurs."

■ Boy Survives Neck Wound

Kevin Panten sat at the base of a tree in Wisconsin's Douglas County, scanning the forest for whitetails on Thanksgiving morning, Nov. 22, 1990. This was Kevin's first deer season.

At about 7:15 a.m. he heard deer moving to his right. Moments later his body rocked to the side, and he felt a jolt in his lower right face and neck.

In a daze, he stood up, stepped onto a nearby trail, and touched his jaw, which was strangely cold. When he pulled his hand down it was covered with blood.

"I never heard the shot," said Kevin, 14, who lives in Slinger, Wis. "I just thought, 'Oh my god, I'm shot!' I set the gun down and started running away screaming."

Seconds later he felt a lump in his esophagus. Thinking it was a clot of blood or a tooth, he spit it out. It was actually the base of a .270 caliber bullet, which had been fired by a companion about 150 yards away.

"The first thing I checked was that my teeth fit together," Kevin said. "I was scared but I never thought I was going to die. It didn't hurt much, either. The only thing that worried me was my Mom finding out."

Doctors first thought he would need a tracheotomy, a metal plate in his jaw, and a bone transplant from his hip.

Another doctor examined the wound and disagreed. He removed a piece of Kevin's jawbone that resembled a quarter-moon, and left the other two-thirds of the jawbone in place. The wound didn't require stitches.

Kevin returned to school a week later, Nov. 29. When contacted in mid-January, he was completely recovered. All that remains is a small scar and a tingling sensation when he touches it. By some miracle, the bullet fragment missed Kevin's spinal column and jugular vein by fractions of an inch. It also did minimal damage to the 31 nerves around the wound.

Kevin doesn't blame his companion for the accident. In fact, neither do conservation wardens with Wisconsin's Department of Natural Resources. Kevin was not in the line of fire. Rather, the rifle had been pointed almost directly away and behind him.

After investigating, the wardens concluded the bullet richocheted at least three times before its base tumbled into Kevin's neck.

"The DNR said you could take

that shot a million times and never hit Kevin again," said his mother, Janet. "Kevin realizes it was really a freak accident."

The wardens found the bullet's base where Kevin spit it out. They gave it back to him. He now keeps it in a plastic case.

News of the shooting made Kevin a celebrity for a few weeks. Newspapers, including some supermarket tabloids, called for his story, but he granted few interviews. He also declined an invitation to appear on the Oprah Winfrey Show.

"Kevin likes deer hunting," his mother said. "That's what he's all about. He didn't want this to get sensationalized. He didn't think everyone would understand."

Kevin has three brothers. All of them hunt, even though neither of his parents do. He expects to go deer hunting again this fall. His parents don't object.

"I've always been more concerned about the long drive it takes to get up there," his mother said. "The hunting itself isn't what worries me."

■ Anti's Poison Deer on Meat Pole

Steve Stamper and Mike Dean of Greencastle, Ind., waited until the last day of the Hoosier muzzleloading season to fill their tags. They and their families love eating deer meat. When they each brought home large does December 9, it appeared they had plenty of venison for the winter.

Both deer were hung overnight behind Stamper's house to cool. The next morning, they went out to look at the deer. What they found shocked them: small droplets of a green liquid on the deer's legs. More was discovered inside the body cavities. The deer had been splashed with antifreeze.

City police and Conservation Officer Floyd Suitors arrived and took samples. They determined that antihunters committed the act.

Stamper phoned the poison control center in Atlanta and discovered that antifreeze is deadly. Even a small amount can cause blindness. He cringed at the thought that his 5year-old son might have eaten it if it had gone unnoticed.

The men were advised to burn the carcasses. If the animals were dumped but not destroyed, other animals could have eaten them.

Authorities have no leads on who might be responsible for the act.

A reward program was set up to catch those involved before they could act again.

"What really scares me is that whoever did this might do it to someone else, and I really hate to think what the outcome could be," Stamper said.

Stamper and Dean contacted several hunting publications and, with help from the Indiana Bow Hunters Association, they have received money toward the reward.

— *John Trout Jr.*

or containing as many tines as the one reported here. The head was mounted and the photograph published through the courtesy of the Kent Canadian Club, Inc., the present owners.

— *Ralph W. Dexter,*
Journal of Mammalogy (1945)

A Virginia Deer With Fifty-four Tines

In November of 1943, a group of railroad section hands discovered the carcass of a white-tailed deer (Odocoileus virginianus) along the right-of-way of the Erie Railroad near Windham Station, Portage County, Ohio. It is believed that the animal was killed by a train. The workmen, noticing the peculiarity of the antlers, cut off the head for preservation. Upon examination it was found that the antlers possess 54 distinct tines over one inch in length and remnants of 6 others that had deteriorated. Normally no more than 10 or 12 points develop. Probably the odd development and configuration of both the beams and the tines of this specimen resulted from repeated physical injury while the antlers were in velvet. The decay of the lower extremities of the antlers would indicate that they may have been rested often on the ground. Published reports show that imperfectly developed antlers on the Virginia deer are more usual than not, but the writer does not know of any record with a rack as grotesque

Buck Killed By Lightning Splinter

In 1933 lightning struck a black oak in the woodlot of the Lloyd Straus farm 3 miles west of Rockford, Ill.

A splinter of oak 8' long and up to 4" thick was torn off and hurled 40 yards through the woods, where it struck a big whitetail buck and killed him.

On Oct. 13, 1936, I saw the bones and skull of the buck, the splinter nearby, and paced the distance to the tree. The splinter fits the wound on the tree.

Straus found the buck dead and deduced the story from the evidence.

— *Aldo Leopold*
Personal Papers

Antlered Fawn

Clinton County - Can a spotted fawn have antlers? Here's one that did. Recently I was called to remove deer from the highway that had met the fate of so many deer. With me at the time was Forest Ranger Clarence Billotte. The deer was a three point buck, in the velvet, but the amazing thing was the fact that its coat was spotted just a like a fawn. I do not infer that it was a 1953 fawn, but it must have been an instance where the last year's fawn broke out in spots again this year. Nice camouflage, but it proved ineffective against one of our modern vehicles.

— *District Game Protector*
Charles F. Keiper
Renovo, Pennsylvania
November, 1953

tail met its demise at the hands of Mother Nature.

— *James Scriven*

Richard P. Smith

■ Blinded Deer

Jim Shope from Rapid River, Michigan, reports that he encountered a white-tailed doe in Delta County during the fall of 1985 that was blinded by tumor-like growths covering its head. The animal was stumbling around aimlessly, unable to see, and was destroyed.

The growths are called fibromas and are frequently caused by virus transmitted from biting insects. Shope said he's seen the growths on deer before, but never that many.

— *Richard P. Smith*

Roland Nisleit

■ Trapped

This unusual photo was taken by my brother, Roland Nisleit. It shows a three- point buck that become trapped among a cluster of trees when he apparently tried to jump through them.

Roland found the deer while on a snowmobile trip in early December 1985. The only noticeable physical damage was on the hindquarter above the tail where a coyote or dog had chewed on him. Having escaped the record deer harvest of 1985, this white-

■ Chopping Block Antler

In the October 1987 issue of Deer & Deer Hunting, I read with interest the article in the "Deer Browse" section regarding the antler that was found wedged in the fork of a tree. It appeared that the buck struggled to free himself and, in the progress, broke the antler as well as part of his skull.

■ Deer Killed By Lightning

In early October 1983 a Marquette, Michigan bow hunter, Sanfred Olson, came upon three dead deer in a field. At the time, Olson was walking across the field after leaving his deer camp to go bow hunting early in the morning.

The three deer were all yearlings - one buck and two does. The deer were apparently killed by lightning during a thunderstorm the previous night. The accompanying photo of one of the does clearly shows the lines on her body that marked the course of electricity followed through her body.

— *Richard P. Smith*

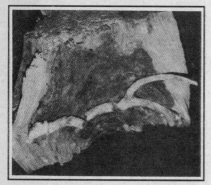

Thomas Indrebo

I have collected deer antlers for many years and a few years ago a friend of mine made an unusual find. I often speculated about the antler he found until I read the article in this magazine. My friend had been using a large section of an oak tree as a chopping block. It appeared to be from a crotch or forked section of the tree. One day the chopping block split apart, revealing a deer antler which had been completely concealed inside the tree. This antler also appeared to be fractured from the skull. The oak tree had been dead for some time prior to being cut down. We estimated the tree to be fifty to sixty years old at the time it died.

— *Thomas Indrebo*

■ Triple-header

On 25 November 1985, Deer & Deer Hunting Field Editor Richard P. Smith photographed a most unusual episode deer behavior. While few deer hunters ever encounter two bucks fighting, Richard observed and photographed an even rarer event - three bucks engaged in combat.

Richard reports that the episode took place on a rather cold day (0°F) in Michigan's Upper Peninsula. Because of the cold temperature, the bucks' faces and heads were coated with ice at daybreak. Prior to the arrival of the third buck (the smallest of the three), the two large bucks would alternately lick the ice on each other's faces and then fight. Mr. Smith suspects the younger buck got drawn in to the site of the fighting by the intensity of the activity.

Richard P. Smith

■ 461 Pounds On The Hoof

This white-tailed buck, shot in 1955 by Horace Hinkley, had a dressed weight of 355 pounds, which puts him at an estimated 461 pounds on the hoof. According to the records of the Biggest Buck in Maine Club, Hinkley's buck still remains the largest buck ever shot in that state. Indeed, it is one of the largest whitetails, in terms of weight, ever shot anywhere.

It was shot on a rainy day in November; the year was 1955. Lennie Rue recalls the tale:

"Horace Hinkley and his wife, Olive, were hunting on the Kennebec River near Bingham, Maine. It was a good hunting day because a hunter could move through the woods silently and there was only a light breeze to move scent around. Mr. and Mrs. Hinkley took stands on opposite sides of a ridge. At about 9:20 that morning, Hinkley fired at a buck but missed. A few minutes later, Olive Hinkley's rifle cracked, and after a few minutes she shouted that she had downed a big buck. Hinkley, certain that there were more deer in a thicket of scrub beech where he had missed the first one, remained where he was and did not respond. Suddenly a huge buck came crashing out of the brush toward him. Hinkley dropped the animal with one shot. It was so heavy that the Hinkleys had to get help to haul it out.

"The buck was not officially weighed until three days later. The weighing was performed by Forrest Brown, an official state sealer of weights and measures, and there were two witnesses. Hog-dressed, and after three days of drying out, it still scaled 355 pounds (160.8 kg.). Bob Elliot, of Maine's Department of Game, originally calculated the live weight to be at least 450 pounds (203.8 kg.) and more probably 480 pounds (217 kg.). Records of the Biggest Bucks in Maine Club officially established the weight at 461-1/2 pounds. The buck's rack was excellent, but not in keeping with its body size. There were eight points on each side, with a spread of twenty-one inches (53 cm.) and a beam length of 24.5 inches (63 cm.)."

Several bucks have come close to this record. One thinks of Dean Coffman who shot a 440-pound Iowa buck in 1962. Or Robert Hogue who reportedly shot a buck in Sawyer County, Wisconsin in 1924, that had a dressed scale weight of 386 pounds (174.8 kg.) and an estimated live weight of 491 pounds (222.4kg.) Unfortunately, Hogue's buck was not officially witnessed. One also thinks of the huge southern whitetail taken in Worth County, Georgia, in 1972 by Boyd Jones. Hog-dressed, it weighed 355 pounds (160.8 kg.) with an estimated live weight of 443 pounds (200.6 kg.).

Minnesota, however, claims the all-time record with Carl J. Lenander's buck shot in 1926. Field-dressed, it scaled 402 pounds (182.1 kg.). The Conservation Department calculated its live weight to be 511 pounds (231.4 kg.), making it the largest whitetail ever officially recorded in North America.

— *Rob Wegner*

Maine Fish and Game Department

■ Old Age is No Friend

Older isn't necessarily better for white-tailed deer. Dinny Slaughter of Marshall, Va., is the operations supervisor of a 4,000-acre breeding farm owned by the Smithsonian Institution. A white-tailed buck lived in a 50-acre woodland/grass enclosure on the farm. Slaughter was able to watch this buck as it grew up and eventually reached age 12.

During the buck's life, it spent most of its time in a thick woods.

Slaughter said people never entered its hideaway, and months sometimes passed without anyone seeing it. The only time it left the woods was the first week of November, when it roamed the fence line looking for does during the rut.

The buck, which was nicknamed, "Slick," always fended for itself. It never begged for

This buck was 12 years old when this picture was taken. It died shortly after from a wide assortment of ailments, including heart disease and arthritis.

food.

The buck's health deteriorated as old age set in. In October of its 12th year, the buck could go no further. Slaughter found it lying down one day and reluctant to get up. The veterinarian came and put it down for good.

An autopsy showed the buck was suffering from heart disease, arthritis, foot rot, skin cuts, hair balls, malnutrition, skin infections, internal and external parasites, and hair and tooth loss.

—*Pat Durkin*
Editor

■ Freak Accident Claims Buck

A freak accident killed an 8-point buck soon after Michigan's 1990 gun season ended. Earl Schuster of Marquette, Mich., witnessed the incident at Little Lake Road on Dec. 5, 1990, about noon.

Schuster said he was driving along when he noticed a buck to his left. It was running parallel to the road on the far side of a barbed-wire fence, and was matching his speed.

A hill blocked Schuster's view of the buck briefly. Soon after it came back into sight, the deer moved for the road and the motorist let up on the gas pedal to avoid a possible collision.

Apparently in a panic to cross the road ahead of the vehicle, the buck didn't attempt to jump the fence. The whitetail plowed into the strands of wire.

"He hit the fence at full stride," Schuster said. "His momentum pushed his head over the fence and his body followed, snapping his neck."

A snow drift at the spot blocked the buck's carcass from view.

"If I hadn't seen it happen, no one would have known the buck was there," Schuster said.

He found someone at a local farm who had an archery deer license and took him to the buck. The hunter then took the carcass. Schuster estimated the buck's weight at about 200 pounds.

A buck that size would be at least 3.5 years old. It's amazing the animal was clever enough to avoid hunters at least two autumns, only to be brought down by a fence.

— *Richard P. Smith*

■ 10 Deer Die in Plunge Off Bridge

Ten white-tailed deer plunged more than 25 feet to their deaths from a bridge in western Henrico County, Va., on Feb. 13, 1991.

The eight does and two young bucks, apparently spooked by traffic, ran across the River Road overpass on Parham Road shortly before 1:30 p.m. and jumped onto Parham, said S.A. Gemmill, a county animal protection officer.

Gemmill said a witness saw the deer run from woods behind All Saints Episcopal Church, and called police from her car telephone. By the time Gemmill arrived, the deer were dead.

Three landed on one side of the bridge and seven on the other. "Luckily there were no rush-hour cars underneath them," Gemmill said.

Officials tagged the deer and gave them to drivers in passing automobiles.

Bob Duncan, wildlife division chief for the Virginia Department of Game and Inland Fisheries, said, "I've heard of similar things happening, but this is certainly the most unusual case in Virginia."

In 1989, Duncan said, 2,213 of the state's estimated 800,000 deer died in traffic-related accidents. He said the River Road case probably will be classified "miscellaneous," a listing that applied to 67 deer deaths in 1989.

Duncan said the bridge deaths weren't a "deer suicide." He speculated that three deer ventured onto the road, the others followed tentatively, and traffic prompted them to flee the road and jump.

"There is a social hierarchy," he said. "There is a lead animal that the others are going to follow."

—*Richmond News Leader*
Feb. 14, 1991

■ Bluffed Buck

For all the strange things the white-tailed buck is known for doing, stepping off a 60 foot bluff and hanging himself is not one of them. But that is exactly what happened to one large buck in Arkansas last deer season.

I first became aware of this freak accident this past season while some of my friends and family were deer hunting on my farm near Batesville, Ark. Marlon Fisher, a neighbor, drove up looking for some of his hunting dogs. After a little small talk, Marlon told us of a strange scene he and his hunting buddies had stumbled upon. A large buck had somehow managed to fall into the crevice of a high bluff and was caught by his antlers as he fell. As the buck's wide rack lodged into the crack he tried to free himself. But the more he struggled to free himself the tighter his antlers wedged into place. His struggles along with his body weight did manage to pull him within a few feet of the ground, but there he hung and met a cruel death. Marlon said the buck was still hanging there, so we asked if he would take us to see this strange sight.

This particular series of bluffs range from just a few feet to well over a 100 feet high, and they run for miles with many cracks and crevices scattered along their length. In several places you can walk up and down the bluffs with ease, and the deer use them frequently. There was one such place not far from where this freak accident took place. Upon closer inspection it was obvious the big buck had struggled for some time, for there were scuff marks on both sides of the crevice. The deer was a magnificent specimen, with a wide, heavy-beamed rack. Apparently he had been hanging there for some time, as the carcass was beginning to decompose and hair was falling off. What could have caused a sure-footed animal, such as the whitetail, to step off such a high bluff? We have all given this question much thought, but may never really know what caused this freak accident.

— *Gary Mize*
Batesville, Arkansas

FIREARM
BALLISTICS

WINCHESTER

WINCHESTER	Bullet Wt.	Bullet	Barrel Length	Velocity in Feet Per Second (fps)						Energy in Foot Pounds (ft-lbs.)		
Cartridge	Grs.	Type	(In.)	Muzzle	100	200	300	400	500	Muzzle	100	200
22-250 Remington	55	PSP	24	3680	3137	2656	2222	1832	1493	1654	1201	861
222 Remington	50	PSP	24	3140	2602	2123	1700	1350	1107	1094	752	500
222 Remington	55	FMJ	24	3020	2675	2355	2057	1783	1537	1114	874	677
223 Remington	53	HP	24	3330	2882	2477	2106	1770	1475	1305	978	722
223 Remington	55	PSP	24	3240	2747	2304	1905	1554	1270	1282	921	648
223 Remington	55	FMJ	24	3240	2877	2543	2232	1943	1679	1282	1011	790
223 Remington	64	PP	24	3020	2621	2256	1920	1619	1362	1296	977	723
225 Winchester	55	PSP	24	3570	3066	2616	2208	1838	1514	1556	1148	836
243 Winchester	80	PSP	24	3350	2955	2593	2259	1951	1670	1993	1551	1194
243 Winchester	100	PP	24	2960	2697	2449	2215	1993	1786	1945	1615	1332
6mm Remington	80	PSP	24	3470	3064	2694	2352	2036	1747	2139	1667	1289
6mm Remington	100	PP	24	3100	2829	2573	2332	2104	1889	2133	1777	1470
25-06 Remington	90	PEP	24	3440	3043	2680	2344	2034	1749	2364	1850	1435
25-06 Remington	120	PEP	24	2990	2730	2484	2252	2032	1825	2382	1985	1644
25-20 Winchester #	86	SP	24	~1460	1194	1030	931	858	798	407	272	203
25-35 Winchester	117	SP	24	2230	1866	1545	1282	1097	984	1292	904	620
250 Savage	100	ST	24	2820	2467	2140	1839	1569	1339	1765	1351	1017
257 Roberts + P	100	ST	24	3000	2633	2295	1982	1697	1447	1998	1539	1169
257 Roberts + P	117	PP	24	2780	2411	2071	1761	1488	1263	2009	1511	1115
264 Winchester Mag.	140	PP	24	3030	2782	2548	2326	2114	1914	2854	2406	2018
270 Winchester	100	PSP	24	3430	3021	2649	2305	1988	1699	2612	2027	1557
270 Winchester	130	PP	24	3060	2802	2559	2329	2110	1904	2702	2267	1890
270 Winchester	130	ST	24	3060	2776	2510	2259	2022	1801	2702	2225	1818
270 Winchester	150	PP	24	2850	2585	2336	2100	1879	1673	2705	2226	1817
280 Remington	140	PP	24	3050	2705	2428	2167	1924	1698	2799	2274	1833
284 Winchester	150	PP	24	2860	2595	2344	2108	1886	1680	2724	2243	1830
7mm Mauser (7x57)	145	PP	24	2660	2413	2180	1959	1754	1564	2279	1875	1530
7mm Remington Mag.	150	PP	24	3110	2830	2568	2320	2085	1866	3221	2667	2196
7mm Remington Mag.	175	PP	24	2860	2645	2440	2244	2057	1879	3178	2718	2313
7.62x39	123	SP	20	2365	2033	1731	1465	1248	1093	1527	1129	818
30 Carbine #	110	HSP	20	1990	1567	1236	1035	923	842	967	600	373
30 Carbine #	110	FMJ	20	1990	1596	1278	1070	952	870	967	622	399
30-30 Winchester	150	HP	24	2390	2018	1684	1398	1177	1036	1902	1356	944
30-30 Winchester	150	PP	24	2390	2018	1684	1398	1177	1036	1902	1356	944
30-30 Winchester	150	ST	24	2390	2018	1684	1398	1177	1036	1902	1356	944

WINCHESTER

Energy in Foot Pounds (ft-lbs)			Trajectory, Short Range Yards						Trajectory, Long Range Yards						
300	400	500	50	100	150	200	250	300	100	150	200	250	300	400	500
603	410	272	0.2	0.5	0	-1.6	-4.4	-8.7	2.3	2.6	1.9	0	-3.4	-15.9	-38.9
321	202	136	0.5	0.9	0	-2.5	-6.9	-13.7	2.2	1.9	0	-3.8	-10.0	-32.3	-73.8
517	388	288	0.5	0.9	0	-2.2	-6.1	-11.7	2.0	1.7	0	-3.3	-8.3	-24.9	-52.5
522	369	256	0.3	0.7	0	-1.9	-5.3	-10.3	1.7	1.4	0	-2.9	-7.4	-22.7	-49.1
443	295	197	0.4	0.8	0	-2.2	-6.0	-11.8	1.9	1.6	0	-3.3	-8.5	-26.7	-59.6
608	461	344	0.4	0.7	0	-1.9	-5.1	-9.9	1.7	1.4	0	-2.8	-7.1	-21.2	-44.6
524	373	264	0.6	0.9	0	-2.4	-6.5	-12.5	2.1	1.8	0	-3.5	-9.0	-27.4	-59.6
595	412	280	0.2	0.6	0	-1.7	-4.6	-9.0	2.4	2.8	2.0	0	-3.5	-16.3	-39.5
906	676	495	0.3	0.7	0	-1.8	-4.9	-9.4	2.6	2.9	2.1	0	-3.6	-16.2	-37.9
1089	882	708	0.5	0.9	0	-2.2	-5.8	-11.0	1.9	1.6	0	-3.1	-7.8	-22.6	-46.3
982	736	542	0.3	0.6	0	-1.6	-4.5	-8.7	2.4	2.7	1.9	0	-3.3	-14.9	-35.0
1207	983	792	0.4	0.8	0	-1.9	-5.2	-9.9	1.7	1.5	0	-2.8	-7.0	-20.4	-41.7
1098	827	611	0.3	0.6	0	-1.7	-4.5	-8.8	2.4	2.7	2.0	0	-3.4	-15.0	-35.2
1351	1100	887	0.5	0.8	0	-2.1	-5.6	-10.7	1.9	1.6	0	-3.0	-7.5	-22.0	-44.8
165	141	122	0	-4.1	-14.4	-31.8	-57.3	-92.0	0	-8.2	-23.5	-47.0	-79.6	-175.9	-319.4
427	313	252	0.6	0	-3.1	-9.2	-19.0	-33.1	2.1	0	-5.1	-13.8	-27.0	-70.1	-142.0
751	547	398	0.2	0	-1.6	-4.9	-10.0	-17.4	2.4	2.0	0	-3.9	-10.1	-30.5	-65.2
872	639	465	0.5	0.9	0	-2.4	-4.9	-12.3	2.9	3.0	1.6	0	-6.4	-23.2	-51.2
806	576	415	0.8	1.1	0	-2.9	-7.8	-15.1	2.6	2.2	0	-4.2	-10.8	-33.0	-70.0
1682	1389	1139	0.5	0.8	0	-2.0	-5.4	-10.2	1.8	1.5	0	-2.9	-7.2	-20.8	-42.2
1179	877	641	0.3	0.6	0	-1.7	-4.6	-9.0	2.5	2.8	2.0	0	-3.4	-15.5	-36.4
1565	1285	1046	0.4	0.8	0	-2.0	-5.3	-10.1	1.8	1.5	0	-2.8	-7.1	-20.6	-42.0
1472	1180	936	0.5	0.8	0	-2.0	-5.5	-10.4	1.8	1.5	0	-2.9	-7.4	-21.6	-44.3
1468	1175	932	0.6	1.0	0	-2.4	-6.4	-12.2	2.2	1.8	0	-3.4	-8.6	-25.0	-51.4
1461	1151	897	0.5	0.8	0.0	-2.2	-5.8	-11.1	1.9	1.6	0	-3.1	-7.8	-23.1	-47.8
1480	1185	940	0.6	1.0	0	-2.4	-6.3	-12.1	2.1	1.8	0	-3.4	-8.5	-24.8	-51.0
1236	990	788	0.2	0	-1.7	-5.1	-10.3	-17.5	1.1	0	-2.8	-7.4	-14.1	-34.4	-66.1
1792	1448	1160	0.4	0.8	0	-1.9	-5.2	-9.9	1.7	1.5	0	-2.8	-7.0	-20.5	-42.1
1956	1644	1372	0.6	0.9	0	-2.3	-6.0	-11.3	2.0	1.7	0	-3.2	-7.9	-22.7	-45.8
586	425	327	5	0	-2.6	-7.6	-15.4	-26.7	3.8	3.1	0	-6.0	-15.4	-46.3	-98.4
262	208	173	0.9	0	-4.5	-13.5	-28.3	-49.9	0	-4.5	-13.5	-28.3	-49.9	-118.6	-228.2
280	221	185	0.9	0	-4.3	-13.0	-26.9	-47.4	2.9	0	-7.2	-19.7	-38.7	-100.4	-200.5
651	461	357	0.5	0	-2.6	-7.7	-16.0	-27.9	1.7	0	-4.3	-11.6	-22.7	-59.1	-120.5
651	461	357	0.5	0	-2.6	-7.7	-16.0	-27.9	1.7	0	-4.3	-11.6	-22.7	-59.1	-120.5
651	461	357	0.5	0	-2.6	-7.7	-16.0	-27.9	1.7	0	-4.3	-11.6	-22.7	-59.1	-120.5

WINCHESTER

WINCHESTER	Bullet Wt.	Bullet	Barrel Length	Velocity in Feet Per Second (fps)						Energy in Foot Pounds (ft-lbs.)		
Cartridge	Grs.	Type	(In.)	Muzzle	100	200	300	400	500	Muzzle	100	200
30-30 Winchester	170	PP	24	2200	1895	1619	1381	1191	1061	1827	1355	989
30-30 Winchester	170	ST	24	2200	1895	1619	1381	1191	1061	1827	1355	989
30-06 Springfield	125	PSP	24	3140	2780	2447	2138	1853	1595	2736	2145	1662
30-06 Springfield	150	PP	24	2920	2580	2265	1972	1704	1466	2839	2217	1708
30-06 Springfield	150	ST	24	2910	2617	2342	2083	1843	1622	2820	2281	1827
30-06 Springfield	165	SP	24	2800	2573	2357	2151	1956	1772	2873	2426	2036
30-06 Springfield	180	PP	24	2700	2348	2023	1727	1466	1251	2913	2203	1635
30-06 Springfield	180	ST	24	2700	2469	2250	2042	1846	1663	2913	2436	2023
30-06 Springfield	220	ST	24	2410	2192	1985	1791	1611	1448	2837	2347	1924
30-40 Krag	180	PP	24	2430	2099	1795	1525	1298	1128	2360	1761	1288
300 Winchester Mag.	150	PP	24	3290	2951	2636	2342	2068	1813	3605	2900	2314
300 Winchester Mag.	180	PP	24	2960	2745	2540	2344	2157	1979	3501	3011	2578
300 Winchester Mag.	220	ST	24	2680	2448	2228	2020	1823	1640	3508	2927	2424
300 H. & H. Magnum	180	ST	24	2880	2640	2412	2196	1991	1798	3315	2785	2325
300 Savage	150	PP	24	2630	2311	2015	1743	1500	1295	2303	1779	1352
300 Savage	150	ST	24	2630	2354	2095	1853	1631	1434	2303	1845	1462
300 Savage	180	PP	24	2350	2025	1728	1467	1252	1098	2207	1639	1193
303 Savage	190	ST	24	1890	1612	1372	1183	1055	970	1507	1096	794
303 British	180	PP	24	2460	2233	2018	1816	1629	1459	2418	1993	1627
307 Winchester	180	PP	24	2510	2179	1874	1599	1362	1177	2519	1898	1404
308 Winchester	150	PP	24	2820	2488	2179	1893	1633	1405	2648	2061	1581
308 Winchester	150	ST	24	2820	2533	2263	2009	1774	1560	2648	2137	1705
308 Winchester	180	PP	24	2620	2274	1955	1666	1414	1212	2743	2066	1527
308 Winchester	180	ST	24	2620	2393	2178	1974	1782	1604	2743	2288	1896
32 Win Special	170	PP	24	2250	1870	1537	1267	1082	971	1911	1320	892
32 Win Special	170	ST	24	2250	1870	1537	1267	1082	971	1911	1320	892
32-20 Winchester #	100	Lead	24	1210	1021	913	834	769	712	325	231	185
8mm Mauser (8x57)	170	PP	24	2360	1969	1622	1333	1123	997	2102	1463	993
338 Winchester Mag.	200	PP	24	2960	2658	2375	2110	1862	1635	3890	3137	2505
338 Winchester Mag.	225	SP	24	2780	2572	2374	2184	2003	1832	3862	3306	2816
348 Winchester	200	ST	24	2520	2215	1931	1672	1443	1253	2820	2178	1656
35 Remington	200	PP	24	2020	1646	1335	1114	985	901	1812	1203	791
35 Remington	200	ST	24	2020	1646	1335	1114	985	901	1812	1203	791
356 Winchester	200	PP	24	2460	2114	1797	1517	1284	1113	2688	1985	1434
356 Winchester	250	PP	24	2160	1911	1682	1476	1299	1158	2591	2028	1571
357 Magnum	158	JSP	20	1830	1427	1138	980	883	809	1175	715	454
358 Winchester	200	ST	24	2490	2171	1876	1610	1379	1194	2753	2093	1563

WINCHESTER

Energy in Foot Pounds (ft-lbs.)			Trajectory, Short Range Yards						Trajectory, Long Range Yards						
300	400	500	50	100	150	200	250	300	100	150	200	250	300	400	500
720	535	425	0.6	0	-3.0	-8.9	-18.0	-31.1	2.0	0	-4.8	-13.0	-25.1	-63.6	-126.7
720	535	425	0.6	0	-3.0	-8.9	-18.0	-31.1	2.0	0	-4.8	-13.0	-25.1	-63.6	-126.7
1269	953	706	0.4	0.8	0	-2.1	-5.6	-10.7	1.8	1.5	0	-3.0	-7.7	-23.0	-48.5
1295	967	716	0.6	1.0	0	-2.4	-6.6	-12.7	2.2	1.8	0	-3.5	-9.0	-27.0	-57.1
-1445	1131	876	0.6	0.9	0	-2.3	-6.3	-12.0	2.1	1.8	0	-3.3	-8.5	-25.0	-51.8
1696	1402	1151	0.7	1.0	0	-2.5	-6.5	-12.2	2.2	1.9	0	-3.6	-8.4	-24.4	-49.6
1192	849	625	0.2	0	-1.8	-5.5	-11.2	-19.5	2.7	2.3	0	-4.4	-11.3	-34.4	-73.7
1666	1362	1105	0.2	0	-1.6	-4.8	-9.7	-16.5	2.4	2.0	0	-3.7	-9.3	-27.0	-54.9
1567	1268	1024	0.4	0	-2.2	-6.4	-12.7	-21.6	1.5	0	-3.5	-9.1	-17.2	-41.8	-79.9
929	673	508	0.4	0	-2.4	-7.1	-14.5	-25.0	1.6	0	-3.9	-10.5	-20.3	-51.7	-103.9
1827	1424	1095	0.3	0.7	0	-1.8	-4.8	-9.3	2.6	2.9	2.1	0	-3.5	-15.4	-35.5
2196	1859	1565	0.5	0.8	0	-2.1	-5.5	-10.4	1.9	1.6	0	-2.9	-7.3	-20.9	-41.9
1993	1623	1314	0.2	0	-1.7	-4.9	-9.9	-16.9	2.5	2.0	0	-3.8	-9.5	-27.5	-56.1
1927	1584	1292	0.6	0.9	0	-2.3	-6.0	-11.5	2.1	1.7	0	-3.2	-8.0	-23.3	-47.4
1012	749	558	0.3	0	-1.9	-5.7	-11.6	-19.9	2.8	2.3	0	-4.5	-11.5	-34.4	-73.0
1143	886	685	0.3	0	-1.8	-5.4	-11.0	-18.8	2.7	2.2	0	-4.2	-10.7	-31.5	-65.5
860	626	482	0.5	0	-2.6	-7.7	-15.6	-27.1	1.7	0	-4.2	-11.3	-21.9	-55.8	-112.0
591	469	397	1.0	0	-4.3	-12.6	-25.5	-43.7	2.9	0	-6.8	-18.3	-35.1	-88.2	-172.5
1318	1060	851	0.3	0	-2.1	-6.1	-12.2	-20.8	1.4	0	-3.3	-8.8	-16.6	-40.4	-77.4
1022	742	554	0.3	0	-2.2	-6.5	-13.3	-22.9	1.5	0	-3.6	-9.6	-18.6	-47.1	-93.7
1193	888	657	0.2	0	-1.6	-4.8	-9.8	-16.9	2.4	2.0	0	-3.8	-9.8	-29.3	-62.0
1344	1048	810	0.2	0	-1.5	-4.5	-9.3	-15.9	2.3	1.9	0	-3.6	-9.1	-26.9	-55.7
1109	799	587	0.3	0	-2.0	-5.9	-12.1	-20.9	2.9	2.4	0	-4.7	-12.1	-36.9	-79.1
1557	1269	1028	0.2	0	-1.8	-5.2	-10.4	-17.7	2.6	2.1	0	-4.0	-9.9	-28.9	-58.8
606	442	356	0.6	0	-3.1	-9.2	-19.0	-33.2	2.0	0	-5.1	-13.8	-27.1	-70.9	-144.3
606	442	356	0.6	0	-3.1	-9.2	-19.0	-33.2	2.0	0	-5.1	-13.8	-27.1	-70.9	-144.3
154	131	113	0	-6.3	-20.9	-44.9	-79.3	-125.1	0	-11.5	-32.3	-63.6	-106.3	-230.3	-413.3
671	476	375	0.5	0	-2.7	-8.2	-17.0	-29.8	1.8	0	-4.5	-12.4	-24.3	-63.8	-130.7
1977	1539	1187	0.5	0.9	0	-2.3	-6.1	-11.6	2.0	1.7	0	-3.2	-8.2	-24.3	-50.4
2384	2005	1677	1.2	1.3	0	-2.7	-7.1	-12.9	2.7	2.1	0	-3.6	-9.4	-25.0	-49.9
1241	925	697	0.3	0	-2.1	-6.2	-12.7	-21.9	1.4	0	-3.4	-9.2	-17.7	-44.4	-87.9
551	431	360	0.9	0	-4.1	-12.1	-25.1	-43.9	2.7	0	-6.7	-18.3	-35.8	-92.8	-185.5
551	431	360	0.9	0	-4.1	-12.1	-25.1	-43.9	2.7	0	-6.7	-18.3	-35.8	-92.8	-185.5
1022	732	550	0.4	0	-2.3	-7.0	-14.3	-24.7	1.6	0	-3.8	-10.4	-20.1	-51.2	-102.3
1210	937	745	0.6	0	-3.0	-8.7	-17.4	-30.0	2.0	0	-4.7	-12.4	-23.7	-58.4	-112.9
337	274	229	0	-2.4	-9.1	-21.0	-39.2	-64.3	0	-5.5	-16.2	-33.1	-57.0	-128.3	-235.8
1151	844	633	0.4	0	-2.2	-6.5	-13.3	-23.0	1.5	0	3.6	-9.7	-18.6	-47.2	-94.1

FEDERAL
PREMIUM CENTERFIRE RIFLE BALLISTICS

CALIBER	BULLETS WGT IN GRAINS	BULLET STYLE	VELOCITY IN FEET PER SECOND (TO NEAREST 10 FEET)					
			MUZZLE	100 YDS.	200 YDS.	300 YDS.	400 YDS.	500 YDS.
223 REM. (5.56X45MM)	55	Boat-Tail HP	3240	2770	2340	1950	1610	1330
22-250 REM.	55	Boat-Tail HP	3680	3280	2920	2590	2280	1990
243 WIN. (6.16X51MM)	100	Boat-Tail SP	2960	2760	2570	2380	2210	2040
243 WIN. (6.16X51MM)	85	Boat-Tail HP	3320	3070	2830	2600	2380	2180
243 WIN. (6.16X51MM)	100	Nosler Partition	2960	2730	2510	2300	2100	1910
6MM REM.	100	Nosler Partition	3100	2830	2570	2330	2100	1890
257 ROBERTS (High-Velocity+P)	120	Nosler Partition	2780	2560	2360	2160	1970	1790
25-06 REM.	117	Boat-Tail SP	2990	2770	2570	2370	2190	2000
6.5X55 SWEDISH	140	Nosler Partition	2850	2640	2440	2250	2070	1890
270 WIN.	150	Boat-Tail SP	2850	2660	2480	2300	2130	1970
270 WIN.	130	Boat-Tail SP	3060	2830	2620	2410	2220	2030
270 WIN.	150	Nosler Partition	2850	2590	2340	2100	1880	1670
7-30 WATERS	120	Boat-Tail SP	2700	2300	1930	1600	1330	1140
7MM MAUSER (7x57mm Mauser)	140	Nosler Partition	2660	2450	2260	2070	1890	1730
7X64 BRENNEKE	160	Nosler Partition	2850	2669	2495	2327	2166	2012
280 REM.	150	Nosler Partition	2890	2620	2370	2140	1910	1710
7MM REM. MAGNUM	150	Boat-Tail SP	3110	2920	2750	2580	2410	2250
7MM REM. MAGNUM	165	Boat-Tail SP	2950	2800	2650	2510	2370	2230
7MM REM. MAGNUM	160	Nosler Partition	2950	2770	2590	2420	2250	2090
7MM REM. MAGNUM	140	Nosler Partition	3150	2930	2710	2510	2320	2130
30-30 WIN.	170	Nosler Partition	2200	1900	1620	1380	1190	1060
308 WIN. (7.62X51MM)	165	Boat-Tail SP	2700	2520	2330	2160	1990	1830
308 WIN. (7.62X51MM)	180	Nosler Partition	2620	2430	2240	2060	1890	1730
30-06 SPRING (7.62X63MM)	165	Boat-Tail SP	2800	2610	2420	2240	2070	1910
30-06 SPRING (7.62X63MM)	180	Nosler Partition	2700	2500	2320	2140	1970	1810
30-06 SPRING (7.62X63MM)	150	Boat-Tail SP	2910	2690	2480	2270	2070	1880
30-06 SPRING (7.62X63MM)	180	Boat-Tail SP	2700	2540	2380	2220	2080	1930
300 H&H MAGNUM	180	Nosler Partition	2880	2620	2380	2150	1930	1730
300 WIN. MAGNUM	200	Boat-Tail SP	2830	2680	2530	2380	2240	2110
300 WIN. MAGNUM	180	Nosler Partition	2960	2700	2450	2210	1990	1780
338 WIN. MAGNUM	210	Nosler Partition	2830	2590	2370	2160	1960	1770
338 WIN. MAGNUM	250	Nosler Partition	2660	2400	2150	1910	1690	1500

FEDERAL
PREMIUM CENTERFIRE RIFLE BALLISTICS

ENERGY IN FOOT/POUNDS (TO NEAREST 5 FOOT/POUNDS)						HEIGHT OF BULLET TRAJECTORY IN INCHES ABOVE OR BELOW LINE OF SIGHT IF ZEROED AT ⊕YARDS. SIGHTS 1.5 INCHES ABOVE BORE LINE									TEST BARREL INCHES
						AVERAGE RANGE				LONG RANGE					
MUZZLE	100 YDS.	200 YDS.	300 YDS.	400 YDS.	500 YDS.	50 YDS.	100 YDS.	200 YDS.	300 YDS.	50 YDS.	100 YDS.	300 YDS.	400 YDS.	500 YDS.	
1280	935	670	465	315	215	-0.3	⊕	-2.7	-10.8	+0.4	+1.4	-6.7	-20.5	-43.4	24
1655	1315	1040	815	630	480	-0.4	⊕	-1.7	-7.6	0	+0.9	-5.0	-15.1	-32.0	24
1950	1690	1460	1260	1080	925	-0.2	⊕	-3.1	-11.4	+0.6	+1.5	-6.8	-19.8	-39.9	24
2080	1770	1510	1280	1070	890	-0.3	⊕	-2.2	-8.8	+0.2	+1.1	-5.5	-16.1	-32.8	24
1945	1650	1395	1170	975	805	-0.2	⊕	-3.2	-11.9	+0.6	+1.6	-7.1	-20.9	-42.5	24
2135	1775	1470	1205	985	790	-0.3	⊕	-2.9	-11.0	+0.5	+1.4	-6.7	-19.8	-39.0	24
2060	1750	1480	1240	1030	855	-0.1	⊕	-3.8	-14.0	+0.8	-1.9	-8.2	-24.0	-48.9	24
2320	2000	1715	1465	1240	1045	-0.2	⊕	-3.0	-11.4	+0.5	+1.5	-6.8	19.9	-40.4	24
2525	2170	1855	1575	1330	1115	-0.2	⊕	-3.5	-12.8	+0.7	+1.7	-7.6	-22.1	-44.5	24
2705	2355	2040	1760	1510	1290	-0.2	⊕	-3.4	-12.5	+0.7	+1.7	-7.4	-21.4	-43.0	24
2700	2320	1980	1680	1420	1190	-0.2	⊕	-2.8	-10.7	+0.5	+1.4	-6.5	-19.0	-38.5	24
2705	2225	1815	1470	1175	930	-0.2	⊕	-3.7	-13.8	+0.8	+1.9	-8.3	-24.4	-50.5	24
1940	1405	990	685	470	345	0	⊕	-5.2	-19.8	+1.2	+2.6	-12.0	-37.6	-81.7	24
2200	1865	1585	1330	1110	930	-0.1	⊕	-4.3	-15.4	+1.0	+2.1	-9.0	-26.1	-52.9	24
2885	2530	2211	1924	1667	1438	-0.2	⊕	-3.4	-12.3	+0.7	+1.7	-7.2	-21.0	-42.0	24
2780	2295	1875	1520	1215	970	-0.2	⊕	-3.6	-13.4	+0.7	+1.8	-8.0	-23.8	-49.2	24
3220	2850	2510	2210	1930	1690	-0.3	⊕	-2.6	-9.8	+0.4	+1.3	-5.9	-17.0	-34.2	24
3190	2865	2570	2300	2050	1825	-0.2	⊕	-3.0	-10.9	+0.5	+1.5	-6.4	-18.4	-36.6	24
3090	2715	2375	2075	1800	1555	-0.2	⊕	-3.1	-11.3	+0.6	+1.5	-6.7	-19.4	-39.0	24
3085	2660	2290	1960	1670	1415	-0.3	⊕	-2.6	-9.9	+0.4	+1.3	-6.0	-17.5	-35.6	24
1830	1355	990	720	535	425	-0.3	⊕	-8.3	-29.8	+2.4	+4.1	-17.4	-52.4	-109.4	24
2670	2310	1990	1700	1450	1230	-0.1	⊕	-4.0	-14.4	+0.9	+2.0	-8.4	-24.3	-49.0	24
2745	2355	2005	1700	1430	1200	-0.1	⊕	-4.4	-15.8	+1.0	+2.2	-9.2	-26.5	-53.6	24
2870	2490	2150	1840	1580	1340	-0.2	⊕	-3.6	-13.2	+0.8	+1.8	-7.8	-22.4	-45.2	24
2910	2510	2150	1830	1550	1350	-0.1	⊕	-4.0	-14.6	+1.9	+2.0	-8.6	-24.6	-49.6	24
2820	2420	2040	1710	1430	1180	-0.2	⊕	-3.3	-14.4	+0.6	+1.7	-7.4	-21.5	-43.7	24
2915	2570	2260	1975	1720	1495	-0.1	⊕	-3.9	-13.9	+0.9	+1.9	-8.1	-23.1	-46.1	24
3315	2750	2260	1840	1480	1190	-0.3	⊕	-3.5	-13.3	+0.7	+1.8	-8.0	-23.4	-48.6	24
3560	3180	2830	2520	2230	1970	-0.2	⊕	-3.4	-12.2	+0.7	+1.7	-7.1	+20.4	-40.5	24
3500	2905	2395	1955	1585	1270	-0.2	⊕	-3.3	-12.4	+0.6	+1.6	-7.5	-22.1	-45.4	24
3735	3140	2620	2170	1785	1455	-0.2	⊕	-3.6	-13.6	+0.8	+1.8	-8.1	-23.6	-48.3	24
3925	3185	2555	2055	1590	1245	-0.1	⊕	-4.6	-16.7	+1.1	+2.3	-9.8	-29.1	-60.2	24

FEDERAL
CLASSIC® CENTERFIRE RIFLE BALLISTICS

CALIBER	BULLET WGT IN GRAINS	BULLET STYLE	VELOCITY IN FEET PER SECOND (TO NEAREST 10 FEET)						ENERGY IN FOOT/POUNDS (TO NEAREST 5 FOOT/POUNDS)		
			MUZZLE	100 YDS.	200 YDS.	300 YDS.	400 YDS.	500 YDS.	MUZZLE	100 YDS.	200 YDS.
222 Rem. (5.56x43mm)	50	Hi-Shok Soft Pint	3140	2600	2120	1700	1350	1110	1095	750	500
	55	Hi-Shok FMJ Boat-tail	3020	2740	2480	2230	1990	1780	1115	915	750
223 Rem. (5.56x45mm)	55	Hi-Shok Soft Point	3240	2750	2300	1910	1550	1270	1280	920	650
	55	Hi-Shok FMJ Boat-tail	3240	2950	2670	2410	2170	1940	1280	1060	875
22-250 Rem.	55	Hi-Shok Soft Point	3680	3140	2660	2220	1830	1490	1655	1200	860
243 Win. (6.16x51mm)	80	Hi-Shok Soft Point	3350	2960	2590	2260	1950	1670	1995	1550	1195
	100	Hi-Shok Soft Point	2960	2700	2450	2220	1990	1790	1945	1615	1330
6mm Rem.	80	Hi-Shok Soft Point	3470	3060	2690	2350	2040	1750	2140	1665	1290
	100	Hi-Shok Soft Point	3100	2830	2570	2330	2100	1890	2135	1775	1470
25-06 Rem.	117	Hi-Shok Soft Point	2990	2730	2480	2250	2030	1830	2320	1985	1645
270 Win.	130	Hi-Shok Soft Point	3060	2800	2560	2330	2110	1900	2700	2265	1890
	150	Hi-Shok Soft Point RN	2850	2500	2180	1890	1620	1390	2705	2085	1585
7mm Mauser	175	Hi-Shok Soft Point RN	2440	2140	1860	1600	1380	1200	2315	1775	1340
(7x57mm Mauser)	140	Hi-Shok Soft Point	2660	2450	2260	2070	1890	1730	2200	1865	1585
280 Rem.	150	Hi-Shok Soft Point	2890	2670	2460	2260	2060	1880	2780	2370	2015
7mm Rem. Magnum	150	Hi-Shok Soft Point	3110	2830	2570	2320	2090	1870	3220	2670	2200
	175	Hi-Shok Soft Point	2860	2650	2440	2240	2060	1880	3180	2720	2310
30 Carbine (7.62x33mm)	110	Hi-Shok Soft Point RN	1990	1570	1240	1040	920	840	965	600	375
7.62x39mm Soviet	123	Hi-Shok Soft Point	2300	2030	1780	1550	1350	1200	1445	1125	860
30-30 Win.	150	Hi-Shok Soft Point FN	2390	2020	1680	1400	1180	1040	1900	1355	945
	170	Hi-Shok Soft Point RN	2200	1900	1620	1380	1190	1060	1830	1355	990
	125	Hi-Shok Hollow Point	2570	2090	1660	1320	1080	960	1830	1210	770

FEDERAL
CLASSIC® CENTERFIRE RIFLE BALLISTICS

ENERGY IN FOOT/POUNDS (TO NEAREST 5 FOOT/POUNDS)			HEIGHT OF BULLET TRAJECTORY IN INCHES ABOVE OR BELOW LINE OF SIGHT IF ZEROED AT ⊕YARDS. SIGHTS 1.5 INCHES ABOVE BORE LINE										TEST BARREL LENGTH INCHES
			AVERAGE RANGE				LONG RANGE						
300 YDS.	400 YDS.	500 YDS.	50 YDS.	100 YDS.	200 YDS.	300 YDS.	50 YDS.	100 YDS.	200 YDS.	300 YDS.	400 YDS.	500 YDS.	
320	200	135	-0.2	⊕	-3.7	-15.3	+0.7	+1.9	⊕	-9.7	-31.6	-71.3	24
610	485	385	-0.2	⊕	-3.1	-12.0	+0.6	+1.6	⊕	-7.3	-21.5	-44.6	24
445	295	195	-0.3	⊕	-3.2	-12.9	+0.5	+1.6	⊕	-8.2	-26.1	-58.3	24
710	575	460	-0.3	⊕	-2.5	-9.9	+0.3	-1.3	⊕	-6.1	-18.3	-37.8	24
605	410	270	-0.4	⊕	-2.1	-9.1	+0.1	+1.0	⊕	-6.0	-19.1	-42.6	24
905	675	495	-0.3	⊕	-2.5	-10.2	+0.3	+1.3	⊕	-6.4	-19.7	-42.2	24
1090	880	710	-0.2	⊕	-3.3	-12.4	+0.6	+1.6	⊕	-7.5	-22.0	-45.4	24
980	735	540	-0.3	⊕	-2.5	-9.3	+0.2	+1.1	⊕	-5.9	-18.25	-39.0	24
1205	985	790	-0.3	⊕	-2.9	-11.0	+0.5	+1.4	⊕	-6.7	-19.8	-40.6	24
1350	1100	885	-0.2	⊕	-3.2	-12.0	+0.6	+1.6	⊕	-7.2	-21.4	-44.0	24
1565	1285	1045	-0.2	⊕	-2.9	-11.2	+0.5	+1.5	⊕	-6.8	-20.0	-41.1	24
1185	870	640	-0.1	⊕	-4.1	-15.5	+0.9	+2.0	⊕	-9.4	-28.6	-61.0	24
1000	740	565	-0.1	⊕	-6.2	-22.6	+1.6	+3.1	⊕	-13.3	-40.1	-84.6	24
1330	1110	930	-0.1	⊕	-4.3	-15.4	+1.0	+2.1	⊕	-9.0	-26.1	-52.9	24
1695	1420	1180	-0.2	⊕	-3.4	-12.6	+0.7	+1.7	⊕	-7.5	-21.8	-44.3	24
1790	1450	1160	-0.3	⊕	-2.9	-11.0	+0.5	+1.4	⊕	-6.7	-19.9	-41.0	24
1960	1640	1370	-0.2	⊕	-3.5	-12.8	+0.7	+1.7	⊕	-7.6	-22.1	-44.9	24
260	210	175	+0.6	⊕	-12.8	-46.9	+3.9	+6.4	⊕	-27.7	-81.8	-167.8	18
655	500	395	+0.2	⊕	-7.0	-25.1	+1.9	+3.5	⊕	-14.5	-43.4	-90.6	20
650	460	355	+0.2	⊕	-7.2	-26.7	+1.9	+3.6	⊕	-15.9	-49.1	-104.5	24
720	535	425	+0.3	⊕	-8.3	-29.8	+2.4	+4.1	⊕	-17.4	-52.4	-109.4	24
480	320	260	+0.1	⊕	-6.6	-26.0	+1.7	+3.3	⊕	-16.0	-50.9	-109.5	24

FEDERAL
CLASSIC® CENTERFIRE RIFLE BALLISTICS

CALIBER	BULLET WGT IN GRAINS	BULLET STYLE	VELOCITY IN FEET PER SECOND (TO NEAREST 10 FEET)						ENERGY IN FOOT/POUNDS (TO NEAREST 5 FOOT/POUNDS)		
			MUZZLE	100 YDS.	200 YDS.	300 YDS.	400 YDS.	500 YDS.	MUZZLE	100 YDS.	200 YDS.
300 Savage	150	Hi-Shok Soft Point	2630	2350	2100	1850	1630	1430	2305	1845	1460
	180	Hi-Shok Soft Point	2350	2140	1940	1750	1570	1410	2205	1825	1495
308 Win. (7.62x51mm)	150	Hi-Shok Soft Point	2910	2620	2340	2080	1840	1620	2820	2280	1825
	180	Hi-Shok Soft Point	2620	2390	2180	1970	1780	1600	2745	2290	1895
	150	Hi-Shok Soft Point	2820	2620	2340	2010	1770	1560	2650	2140	1705
(7.62x63mm)	180	Hi-Shok Soft Point	2700	2470	2250	2040	1850	1660	2915	2435	2025
	125	Hi-Shok Soft Point	3140	2780	2450	2140	1850	1600	2735	2145	1660
	220	Hi-Shok Soft Point RN	2410	2130	1870	1630	1420	1250	2835	2215	1705
	180	Hi-Shok Soft Point RN	2700	2350	2020	1730	1470	1250	2915	2200	1630
300 Win. Magnum	180	Hi-Shok Soft Point	2960	2750	2540	2340	2160	1980	3500	3010	2580
303 British	180	Hi-Shok Soft Point	2460	2230	2020	1820	1630	1460	2420	1995	1625
	150	Hi-Shok Soft Point	2690	2440	2210	1980	1780	1590	2400	1980	1620
32 Win. Special	170	Hi-Shok Soft Point	2250	1920	1630	1370	1180	1040	1910	1395	1000
8mm Mauser (8x57mm JS Mauser)	170	Hi-Shok Soft Point	2360	1970	1620	1330	1120	1000	2100	1465	995
338 Win. Magnum	225	Hi-Shok Soft Point	2780	2570	2370	2180	2000	1830	3860	3305	2815
357 Magnum	180	Hi-Shok Hollow Point	1550	1160	980	860	770	680	960	535	385
35 Rem.	200	Hi-Shok Soft Point	2080	1700	1380	1140	1000	910	1920	1280	840

FEDERAL
CLASSIC® CENTERFIRE RIFLE BALLISTICS

ENERGY IN FOOT/POUNDS (TO NEAREST 5 FOOT/POUNDS)			HEIGHT OF BULLET TRAJECTORY IN INCHES ABOVE OR BELOW LINE OF SIGHT IF ZEROED AT ⊕YARDS. SIGHTS 1.5 INCHES ABOVE BORE LINE										TEST BARREL LENGTH INCHES
			AVERAGE RANGE				LONG RANGE						
300 YDS.	400 YDS.	500 YDS.	50 YDS.	100 YDS.	200 YDS.	300 YDS.	50 YDS.	100 YDS.	200 YDS.	300 YDS.	400 YDS.	500 YDS.	
1145	885	685	0	⊕	-4.8	-17.6	+1.2	+2.4	⊕	-10.4	-30.9	-64.4	24
1215	985	800	+0.1	⊕	-6.1	-21.6	+1.7	+3.1	⊕	-12.4	-36.1	-73.8	24
1445	1130	875	-0.2	⊕	-3.6	-13.6	+0.7	+1.8	⊕	-8.2	-24.4	-50.9	24
1555	1270	1030	-0.1	⊕	-4.6	-16.5	+1.1	+2.3	⊕	-9.7	-28.3	-57.8	24
1345	1050	810	-0.1	⊕	-3.9	-14.7	+0.8	+2.0	⊕	-8.8	-26.3	-54.8	24
1665	1360	1105	-0.1	⊕	-4.2	-15.3	+1.0	+2.1	⊕	-9.0	+26.4	-54.0	24
1270	955	705	-0.3	⊕	-3.0	-11.9	+0.5	+1.5	⊕	-7.3	-22.3	-47.5	24
1300	985	760	-0.1	⊕	-6.2	-22.4	+1.7	+3.1	⊕	-13.1	-39.3	-82.2	24
1190	860	620	-0.1	⊕	-4.9	-18.3	+1.1	+2.4	⊕	-11.0	-33.6	-71.9	24
2195	1860	1565	-0.2	⊕	-3.1	-11.7	+0.6	+1.6	⊕	-7.0	-20.3	-41.1	24
1315	1060	850	0	⊕	-5.5	-19.6	+1.4	+2.8	⊕	-11.3	-33.2	-68.1	24
1310	1055	840	-0.1	⊕	-4.4	-15.9	+1.0	+2.2	⊕	-9.4	-27.6	-56.8	24
710	520	410	+0.3	⊕	-8.0	-29.2	+2.3	+4.0	⊕	-17.2	-52.3	-109.8	24
670	475	375	+0.2	⊕	-7.6	-28.5	+2.1	+3.8	⊕	-17.1	-52.9	-111.9	24
2380	2000	1670	-0.1	⊕	-3.8	-13.7	+0.8	+1.9	⊕	-8.1	-23.5	-47.5	24
295	235	185	⊕	-3.4	-29.7	-88.2	+1.7	⊕	-22.8	-77.9	-173.8	-321.4	18
575	445	370	+0.5	⊕	-10.7	-39.3	+3.2	+5.4	⊕	-23.3	-70.0	-144.0	24

REMINGTON
BALLISTICS

CALIBER	Wt.-Grs.	BULLET Style	VELOCITY-Feet Per Second						ENERGY-Foot-Pounds			
			Muzzle	100 Yds.	200 Yds.	300 Yds.	400 Yds.	500 Yds.	Muzzle	100 Yds.	200 Yds.	300 Yds.
220 SWIFT	50	Pointed Soft Point	3780	3158	2617	2135	1710	1357	1586	1107	760	506
222 REM.	50	Pointed Soft Point	3140	2602	2123	1700	1350	1107	1094	752	500	321
	50	Hollow Point Power-Lokt®	3140	2635	2182	1777	1432	1172	1094	771	529	351
222 REM. MAG.	55	Pointed Soft Point	3240	2748	2305	1906	1556	1272	1282	922	649	444
223 REM.	55	Pointed Soft Point	3240	2747	2304	1905	1554	1270	1282	921	648	443
	55	Hollow Point Power-Lokt®	3240	2773	2352	1969	1627	1341	1282	939	675	473
	55	Metal Case	3240	2759	2326	1933	1587	1301	1282	929	660	456
	60	Hollow Point Match	3100	2712	2355	2026	1726	1463	1280	979	739	547
22-250 REM.	55	Pointed Soft Point	3680	3137	2656	2222	1832	1493	1654	1201	861	603
	55	Hollow Point Power Lokt®	3680	3209	2785	2400	2046	1725	1654	1257	947	703
243 WIN.	80	Pointed Soft Point	3350	2955	2593	2259	1951	1670	1993	1551	1194	906
	80	Hollow Point Power-Lokt®	3350	2955	2593	2259	1951	1670	1993	1551	1194	906
	100	Pointed Soft Point Core-Lokt®	2960	2697	2449	2215	1993	1786	1945	1615	1332	1089
	105	Extended Range	2920	2689	2470	2261	2062	1874	1988	1686	1422	1192
6MM REM.	80	Pointed Soft Point	3470	3064	2694	2352	2036	1747	2139	1667	1289	982
	100	Pointed Soft Point Core-Lokt®	3100	2829	2573	2332	2104	1889	2133	1777	1470	1207
	105	Extended Range	3060	2822	2596	2381	2177	1982	2183	1856	1571	1322
6MM BR REM.	100	Pointed Soft Point	2550	2310	2083	1870	1671	1491	1444	1185	963	776
25-20 WIN.	86	Soft Point	1460	1194	1030	931	858	797	407	272	203	165
250 SAV.	100	Pointed Soft Point	2820	2504	2210	1936	1684	1461	1765	1392	1084	832
257 ROBERTS	117	Soft Point Core-Lokt®	2650	2291	1961	1663	1404	1199	1824	1363	999	718
	122	Extended Range	2600	2331	2078	1842	1625	1431	1831	1472	1170	919
25-06 REM.	100	Pointed Soft Point Core-Lokt®	3230	2893	2580	2287	2014	1762	2316	1858	1478	1161
	120	Pointed Soft Point Core-Lokt®	2990	2730	2484	2252	2032	1825	2382	1985	1644	1351

REMINGTON
BALLISTICS

ENERGY Foot-Pounds		SHORT RANGE TRAJECTORY						LONG RANGE TRAJECTORY							Barrel Length
00 Yds.	500 Yds.	50 Yds.	100 Yds.	150 Yds.	200 Yds.	250 Yds.	300 Yds.	100 Yds.	150 Yds.	200 Yds.	250 Yds.	300 Yds.	400 Yds.	500 Yds.	
25	204	0.2	0.5	0.0	-1.6	-4.4	-8.8	1.3	1.2	0.0	-2.5	-6.5	-20.7	-47.0	24"
2	136	0.5	0.9	0.0	-2.5	-6.9	-13.7	2.2	1.9	0.0	-3.8	-10.0	-32.3	-73.8	24"
8	152	0.5	0.9	0.0	-2.4	-6.6	-13.1	2.1	1.8	0.0	-3.6	-9.5	-30.2	-68.1	
6	198	0.4	0.8	0.0	-2.2	-6.0	-11.8	1.9	1.6	0.0	-3.3	-8.5	-26.7	-59.5	24"
5	197	0.4	0.8	0.0	-2.2	-6.0	-11.8	1.9	1.6	0.0	-3.3	-8.5	-26.7	-59.6	
3	220	0.4	0.8	0.0	-2.1	-5.8	-11.4	1.8	1.6	0.0	-3.2	-8.2	-25.5	-56.0	24"
7	207	0.4	0.8	0.0	-2.1	-5.9	-11.6	1.9	1.6	0.0	-3.2	-8.4	-26.2	-57.9	
7	285	0.5	0.8	0.0	-2.2	-6.0	-11.5	1.9	1.6	0.0	-3.2	-8.3	-25.1	-63.6	
0	272	0.2	0.5	0.0	-1.6	-4.4	-8.7	2.3	2.6	1.9	0.0	-3.4	-15.9	-38.9	24"
1	363	0.2	0.5	0.0	-1.5	-4.1	-8.0	2.1	2.5	1.8	0.0	-3.1	-14.1	-33.4	
6	495	0.3	0.7	0.0	-1.8	-4.9	-9.4	2.6	2.9	2.1	0.0	-3.6	-16.2	-37.9	
6	495	0.3	0.7	0.0	-1.8	-4.9	-9.4	2.6	2.9	2.1	0.0	-3.6	-16.2	-37.9	24"
2	708	0.5	0.9	0.0	-2.2	-5.8	-11.0	1.9	1.6	0.0	-3.1	-7.8	-22.6	-46.3	
2	819	0.5	0.9	0.0	-2.2	-5.8	-11.0	2.0	1.6	0.0	-3.1	-7.7	-22.2	-44.8	
6	542	0.3	0.6	0.0	-1.6	-4.5	-8.7	2.4	2.7	1.9	0.0	-3.3	-14.9	-35.0	
3	792	0.4	0.8	0.0	-1.9	-5.2	-9.9	1.7	1.5	0.0	-2.8	-7.0	-20.4	-41.7	
05	916	0.4	0.8	0.0	-2.0	-5.2	-9.8	1.7	1.5	0.0	-2.7	-6.9	-20.0	-40.4	
0	494	0.3	0.0	-1.9	-5.6	-11.4	-19.3	2.8	2.3	0.0	-4.3	-10.9	-31.7	-65.1	15"
1	121	0.0	-4.1	-14.4	-31.8	-57.3	-92.0	0.0	-8.2	-23.5	-47.0	-79.6	-175.9	-319.4	24"
0	474	0.2	0.0	-1.6	-4.7	-9.6	-16.5	2.3	2.0	0.0	-3.7	-9.2	-28.3	-59.5	24"
2	373	0.3	0.0	-1.9	-5.8	-11.9	-20.7	2.9	2.4	0.0	-4.7	-12.0	-36.7	-79.2	24"
5	555	0.3	0.0	-1.9	-5.5	-11.2	-19.1	2.8	2.3	0.0	-4.3	-10.9	-32.0	-66.4	
1	689	0.4	0.7	0.0	-1.9	-5.0	-9.7	1.6	1.4	0.0	-2.7	-6.9	-20.5	-42.7	
00	887	0.5	0.8	0.0	-2.1	-5.6	-10.7	1.9	1.6	0.0	-3.0	-7.5	-22.0	-44.8	24"

REMINGTON
BALLISTICS

CALIBER	Wt.-Grs.	BULLET Style	VELOCITY-Feet Per Second						ENERGY-Foot-Pounds			
			Muzzle	100 Yds.	200 Yds.	300 Yds.	400 Yds.	500 Yds.	Muzzle	100 Yds.	200 Yds.	300 Yds.
25-06 REM.	122	Extended Range	2930	2706	2492	2289	2095	1911	2325	1983	1683	1419
264 WIN. MAG.	140	Pointed Soft Point Core-Lokt®	3030	2782	2548	2326	2114	1914	2854	2406	2018	1682
270 WIN.	100	Pointed Soft Point	3320	2924	2561	2225	1916	1636	2448	1898	1456	1099
	130	Pointed Soft Point Core-Lokt®	3060	2776	2510	2259	2022	1801	2702	2225	1818	1472
	130	Bronze Point	3060	2802	2559	2329	2110	1904	2702	2267	1890	1565
	150	Soft Point Core Lokt®	2850	2504	2183	1886	1618	1385	2705	2087	1587	1185
	135	Extended Range	3000	2780	2570	2369	2178	1995	2697	2315	1979	1682
	140	Extended Range Boat-Tail	2960	2749	2548	2355	2171	1995	2723	2349	2018	1724
7MM BR REM.	140	Pointed Soft Point	2215	2012	1821	1643	1481	1336	1525	1259	1031	839
7MM MAUSER (7x57)	140	Pointed Soft Point	2660	2435	2221	2018	1827	1648	2199	1843	1533	1266
7MM-08 REM.	140	Pointed Soft Point	2860	2625	2402	2189	1988	1798	2542	2142	1793	1490
	120	Hollow Point	3000	2725	2467	2223	1992	1778	2398	1979	1621	1316
	154	Extended Range	2715	2510	2315	2128	1950	1781	2520	2155	1832	1548
280 REM.	140	Pointed Soft Point	3000	2758	2528	2309	2102	1905	2797	2363	1986	1657
	150	Pointed Soft Point Core Lokt®	2890	2624	2373	2135	1912	1705	2781	2293	1875	1518
	165	Soft Point Core Lokt®	2820	2510	2220	1950	1701	1479	2913	2308	1805	1393
	120	Hollow Point	3150	2866	2599	2348	2110	1887	2643	2188	1800	1468
	165	Extended Range	2820	2623	2434	2253	2080	1915	2913	2520	2171	1860
7MM REM. MAG.	150	Pointed Soft Pint Core-Lokt®	3110	2830	2568	2320	2085	1866	3221	2667	2196	1792
	175	Pointed Soft Point Core-Lokt®	2860	2645	2440	2244	2057	1879	3178	2718	2313	1956
	140	Pointed Soft Point	3175	2923	2684	2458	2243	2039	3133	2655	2240	1878
	165	Extended Range	2900	2699	2507	2324	2147	1979	3081	2669	2303	1978
7MM WBY MAG.	140	Pointed Soft Point	3225	2970	2729	2501	2283	2077	3233	2741	2315	1943

ENERGY-Foot-Pounds		SHORT RANGE TRAJECTORY						LONG RANGE TRAJECTORY							Barrel Length
400 Yds.	500 Yds.	50 Yds.	100 Yds.	150 Yds.	200 Yds.	250 Yds.	300 Yds.	100 Yds.	150 Yds.	200 Yds.	250 Yds.	300 Yds.	400 Yds.	500 Yds.	
1189	989	0.5	0.9	0.0	-2.2	-5.7	-10.8	1.9	1.6	0.0	-3.0	-7.5	-21.7	-43.9	
1389	1139	0.5	0.8	0.0	-2.0	-5.4	-10.2	1.8	1.5	0.0	-2.9	-7.2	-20.8	-42.2	24"
815	594	0.3	0.7	0.0	-1.8	-5.0	-9.7	2.7	3.0	2.2	0.0	-3.7	-16.6	-39.1	
1180	936	0.5	0.8	0.0	-2.0	-5.5	-10.4	1.8	1.5	0.0	-2.9	-7.4	-21.6	-44.3	
1285	1046	0.4	0.8	0.0	-2.0	-5.3	-10.1	1.8	1.5	0.0	-2.8	-7.1	-20.6	-42.0	24"
872	639	0.7	1.0	0.0	-2.6	-7.1	-13.6	2.3	2.0	0.0	-3.8	-9.7	-29.2	-62.2	
1421	1193	0.5	0.8	0.0	-2.0	-5.3	-10.1	1.8	1.5	0.0	-2.8	-7.1	-20.4	-41.0	
1465	1237	0.5	0.8	0.0	-2.1	-5.5	-10.3	1.9	1.5	0.0	-2.9	-7.2	-20.7	-41.6	
681	555	0.5	0.0	-2.7	-7.7	-15.4	-25.9	1.8	0.0	-4.1	-10.9	-20.6	-50.0	-95.2	15"
1037	844	0.2	0.0	-1.7	-5.0	-10.0	-17.0	2.5	2.0	0.0	-3.8	-9.6	-27.7	-56.3	24"
1228	1005	0.6	0.9	0.0	-2.3	-6.1	-11.6	2.1	1.7	0.0	-3.2	-8.1	-23.5	-47.7	
1058	842	0.5	0.8	0.0	-2.1	-5.7	-10.8	1.9	1.6	0.0	-3.0	-7.6	-22.3	-45.8	24"
1300	1085	0.7	1.0	0.0	-2.5	-6.7	-12.6	2.3	1.9	0.0	-3.5	-8.8	-25.3	-51.0	
1373	1128	0.5	0.8	0.0	-2.1	-5.5	-10.4	1.8	1.5	0.0	-2.9	-7.3	-21.1	-42.9	
1217	968	0.6	0.9	0.0	-2.3	-6.2	-11.8	2.1	1.7	0.0	-3.3	-8.3	-24.2	-49.7	
1060	801	0.2	0.0	-1.5	-4.6	-9.5	-16.4	2.3	1.9	0.0	-3.7	-9.4	-28.1	-58.8	24"
1186	949	0.4	0.7	0.0	-1.9	-5.1	-9.7	2.8	3.0	2.2	0.0	-3.6	-15.7	-35.6	
1585	1343	0.6	0.9	0.0	-2.3	-6.1	-11.4	2.1	1.7	0.0	-3.2	-8.0	-22.8	-45.6	
1448	1160	0.4	0.8	0.0	-1.9	-5.2	-9.9	1.7	1.5	0.0	-2.8	-7.0	-20.5	-42.1	
1644	1372	0.6	0.9	0.0	-2.3	-6.0	-11.3	2.0	1.7	0.0	-3.2	-7.9	-22.7	-45.8	24"
1564	1292	0.4	0.7	0.0	-1.8	-4.8	-9.1	2.6	2.9	2.0	0.0	-3.4	-14.5	-32.6	
1689	1434	0.5	0.9	0.0	-2.1	-5.7	-10.7	1.9	1.6	0.0	-3.0	-7.5	-21.4	-42.9	
1621	1341	0.3	0.7	0.0	-1.7	-4.6	-8.8	2.5	2.8	2.0	0.0	-3.2	-14.0	-31.5	

REMINGTON
BALLISTICS

CALIBER	Wt.-Grs.	BULLET Style	VELOCITY-Feet Per Second						ENERGY-Foot-Pounds			
			Muzzle	100 Yds.	200 Yds.	300 Yds.	400 Yds.	500 Yds.	Muzzle	100 Yds.	200 Yds.	300 Yds.
7MM WBY MAG.	175	Pointed Soft Point Core Lokt®	2910	2693	2486	2288	2098	1918	3293	2818	2401	2033
	165	Exteneded Range	2950	2747	2553	2367	2189	2019	3188	2765	2388	2053
30 CARBINE	110	Soft Point	1990	1567	1236	1035	923	842	967	600	373	262
30 REM.	170	Soft Point Core Lokt®	2120	1822	1555	1328	1153	1036	1696	1253	913	666
30-30 WIN. ACCELERATOR®	55	Soft Point	3400	2693	2085	1570	1187	986	1412	886	521	301
30-30 WIN.	150	Soft Point Core Lokt®	2390	1973	1605	1303	1095	974	1902	1296	858	565
	170	Soft Point Core Lokt®	2200	1895	1619	1381	1191	1061	1827	1355	989	720
	170	Hollow Point Core Lokt®	2200	1895	1619	1381	1191	1061	1827	1355	989	720
	160	Extended Range	2300	1997	1719	1473	1268	1116	1879	1416	1050	771
300 SAVAGE	180	Soft Pint Core Lokt®	2350	2025	1725	1467	1252	1098	2207	1639	1193	860
	150	Pointed Soft Point Core Lokt®	2630	2354	2095	1853	1631	1432	2303	1845	1462	1143
30-40 KRAG	180	Pointed Soft Pint Core-Lokt®	2430	2213	2007	1813	1632	1468	2360	1957	1610	1314
308 WIN. ACCELERATOR®	55	Pointed Soft Point	3770	3215	2726	2286	1888	1541	1735	1262	907	638
308 WIN.	150	Pointed Soft Point Core-Lokt®	2820	2533	2263	2009	1774	1560	2648	2137	1705	1344
	180	Soft Point Core-Lokt®	2620	2274	1955	1666	1414	1212	2743	2066	1527	1109
	180	Pointed Soft Point Core-Lokt®	2620	2393	2178	1974	1782	1604	2743	2288	2896	1557
	168	Boat-Tail H.P. Match	2680	2493	2314	2143	1979	1823	2678	2318	1998	1713
	165	Extended Range Boat-Tail	2700	2497	2303	2117	1941	1773	2670	2284	1942	1642
	178	Extended Range	2620	2415	2220	2034	1857	1691	2713	2306	1948	1635
30-06 ACCEL-ERATOR®	55	Pointed Soft Point	4080	3485	2965	2502	2083	1709	2033	1483	1074	764
30-06 SPRING-FIELD	125	Pointed Soft Point	3140	2780	2447	2138	1853	1595	2736	2145	1662	1269
	150	Pointed Soft Point Core-Lokt®	2910	2617	2342	2083	1843	1622	2820	2281	1827	1445
	150	Bronze Point	2910	2656	2416	2189	1974	1773	2820	2349	1944	1596

REMINGTON
BALLISTICS

ENERGY-Foot-Pounds		SHORT RANGE TRAJECTORY						LONG RANGE TRAJECTORY							Barrel Length
400 Yds.	500 Yds.	50 Yds.	100 Yds.	150 Yds.	200 Yds.	250 Yds.	300 Yds.	100 Yds.	150 Yds.	200 Yds.	250 Yds.	300 Yds.	400 Yds.	500 Yds.	
1711	1430	0.5	0.9	0.0	-2.2	-5.7	-18.8	1.9	1.6	0.0	-3.0	-7.6	-21.8	-44.0	24"
1756	1493	0.5	0.8	0.0	-2.1	-5.5	-10.3	1.9	1.6	0.0	-2.9	-7.2	-20.6	-41.3	
208	173	0.9	0.0	-4.5	-13.5	-28.3	-49.9	0.0	-4.5	-13.5	-28.3	-49.9	-118.6	-228.2	20"
502	405	0.7	0.0	-3.3	-9.7	-19.6	-33.8	2.2	0.0	-5.3	-14.1	-27.2	-69.0	-136.9	24"
172	119	0.4	0.8	0.0	-2.4	-6.7	-13.8	2.0	1.8	0.0	-3.8	-10.2	-35.0	-84.4	24"
399	316	0.5	0.0	-2.7	-8.2	-17.0	-30.0	1.8	00	-4.6	-12.5	-24.6	-65.3	134.9	
535	425	0.6	0.0	-3.0	-8.9	-18.0	-31.1	2.0	0.0	-4.8	-13.0	-25.1	-63.6	-126.7	24"
535	425	0.6	0.0	-3.0	-8.9	-18.0	-31.1	2.0	0.0	-4.8	-13.0	-25.1	-63.3	-126.7	
571	442	0.5	0.0	-2.7	-7.9	-16.1	-27.6	1.8	0.0	-4.3	-11.6	-22.3	-56.3	-111.9	
626	782	0.5	0.0	-2.6	-7.7	-15.6	-27.1	1.7	0.0	-4.2	-11.3	-21.9	-55.8	-112.0	24"
806	685	0.3	0.0	-1.8	-5.4	11.0	18.8	2.7	2.2	0.0	-4.2	-10.7	-31.5	-65.5	
1064	861	0.4	0.0	-2.1	6.2	12.5	-21.1	1.4	0.0	-3.4	-8.9	-16.8	-40.9	-78.1	24"
435	290	0.2	0.5	0.0	-1.5	-4.2	-8.2	2.2	2.5	1.8	0.0	-3.2	-15.0	-36.7	24"
1048	810	0.2	0.0	-1.5	-4.5	-9.3	-15.9	2.3	1.9	0.0	-3.6	-9.1	-26.9	-55.7	
799	587	0.3	0.0	-2.0	-5.9	-12.1	-20.9	2.9	2.4	0.0	-4.7	-12.1	-36.9	-79.1	
1269	1028	0.2	0.0	-1.8	-5.2	-10.4	-17.7	2.6	2.1	0.0	-4.0	-9.9	-28.9	-58.8	24"
1460	1239	0.2	0.0	-1.6	-4.7	-9.4	-15.9	2.4	1.9	0.0	-3.5	-8.9	-25.3	-50.6	
1379	1152	0.2	0.0	-1.6	-4.7	-9.4	-16.0	2.3	1.9	0.0	-3.5	-8.9	-25.6	-51.5	
1363	1130	0.2	0.0	-1.7	-5.1	-10.2	-17.2	2.5	2.1	0.0	-3.8	-9.6	-27.6	-55.8	
530	356	0.4	1.0	0.9	0.0	-1.9	-5.0	1.8	2.1	1.5	0.0	-2.7	-12.5	-30.5	24"
953	706	0.4	0.8	0.0	-2.1	-5.6	-10.7	1.8	1.5	0.0	-3.0	-7.7	-23.0	-48.5	
1131	876	0.6	0.9	0.0	-2.3	-6.3	-12.0	2.1	1.8	0.0	-3.3	-8.5	-25.0	-51.8	
1298	1047	0.6	0.9	0.0	-2.2	-6.0	-11.4	2.0	1.7	0.0	-3.2	-8.0	-23.3	-47.5	

REMINGTON
BALLISTICS

CALIBER	Wt.-Grs.	BULLET Style	VELOCITY-Feet Per Second						ENERGY-Foot-Pounds			
			Muzzle	100 Yds.	200 Yds.	300 Yds.	400 Yds.	500 Yds.	Muzzle	100 Yds.	200 Yds.	300 Yds.
30-06 SPRING-FIELD	165	Pointed Soft Point Core Lokt®	2800	2534	2283	2047	1825	1621	2872	2352	1909	1534
	180	Soft Point Core-Lokt®	2700	2348	2023	1727	1466	1251	2913	2203	1635	1192
	180	Pointed Soft Point Core Lokt®	2700	2469	2250	2042	1846	1663	2913	2436	2023	1666
	180	Bronze Point	2700	2485	2280	2084	1899	1725	2913	2468	2077	1736
	220	Soft Point Core-Lokt®	2410	2130	1870	1632	1422	1246	2837	2216	1708	1301
	168	Boat-Tail H.P. Match	2710	2522	2346	2169	2003	1845	2739	2372	2045	1754
	152	Extended Range	2910	2654	2413	2184	1968	1765	2858	2378	1965	1610
	165	Extended Range Boat-Tail	2800	2592	2394	2204	2023	1852	2872	2462	2100	1780
	178	Extended Range	2720	2511	2311	2121	1939	1768	2924	2491	2111	1777
300 H&H MAG.	180	Pointed Soft Point Core-Lokt®	2880	2640	2412	2196	1990	1798	3315	2785	2325	1927
300 WIN. MAG.	150	Pointed Soft Point Core-Lokt®	3290	2951	2636	2342	2068	1813	3605	2900	2314	1827
	180	Pointed Soft Point Core-Lokt®	2960	2745	2540	2344	2157	1979	3501	3011	2578	2196
	200	Swift A-Frame™ PSP	2825	2595	2376	2167	1970	1783	3544	2989	2506	2086
	178	Extended Range	2980	2769	2568	2375	2191	2015	3509	3030	2606	2230
	190	Extended Range Boat-Tail	2885	2691	2506	2327	2156	1993	3511	3055	2648	2285
300 WBY MAG.	180	Pointed Soft Point Core-Lokt®	3120	2866	2627	2400	2184	1979	3890	3284	2758	2301
	220	Soft Piont Core Lokt®	2850	2541	2283	1984	1736	1512	3967	3155	2480	1922
	178	Extended Range	3120	2902	2695	2497	2308	2126	3847	3329	2870	2464
	190	Extended Range Boat-Tail	3030	2830	2638	2455	2279	2110	3873	3378	2936	2542
303 BRITISH	180	Soft Point Core-Lokt®	2460	2124	1817	1542	1311	1137	2418	1803	1319	950
7.62x39MM	125	Pointed Soft Point	2365	2062	1783	1533	1320	1154	1552	1180	882	652
32-20 WIN.	100	Lead	1210	1021	913	834	769	712	325	231	185	154
	100	Soft Point	1210	1021	913	834	769	712	325	231	185	154
32 WIN. SPECIAL	170	Soft Point Core-Lokt®	2250	1921	1626	1372	1175	1044	1911	1393	998	710

REMINGTON
BALLISTICS

ENERGY Foot-Pounds		SHORT RANGE TRAJECTORY						LONG RANGE TRAJECTORY							Barrel Length
400 Yds.	500 Yds.	50 Yds.	100 Yds.	150 Yds.	200 Yds.	250 Yds.	300 Yds.	100 Yds.	150 Yds.	200 Yds.	250 Yds.	300 Yds.	400 Yds.	500 Yds.	
1220	963	0.7	1.0	0.0	-2.5	-6.7	-12.7	2.3	1.9	0.0	-3.6	-9.0	-26.3	-54.1	
859	625	0.2	0.0	-1.8	-5.5	-11.2	-19.5	2.7	2.3	0.0	-4.4	-11.3	-34.4	-73.7	
1362	1105	0.2	0.0	-1.6	-4.8	-9.7	-16.5	2.4	2.0	0.0	-3.7	-9.3	-27.0	-54.9	24"
1441	1189	0.2	0.0	-1.6	-4.7	-9.6	-16.2	2.4	2.0	0.0	-3.6	-9.1	-26.2	53.0	
988	758	0.4	0.0	-2.3	-6.8	-13.8	-23.6	1.5	0.0	-3.7	-9.9	-19.0	-47.4	-93.1	
1497	1270	0.7	1.0	-0.0	-2.5	-6.6	-12.4	2.3	1.9	-0.0	-3.5	-8.6	-24.7	-49.4	
1307	1052	0.6	0.9	0.0	-2.3	-6.0	-11.4	2.0	1.7	0.0	-3.2	-8.0	-23.3	-47.7	
1500	1256	0.6	1.0	0.0	-2.4	-6.2	-11.8	2.1	1.8	0.0	-3.3	-8.2	-23.6	-47.5	
1486	1235	0.7	1.0	0.0	-2.6	-6.7	-12.7	2.3	1.9	0.0	-3.5	-8.8	-25.4	-51.2	
1583	1292	0.6	0.9	0.0	-2.3	-6.0	-11.5	2.1	1.7	0.0	-3.2	-8.0	-23.3	-47.4	24"
1424	1095	0.3	0.7	0.0	-1.8	-4.8	-9.3	2.6	2.9	2.0	0.0	-3.5	-15.4	-35.5	
1859	1565	0.5	0.8	0.0	-2.1	-5.5	-10.4	1.9	1.6	0.0	-2.9	-7.3	-20.9	-41.9	24"
1722	1412	0.6	1.0	0.0	-2.4	-6.3	-11.9	2.1	1.8	0.0	-3.3	-8.3	-24.0	-48.8	
1897	1605	0.5	0.8	0.0	-2.0	-5.4	-10.2	1.8	1.5	0.0	-2.9	-7.1	-20.4	-40.9	
1961	1675	0.5	0.9	0.0	-2.2	-5.7	-10.7	1.9	1.6	0.0	-3.0	-7.5	-21.4	-42.9	
1905	1565	0.4	0.7	0.0	-1.9	-5.0	-9.5	2.7	3.0	2.1	0.0	-3.5	-15.2	-34.2	
1471	1117	0.6	1.0	0.0	-2.5	-6.7	-12.9	2.3	1.9	0.0	-3.6	-9.1	-27.2	-56.8	24"
2104	1787	0.4	0.7	0.0	-1.8	-4.8	-9.1	2.6	2.9	2.0	0.0	-3.3	-14.3	-31.8	
2190	1878	0.4	0.8	0.0	-1.9	-5.1	-9.6	1.7	1.4	0.0	-2.7	-6.7	-19.2	-38.4	
687	517	0.4	0.0	-2.3	-6.9	-14.1	-24.4	1.5	0.0	-3.8	-10.2	-19.8	-50.5	-101.5	24"
483	370	0.4	0.0	-2.5	-7.6	-14.3	-25.7	1.7	0.0	-4.8	-10.8	-20.7	-52.3	-104.0	24"
131	113	0.0	-6.3	-20.9	-44.9	-79.3	-125.1	0.0	-11.5	-32.3	-63.8	-106.3	-230.3	-413.3	24"
131	113	0.0	-6.3	-20.9	-44.9	-79.6	-125.1	0.0	-11.5	-32.3	-63.6	-106.3	-230.3	-413.3	
521	411	0.6	0.0	-2.9	-8.6	-17.6	-30.5	1.9	0.0	-4.7	-12.7	-24.7	-63.2	-126.9	24"

REMINGTON
BALLISTICS

CALIBER	Wt.-Grs.	BULLET Style	VELOCITY-Feet Per Second						ENERGY-Foot-Pounds			
			Muzzle	100 Yds.	200 Yds.	300 Yds.	400 Yds.	500 Yds.	Muzzle	100 Yds.	200 Yds.	300 Yds.
8MM MAUSER	170	Soft Point Core-Lokt®	2360	1969	1622	1333	1123	997	2102	1463	993	671
8MM REM. MAG.	185	Pointed Soft Point Core-Lokt®	3080	2761	2464	2186	1927	1688	3896	3131	2494	1963
338 WIN. MAG.	225	Pointed Soft Point	2780	2572	2374	2184	2003	1832	3860	3305	2815	2383
	250	Pointed Soft Point	2660	2456	2261	2075	1898	1731	3927	3348	2837	2389
	225	Swift A-Frame™PSP	2785	2517	2266	2029	1808	1605	3871	3165	2565	2057
35 REM.	150	Pointed Soft Point Core-Lokt®	2300	1874	1506	1218	1039	934	1762	1169	755	494
	200	Soft Point Core-Lokt®	2080	1698	1376	1140	1001	911	1921	1280	841	577
250 REM. MAG.	200	Pointed Soft Point Core-Lokt®	2710	2410	2130	1870	1631	1421	3261	2579	2014	1553
35 WHELEN	200	Pointed Soft Point	2675	2378	2100	1842	1606	1399	3177	2510	1958	1506
	250	Soft Point	2400	2066	1761	1492	1269	1107	3197	2369	1722	1235
	250	Pointed Soft Point	2400	2197	2005	1823	1652	1496	3197	2680	2230	1844

REMINGTON
BALLISTICS

ENERGY-Foot-Pounds		SHORT RANGE TRAJECTORY						LONG RANGE TRAJECTORY							Barrel Length
400 Yds.	500 Yds.	50 Yds.	100 Yds.	150 Yds.	200 Yds.	250 Yds.	300 Yds.	100 Yds.	150 Yds.	200 Yds.	250 Yds.	300 Yds.	400 Yds.	500 Yds.	
476	375	0.5	0.0	-2.7	-8.2	-17.0	-29.8	1.8	0.0	-4.5	-12.4	-24.3	-63.8	-130.7	24"
1525	1170	0.5	0.8	0.0	-2.1	-5.6	-10.7	1.8	1.6	0.0	-3.0	-7.6	-22.5	-46.8	24"
2004	1676	0.6	1.0	0.0	-2.4	-6.3	-12.0	2.2	1.8	0.0	-3.3	-8.4	-24.0	-48.4	
1999	1663	0.2	0.0	-1.7	-4.9	-9.8	-16.6	2.4	2.0	0.0	-3.7	-6.3	-26.6	-53.6	24"
1633	1286	0.2	0.0	-1.5	-4.6	-9.4	-16.0	2.3	1.9	0.0	.-3.6	-9.1	-26.7	-54.9	
359	291	0.6	0.0	-3.0	-9.2	-19.1	-33.9	2.0	0.0	-5.1	-14.1	-27.8	-74.0	-152.3	24"
445	369	0.8	0.0	-3.8	-11.3	-23.5	-41.2	2.5	0.0	-6.3	-17.1	-33.6	-87.7	-176.4	
1181	897	0.2	0.0	-1.7	-5.1	-10.4	-17.9	2.6	2.1	0.0	-4.0	-10.3	-30.5	-64.0	20"
1145	869	0.2	0.0	-1.8	-5.3	-10.8	-18.5	2.6	2.2	0.0	-4.2	-10.6	-31.5	-65.9	
892	680	0.4	0.0	-2.5	-7.6	-15.0	-26.0	1.6	0.0	-4.0	-10.9	-21.0	-53.8	-108.2	24"
1515	1242	0.4	0.0	-2.2	-6.3	-12.6	-21.3	1.4	0.0	-.34	-9.0	-17.0	-41.0	-77.8	

FEDERAL
CLASSIC® SABOT SLUGS

CONT.

GAUGE	SHELL LENGTH	SLUG TYPE	SLUG WEIGHT IN OUNCES	VELOCITY IN FEET PER SECOND				
				MUZZLE	50 YDS.	75 YDS.	100 YDS.	125 YDS.
12	3	Sabot HP	1	1550	1410	1290	1190	1100
12	2-3/4	Sabot HP	1	1450	1320	1220	1130	1060

FEDERAL
CLASSIC® RIFLED SLUGS

CONT.

GAUGE	SHELL LENGTH	SLUG TYPE	SLUG WEIGHT IN OUNCES	VELOCITY IN FEET PER SECOND				
				MUZZLE	25 YDS.	50YDS.	75YDS.	100 YDS.
10	3-1/2	Hollow Point	1-3/4	1280	1130	1080	1020	970
12	3	Hollow Point	1-1/4	1600	1450	1320	1210	1130
12	2-3/4	Hollow Point	1-1/4	1520	1380	1260	1160	1090
12	2-3/4	Hollow Point	1	1610	1460	1330	1220	1140
16	2-3/4	Hollow Point	4/5	1600	1360	1180	1060	990
20	2-3/4	Hollow Point	3/4	1600	1420	1270	1150	1070
410	2-1/2	Hollow Point	1/5	1830	1560	1340	1160	1060

WINCHESTER
SUPER-X® BRI SABOT SLUG LOADS

Gauge	Length of Shell In.	Velocity fps @ 3 ft.	Oz. Shot	Standard Shot Sizes
New 12	2-3/4	1200	1	Sabot Slug
New 12	3	1300	1	Sabot Slug
New 20	2-3/4	1400	5/8	Sabot Slug

WINCHESTER
SUPER-X® HOLLOW POINT RIFLED SLUG LOADS

Gauge	Length Of Shell In.	Velocity fps @ 3 ft.	Oz. Shot	Standard Shot Sizes
12	2-3/4	1600	1	Rifled Slug
16	2-3/4	1570	4/5	Rifled Slug
20	2-3/4	1570	3/4	Rifled Slug
410	2-1/2	1815	1/5	Rifled Slug

FEDERAL
CLASSIC® SABOT SLUGS

CONT.

ENERGY IN FOOT/POUNDS					HEIGHT OF SLUG TRAJECTORY IN INCHES ABOVE OR BELOW LINE OF SIGHT IF ZEROED AT ⊕ YARDS. SIGHTS .5 INCHES ABOVE BORE LINE.				TEST BARREL LENGTH INCHES
MUZZLE	25 YDS.	50YDS.	75YDS.	100 YDS.	50 YDS.	75 YDS.	100 YDS.	125 YDS.	
2400	1990	1665	1405	1220	+1.9	+1.7	⊕	-3.9	30
2100	1750	1475	1270	1130	+2.2	+2.0	⊕	-3.9	30

FEDERAL
CLASSIC® RIFLED SLUGS

CONT.

ENERGY IN FOOT/POUNDS					HEIGHT OF SLUG TRAJECTORY IN INCHES ABOVE OR BELOW LINE OF SIGHT IF ZEROED AT ⊕ YARDS. SIGHTS .5 INCHES ABOVE BORE LINE.				TEST BARREL LENGTH INCHES
MUZZLE	25 YDS.	50YDS.	75YDS.	100 YDS.	25 YDS.	50 YDS.	75 YDS.	100 YDS.	
2785	2295	1980	1775	1605	+0.5	⊕	-2.3	-6.7	32
3110	2555	2120	1785	1540	+.03	⊕	-1.5	-4.4	30
2805	2310	1930	1645	1450	+0.3	⊕	-1.7	-4.9	28
2520	2075	1725	1455	1255	+0.3	⊕	-1.5	-4.3	30
1990	1435	1075	875	755	+0.3	⊕	-1.8	-5.4	28
1865	1465	1175	965	835	+0.3	⊕	-1.6	-4.8	26
650	475	345	265	215	+0.2	⊕	-1.4	-4.3	26

REMINGTON
SLUGGER® RIFLED SLUG LOADS

Gauge	Shell Length	Slug Wt. (oz).	Velocity (ft/sec.)			Energy (ft-lb.)	Drop (in.)
			Muz.	50 yds.	100 yds.	Muz.	100 yds.
12	3"	1	1760	1345	1075	3009	-8.3
12	2-3/4"	1	1680	1285	1045	2741	-9.0
12	2-3/4"	1	1560	1176	977	2364	-10.7
16	2-3/4"	4/5	1600	1175	965	1989	-10.6
20	2-3/4"	5/8	1580	1230	1034	1515	-9/8
.410	2-1/2"	1/5	1830	1335	1040	651	-8.2

REMINGTON
PREMIER® COPPER SOLID SABOT SLUG

Gauge	Shell Length	Slug Wt. (oz.)	Velocity (ft./sec.)			Energy (ft.-lb.)			Drop (in.)	
			Muz.	50 yds.	100 yds.	Muz.	50 yds.	100 yds.	50 yds.	100 yds.
12	2-3/4"	1	1450	1316	1203	2054	1692	1413	0.0†	-4.2

†0.0 indicates yardage at which shotgun was sighted in.

Quick Reference Shaft Selection Chart

The Quick Reference chart below is designed to give a good approximation of the shaft sizes needed to shoot from the average equipment set-up described on the chart. This abbreviated version is not intended to replace the complete Easton Hunting Shaft Selection Chart, available from Easton, 5040 W. Harold Gatty Drive, Salt Lake City, UT 84116-2897.

First, locate your arrow length. Then go down that column until you find your bow weight. Go across that row to the right and you will find 3-5 sizes that will shoot from that equipment set-up. You can select from one of the 3-5 weight groups shown - from the blinding speed of the A/C/C to the extreme stability and durability of the standard aluminum sizes.

If you shoot a recurve bow, compound bow with round wheel or speed cams, use a mechanical release, or use other than 125 grain weight points. Write for Technical Bulletins #15 and #16.

QUICK REFERENCE
EASTON HUNTING SHAFT SIZE SELECTION CHART

SIZE SELECTION BASED ON: * COMPOUND BOW WITH ENERGY WHEELS
* FINGER RELEASE
* 125 GRAIN BROADHEAD OR FIELD POINT

ARROW LENGTH					SHAFT WEIGHT GROUP & SIZE				
28"	29"	30"	31"	32"	SuperLite A/C/C	UltraLite Aluminum	SuperLite Aluminum	Lite Aluminum	Standard Aluminum
34-39#					3L-18	2112	2013	1916	
39-44#	34-39#				3-18	2112	2113	2016	
44-49#	39-44#	34-39#			3-28	2112	2114	2115	2018
49-54#	44-49#	39-44#	34-39#		3-28	2112	2213	2115	2018
54-59#	49-54#	44-49#	39-44#	34-39#	3-39	2312	2213	2215	2117
59-64#	54-59#	49-54#	44-49#	39-44#	3-49	2312	2314	2215	2117
64-70#	59-64#	54-59#	49-54#	44-49#	3-49	2312	2314	2216	2219
70-76#	64-70#	59-64#	54-59#	49-54#	3-60	2512	2413	2315	2219
76-82#	70-76#	64-70#	59-64#	54-59#	3-60	2512	2413	2315	2219
82-88#	76-82#	70-76#	64-70#	59-64#	3-71	2512	2514		2317
88-94#	82-88#	76-82#	70-76#	64-70#	3-71		2514		2317
94-100#	88-94#	82-88#	76-82#	70-76#	3-71		2514		2419

COMPOUND BOW - Energy Wheel Peak Bow Weight

■ STATE DEER HUNTING STATISTICS
Alphabetical Order By Statistics

STATE [1]	ESTIMATED DEER POPULATION	RESIDENT DEER HUNTERS[2]	RESIDENT DEER HUNTERS[3]	NON SEASON BAG LIMIT[4]	TOTAL DEER HARVEST[5]
Alabama	1,500,000	205,000	16,400	1/day	292,125
Arizona [6,7,9]	215,000	80,285	4,220	1	18,582
Arkansas	700,000	Unknown	Unknown	3	110,000
California [6,7]	725,000	244,000	600	2	35,600
Colorado [6,7]	657,000	148,000	90,000	1	79,384
Connecticut	55,000	30,000	2,000	15	11,311
Delaware	15,000	15,000	400	2	5,333
Florida	750,000	145,138	2,414	2/day	75,000
Georgia	1,210,000	340,000	16,000	5	351,000
Idaho [7]	Unknown	145,038	15,967	1	76,822
Illinois	Unknown	217,000	Combined	2	100,270
Indiana	312,000	170,000	4,000	4	98,366
Iowa	200,000	210,000	1,200	1	84,000
Kansas [7]	300,000	75,000	Not allowed	2	47,000
Kentucky	401,000	210,000	2,100	2	119,361
Louisiana	650,000	187,000	1,732	6	204,082
Maine	290,000	174,000	32,000	1	26,736
Maryland	200,000	120,000	Combined	6	46,623
Massachusetts	55,000	70,000	Combined	2	9,455
Michigan	1,600,000	760,000	20,000	4	400,000
Minnesota	1,100,000	499,000	8,000	1	220,200
Mississippi	1,500,000	250,000	20,000	8	265,000
Missouri	800,000	561,560	11,164	3	163,330
Montana [7]	900,000	142,713	27,433	3	144,253
Nebraska [7]	200,000	69,143	1,870	2	34,045
Nevada [6,7]	180,000	24,052	2,532	1	12,695
New Hampshire	45,000	82,759	12,629	2	8,792
New Jersey	146,000	115,000	2,500	12	45,416
New Mexico[6,7]	225,000	77,191	7,824	1	19,790
New York	850,000	721,452	Combined	2	212,633

STATE [1]	ESTIMATED DEER POPULATION	RESIDENT DEER HUNTERS[2]	RESIDENT DEER HUNTERS[3]	NON SEASON BAG LIMIT[4]	TOTAL DEER HARVEST[5]
North Carolina	660,000	275,000	Combined	5	104,821
North Dakota[7]	170,000	81,926	1,189	3	58,488
Ohio	282,500	274,870	Combined	1	119,614
Oklahoma [7]	277,500	199,628	1,073	5	47,286
Oregon [6,7,8]	693,900	300,000	Combined	1	78,000
Pennsylvania	1,048,600	965,000	70,000	1	388,015
Rhode Island	4,800	11,000	400	2	1,141
South Carolina	750,000	150,000	Combined	7	130,000
South Dakota[7]	330,000	78,700	4,050	25	55,530
Tennessee	700,000	185,000	5,000	23	121,596
Texas [7]	3,260,000	607,000	Combined	6	481,900
Utah [6,7]	400,000	185,000	23,000	1	67,111
Vermont	125,000	92,000	16,500	3	11,584
Virginia	900,000	270,000	15,000	3	179,344
Washington[7,8]	398,880	193,342	1,138	1	57,112
West Virginia	800,000	260,000	41,000	6	176,984
Wisconsin	1,350,000	691,600	27,260	2	419,617
Wyoming [7]	726,000	62,638	37,931	2	91,656

Alphabetical Order By Statistics

1--Several western states that have more than one species of deer usually allow hunters to buy one license that will generally allow them to hunt multiple deer species within that state.

2--Based on actual license sales, or best estimates by the respective state Game & Fish Department based on a combination of license sales and hunter surveys.

3--Non-resident hunter numbers are unknown in some states, and not allowed in others. Some states provide this data "combined" with the resident hunter numbers.

4--State bag limit is defined here as the general statewide bag limit, or that which is available for the majority of hunters within that state.

5--Deer harvest is the actual registered harvest recorded, or the best estimates by the respective state Game & Fish Department based on a combination of license sales and hunter surveys.

6--Very limited number of whitetails, if any, in the state.

7--Mule deer are present, and included in the estimated deer population figures, and/or the deer harvest figures.

8--Black tailed deer are present, and included in the estimated deer population figures, and/or the deer harvest figures.

9--Coues deer are present, and included in the estimated deer population figures, and/or the deer harvest figures.

■ KEY DEER HUNTING STATISTICS
Descending Numerical Order By State

STATE	ESTIMATED DEER POPULATION	STATE	RESIDENT DEER HUNTERS	STATE	TOTAL DEER HARVEST
Texas	3,260,000	Pennsylvania	965,000	Texas	481,900
Michigan	1,600,000	Michigan	760,000	Wisconsin	419,617
Alabama	1,500,000	New York	721,452	Michigan	400,000
Mississippi	1,500,000	Wisconsin	691,600	Pennsylvania	388,015
Wisconsin	1,350,000	Texas	607,000	Georgia	351,000
Georgia	1,210,000	Missouri	561,560	Alabama	292,125
Minnesota	1,100,000	Minnesota	499,000	Mississippi	265,000
Pennsylvania	1,048,600	Georgia	340,000	Minnesota	220,200
Montana	900,000	Oregon	300,000	New York	212,633
Virginia	900,000	North Carolina	275,000	Louisiana	204,082
New York	850,000	Ohio	274,870	Virginia	179,344
Missouri	800,000	Virginia	270,000	West Virginia	176,984
West Virginia	800,000	West Virginia	260,000	Missouri	163,330
Florida	750,000	Mississippi	250,000	Montana	144,253
South Carolina	750,000	California	244,000	South Carolina	130,000
Wyoming	726,000	Illinois	217,000	Tennessee	121,596
California	725,000	Kentucky	210,000	Ohio	119,614
Arkansas	700,000	Alabama	205,000	Kentucky	119,361
Tennessee	700,000	Oklahoma	199,628	Arkansas	110,000
Oregon	693,900	Washington	193,342	North Carolina	104,821
North Carolina	660,000	Louisiana	187,000	Illinois	100,270
Colorado	657,000	Tennessee	185,000	Indiana	98,366
Louisiana	650,000	Utah	185,000	Wyoming	91,656
Kentucky	401,000	Maine	174,000	Iowa	84,000
Utah	400,000	Indiana	170,000	Colorado	79,384
Washington	398,880	South Carolina	150,000	Oregon	78,000
South Dakota	330,000	Colorado	148,000	Idaho	76,822
Indiana	312,000	Florida	145,138	Florida	75,000
Kansas	300,000	Idaho	145,038	Utah	67,111
Maine	290,000	Montana	142,713	North Dakota	58,488
Ohio	282,500	Maryland	120,000	Washington	57,112
Oklahoma	277,500	New Jersey	115,000	South Dakota	55,530
New Mexico	225,000	Vermont	92,000	Oklahoma	47,286
Arizona	215,000	New Hampshire	82,759	Kansas	47,000
Iowa	200,000	North Dakota	81,926	Maryland	46,623
Maryland	200,000	Arizona	80,285	New Jersey	45,416
Nebraska	200,000	South Dakota	78,700	California	35,600
Nevada	180,000	New Mexico	77,191	Nebraska	34,045
North Dakota	170,000	Kansas	75,000	Maine	26,736
New Jersey	146,000	Massachusetts	70,000	New Mexico	19,790
Vermont	125,000	Nebraska	69,143	Arizona	18,582
Connecticut	55,000	Wyoming	62,638	Nevada	12,695
Massachusetts	55,000	Connecticut	30,000	Vermont	11,584
New Hampshire	45,000	Nevada	24,052	Connecticut	11,311
Delaware	15,000	Delaware	15,000	Massachusetts	9,455
Rhode Island	4,800	Rhode Island	11,000	New Hampshire	8,792
Idaho	Unknown	Arkansas	Unknown	Delaware	5,333
Illinois	Unknown	Iowa		Rhode Island	1,141

■ FIREARM HUNTING INFORMATION
Alphabetical Order By State

STATE	FIREARM SEASON DATES[1]	FIREARM SEASON DATES[2]	RESIDENT FIREARMS HUNTERS[2]	HOW MANY NON-RESIDENT FIREARMS HUNTERS[3]	HOW MANY HARVESTED BY FIREARMS	DEER RIFLES PERMITTED[4]	SHOTGUNS PERMITTED[4]	HANDGUNS PERMITTED[4]	MUZZLELOADERS PERMITTED[4]
Alabama	11/23-1/31	70	193,000	16,000	266,500	Yes	Yes	Yes	Yes
Arizona	10/30-12/31	40	59,698	3,408	17,444	Yes	Yes	Yes	Yes
Arkansas	11/9-12/15	37	Unknown	Unknown	84,000	Yes	Yes	Yes	Yes
California	8/8-12/13	93	190,600	Combined	32,300	Yes	Yes	Yes	Yes
Colorado	10/10-10/27	26	129,745	79,524	71,785	Yes	Yes	Yes	Yes
Connecticut	11/23-12/12	18	25,200	1,800	9,674	Yes	Yes	No	Yes
Delaware	11/15-1/8	10	14,000	300	4,348	No	Yes	No	Yes
Florida	10/26-2/19	72	145,138	2,414	Unknown	Yes	Yes	Yes	Yes
Georgia	10/26-1/12	79	340,000	16,000	314,000	Yes	Yes	Yes	Yes
Idaho	10/5-12/1	30	145,038	15,967	64,000	Yes	Yes	Yes	Yes
Illinois	11/20-12/6	7	151,572	Combined	82,190	No	Yes	Yes	Yes
Indiana	11/16-12/1	16	158,000	3,000	64,429	No	Yes	Yes	Yes
Iowa	12/5-12/20	14	160,000	1,200	75,000	No	Yes	No	Yes
Kansas	12/1-12/15	12	50,000	Not allowed	40,000	Yes	Yes	Yes	Yes
Kentucky	11/14-12/3	20	186,900	1,869	96,283	Yes	Yes	Yes	Yes
Louisiana	11/2-1/20	80	185,211	1,732	184,054	Yes	Yes	Yes	Yes
Maine	11/2-11/30	25	174,000	32,000	26,113	Yes	Yes	Yes	Yes
Maryland	11/30-12/7	7	102,000	Combined	31,426	Yes	Yes	Yes	Yes
Massachusetts	12/2-12/11	9	70,000	Combined	7,169	No	Yes	No	Yes
Michigan	11/15-11/30	16	720,000	15,000	275,000	Yes	Yes	Yes	Yes
Minnesota	11/7-11/27	16	425,000	7,000	206,275	Yes	Yes	Yes	Yes
Mississippi	11/23-1/22	47	180,000	20,000	200,000	Yes	Yes	Yes	Yes
Missouri	11/14-11/22	9	426,602	9,539	147,188	Yes	Yes	Yes	Yes
Montana [5]	10/25-11/29	36	140,000	23,000	141,853	Yes	Yes	Yes	Yes
Nebraska	11/9-11/17	9	52,674	1,277	29,368	Yes	Yes	Yes	Yes
Nevada	10/5-11/3	30	21,889	1,722	11,965	Yes	Yes	Yes	Yes
New Hampshire	11/11-12/6	26	67,627	9,608	6,435	Yes	Yes	Yes	Yes
New Jersey	12/9-1/25	8	110,000	2,500	25,510	No	Yes	No	Yes
New Mexico	10/1-11/17	35	68,204	6,166	Unknown	Yes	Yes	Yes	Yes
New York	10/24-12/8	67	700,000	Combined	191,533	Yes	Yes	Yes	Yes
North Carolina	10/12-1/1	71	260,000	14,000	88,721	Yes	Yes	Yes	Yes
North Dakota	11/8-11/24	16	70,604	636	54,251	Yes	Yes	Yes	Yes
Ohio[6]	12/2-12/7	6	274,870	Combined	93,063	No	Yes	Yes	Yes
Oklahoma	11/23-12/1	9	144,662	Combined	30,406	Yes	Yes	Yes	Yes

STATE	FIREARM SEASON DATES[1]	FIREARM SEASON DATES[2]	RESIDENT FIREARMS HUNTERS[2]	HOW MANY NON-RESIDENT FIREARMS HUNTERS[3]	HOW MANY HARVESTED BY FIREARMS	DEER RIFLES PERMITTED[4]	SHOTGUNS PERMITTED[4]	HANDGUNS PERMITTED[4]	MUZZLELOADERS PERMITTED[4]
Oregon[5]	9/28-12/2	24	230,000	Combined	73,000	Yes	Yes	Yes	Yes
Pennsylvania	12/2-12/18	15	950,000	60,000	356,134	Yes	Yes	Yes	Yes
Rhode Island	12/5-12/13	9	5,458	144	376	No	Yes	No	Yes
South Carolina[5]	8/15-1/1	140	147,500	Combined	Unknown	Yes	Yes	Yes	Yes
South Dakota	11/1-12/6	30	66,850	3,535	52,110	Yes	Yes	Yes	Yes
Tennessee	11/21-1/1	40	150,000	5,000	87,532	Yes	Yes	Yes	Yes
Texas[5]	11/7-1/10	58	585,247	Combined	466,700	Yes	Yes	Yes	Yes
Utah	10/17-10/27	11	144,053	20,000	45,785	Yes	Yes	Yes	Yes
Vermont	11/14-11/29	16	92,000	16,500	9,825	Yes	Yes	Yes	Yes
Virginia	11/16-1/2	42	270,000	15,000	158,546	Yes	Yes	Yes	Yes
Washington	10/17-11/1	16	165,438	938	50,576	Yes	Yes	Yes	Yes
West Virginia	11/23-12/12	15	260,000	41,000	138,051	Yes	Yes	Yes	Yes
Wisconsin[5]	11/21-11/29	9	650,000	26,000	352,520	Yes	Yes	Yes	Yes
Wyoming[5]	10/1-11/30	61	62,638	37,931	90,419	Yes	Yes	Yes	Yes

1--Dates for the firearm season as listed here are in the broadest context due to space limitations. These dates reflect the first day to the last day of firearm activity within the state. While some states have statewide seasons, others have varying seasons for different management units within their state.

2--Length of each season is the total available hunting days in each state. Some states do not allow hunting on Sundays, while some states break seasons into "early" and "late" seasons.

3--"Combined" means that the non-resident hunter figure is included with the resident hunter figure.

4--Indicates types of weapons that may be used to hunt deer at some time period during the year. Check regulations for restrictions.

5--The number of resident hunters, non-resident hunters, and total deer harvest include both the firearm totals and the muzzleloader totals. South Carolina also includes the number of deer harvested by bow in the firearm harvest total.

■ BOW HUNTING INFORMATION
Alphabetical Order By State

STATE	BOW SEASON DATES[1]	BOW SEASON DAYS[2]	HOW MANY RESIDENT BOW HUNTERS[3]	HOW MANY NON-RESIDENT BOW HUNTERS[3]	DEER HARVESTED BY BOW[4]	ARE CROSSBOWS PERMITTED?[5]	BOW BAG LIMIT[6]	IS SPECIAL LICENSE NEEDED?[7]	MAY BOWS BE USED DURING FIREARMS SEASON?[8]
Alabama	10/15-1/31	118	46,000	4,000	19,475	Handicapped	1/day	No	Yes
Arizona	8/21-1/31	73	19,518	807	902	No	1	Yes	Yes
Arkansas	10/1-2/29	152	Unknown	Unknown	11,500	Yes	3	No	Yes
California	7/11-10/25	90	20,000	Combined	2,800	Yes	2	No	Yes
Colorado	8/29-11/27	72	13,600	9,200	5,400	Yes	1	Yes	Yes
Connecticut	9/15-12/31	63	10,000	2,000	1,205	No	4	Yes	No
Delaware	9/2-1/31	111	4,000	100	362	Handicapped	2	No	No
Florida	9/7-11/17	30	46,696	Combined	Unknown	Yes	2/day	Yes	Yes
Georgia	9/21-10/25	35	66,600	3,000	37,000	Handicapped	5	Yes	Yes
Idaho	8/30-9/24	26	21,251	Combined	10,372	Yes	1	Yes	Yes
Illinois	10/1-12/31	85	100,148	Combined	18,000	Handicapped	3	Yes	No
Indiana	10/12-12/31	60	80,000	1,000	21,581	Handicapped	2	Yes	No
Iowa	10/1-1/10	86	31,000	430	9,000	Handicapped	1	Yes	No
Kansas	10/1-12/31	79	15,000	Not Allowed	6,000	Handicapped	1	Yes	No
Kentucky	10/1-1/15	107	100,800	1,000	8,755	Yes	2	No	Yes
Louisiana	10/1-1/20	112	44,616	227	17,706	Handicapped	6	Yes	Yes
Maine	10/1-11/1	28	9,287	1,038	500	No	1	Yes	Yes
Maryland	9/14-1/31	118	53,000	Combined	10,454	Handicapped	2	Yes	Yes
Massachusetts	11/4-12/23	18	18,000	Combined	1,378	No	2	Yes	Yes
Michigan	10/10-1/1	76	304,000	6,000	100,000	No	3	Yes	Yes
Minnesota	9/19-12/31	104	74,000	1,000	12,964	Handicapped	1	Yes	Yes
Mississippi	10/1-11/22	53	61,000	10,000	29,000	Handicapped	8	Yes	Yes
Missouri	10/1-12/31	83	90,296	1,425	14,185	Handicapped	2	Yes	Yes
Montana	9/5-10/18	44	22,000	9,000	2,400	Yes	3	Yes	Yes
Nebraska	9/15-12/31	99	11,700	511	3,211	Handicapped	2	Yes	No
Nevada	8/10-9/6	28	1,854	530	477	No	1	Yes	Yes
New Hampshire	9/12-12/13	93	15,132	3,021	732	Handicapped	1	Yes	Yes
New Jersey	9/28-1/29	82	51,000	2,000	15,480	No	6	Yes	No
New Mexico	8/31-1/9	79	4,527	586	611	No	1	No	No
New York	9/27-12/13	55	171,647	Combined	19,008	Handicapped	2	Yes	Yes
North Carolina	9/7-11/21	66	100,000	Combined	6,700	No	5	Yes	Yes
North Dakota	8/30-12/31	124	10,669	553	3,889	Handicapped	1	Yes	Yes
Ohio	10/5-1/31	96	137,500	Combined	17,138	Yes	1	No	Yes

STATE	BOW SEASON DATES[1]	BOW SEASON DAYS[2]	HOW MANY RESIDENT BOW HUNTERS[3]	HOW MANY NON-RESIDENT BOW HUNTERS[3]	DEER HARVESTED BY BOW[4]	ARE CROSSBOWS PERMITTED?[5]	BOW BAG LIMIT[6]	IS SPECIAL LICENSE NEEDED?[7]	MAY BOWS BE USED DURING FIREARMS SEASON?[8]
Oklahoma	10/1-12/31	78	49,374	Combined	7,089	Handicapped	2	Yes	Yes
Oregon	8/24-9/22	30	25,000	Combined	5,000	No	1	Yes	No
Pennsylvania	10/5-1/11	39	278,000	17,000	23,243	Handicapped	1	Yes	No
Rhode Island	10/1-1/31	122	1,839	250	291	No	2	Yes	Yes
South Carolina[8]	10/1-12/12	23	25,000	5,000	Combined	Yes (most)	7	No	Yes
South Dakota	10/1-12/31	92	11,350	500	3,100	Handicapped	5	Yes	Yes
Tennessee	9/26-11/15	42	60,000	2,500	17,032	Yes	9	Yes	No
Texas	10/1-11/1	32	80,000	Combined	15,200	Handicapped	6	Yes	Yes
Utah	8/22-9/7	17	28,300	600	4,052	No	1	Yes	Yes
Vermont	10/3-12/13	32	17,683	4,007	1,591	Handicapped	2	Yes	Yes
Virginia	10/10-1/9	55	63,000	2,200	13,438	No	2	Yes	Yes
Washington	9/16-12/15	49	20,716	154	4,367	No	1	No	Yes
West Virginia	10/17-12/31	65	125,000	18,000	27,448	No	5	No	Yes
Wisconsin	9/19-12/31	85	208,000	6,300	67,097	Handicapped	1	Yes	No
Wyoming	9/1-9/30	30	5,474	969	1,237	Yes	2	Yes	Yes

1--Dates for the bow hunting season as listed here are in the broadest context due to space limitations. These dates reflect the first day to the last day of bow hunting activity within the state. While some states have statewide seasons, others have varying seasons for different management units within their state.

2--Length of each season is the total available hunting days in each state. Some states do not allow hunting on Sundays, while some states break seasons into "early" or "late" seasons.

3--"Combined" means that the non-resident hunter figure is included with the resident hunter figure.

4--"Combined" means that the deer harvested by bow are included with the number of deer harvested by regular firearms. The grand total may be found in the chart entitled "Firearm Hunting Information."

5--Indicates states that allow the use of a crossbow to hunt deer. Some states classify a crossbow as a firearm, some as a bow, others outlaw them, while others only allow handicapped persons with a special permit to use them.

6--Indicates the general statewide bag limit for the majority of bow hunters in the state.

7--States that require the purchase of a special bow hunting license or stamp.

8--Rules of regular firearms season will usually apply. Use of blaze orange, and getting a special permit may be required, among other restrictions.

■ MUZZLELOADER HUNTING INFORMATION
Alphabetical Order By State

STATE	MUZZLELOADER SEASON DATES[1]	MUZZLELOADER SEASON DAYS[2]	IS THERE A SPECIAL MUZZLELOADER SEASON?[3]	MAY MUZZLELOADERS BE USED TO HUNT DEER DURING REGULAR FIREARMS SEASON?[4]	ARE THERE SPECIAL MUZZLELOADER RESTRICTIONS?[5]	HOW MANY RESIDENT MUZZLELOADER HUNTERS ARE THERE?[6]	HOW MANY NON-RESIDENT MUZZLELOADER HUNTERS?[7]	HOW MANY DEER HARVESTED BY MUZZLELOADER[8]
Alabama	11/23-1/31	70	No	Yes	Yes	20,500	1,640	6,150
Arizona	10/30-12/31	40	Yes	Yes	Yes	1,069	5	236
Arkansas	10/19-12/1	24	Yes	Yes	Yes	Unknown	Unknown	14,500
California	9/26-12/20	86	Yes	Yes	Yes	1,300	Combined	500
Colorado	9/12-9/20	9	Yes	Yes	Yes	4,700	1,300	2,200
Connecticut	12/14-12/26	12	Yes	No	Yes	5,000	300	432
Delaware	10/10-1/22	6	Yes	Yes	Yes	4,000	100	623
Florida	10/11-11/24	3	Yes	Yes	No	31,323	Combined	Unknown
Georgia	10/26-1/12	79	No	Yes	Yes	20,000	Combined	Combined
Idaho	11/10-12/9	29	Yes	Yes	Yes	10,372	Combined	2,450
Illinois	12/11-12/13	3	Yes	Yes	Yes	402	Combined	80
Indiana	12/7-12/15	9	Yes	Yes	Yes	53,000	1,000	12,356
Iowa	10/10-1/10	30	Yes	Yes	No	18,000	50	5,500
Kansas	9/21-12/15	21	Yes	Yes	Yes	2,010	Not allowed	1,000
Kentucky	10/17-12/18	20	Yes	Yes	Yes	36,000	500	14,323
Louisiana	12/2-12/6	5	Yes	Yes	Yes	9,576	62	2,322
Maine	12/2-12/7	6	Yes	Yes	Yes	2,814	94	123
Maryland	12/21-1/4	13	Yes	Yes	Yes	38,000	Combined	4,743
Massachusetts	12/16-12/18	3	Yes	No	Yes	15,000	Combined	908
Michigan	12/4-12/20	17	Yes	Yes	Yes	149,000	1,000	25,000
Minnesota	11/28-12/13	16	Yes	Yes	Yes	2,500	Combined	961
Mississippi	12/2-12/15	14	Yes	Yes	Yes	69,000	10,000	36,000
Missouri	11/14-12/13	18	Yes	Yes	Yes	10,662	Not allowed	1,957
Montana	10/25-11/29	36	No	Yes	No	Combined	Combined	Combined
Nebraska	12/7-12/22	16	Yes	Yes	Yes	3,770	82	1,466
Nevada	9/7-9/22	16	Yes	Yes	Yes	560	29	253
New Hampshire	10/31-11/10	11	Yes	Yes	Yes	17,079	2,252	1,625
New Jersey	12/16-1/4	13	Yes	Yes	Yes	18,000	Combined	4,426
New Mexico	9/14-9/22	9	Yes	No	Yes	4,460	1,072	1,591
New York	10/17-12/15	14	Yes	Yes	Yes	34,295	Combined	2,092
North Carolina	10/5-11/21	18	Yes	Yes	No	96,000	Combined	9,400

STATE	MUZZLELOADER SEASON DATES[1]	MUZZLELOADER SEASON DAYS[2]	IS THERE A SPECIAL MUZZLELOADER SEASON?[3]	MAY MUZZLELOADERS BE USED TO HUNT DEER DURING REGULAR FIREARMS SEASON?[4]	ARE THERE SPECIAL MUZZLELOADER RESTRICTIONS?[5]	HOW MANY RESIDENT MUZZLELOADER HUNTERS ARE THERE?[6]	HOW MANY NON-RESIDENT MUZZLELOADER HUNTERS?[7]	HOW MANY DEER HARVESTED BY MUZZLELOADER[8]
North Dakota	11/29-12/9	7	Yes	Yes	Yes	653	Not allowed	348
Ohio	10/21-12/7	15	Yes	Yes	Yes	Combined	Combined	9,413
Oklahoma	10/26-11/3	9	Yes	Yes	Yes	38,670	Combined	9,791
Oregon	9/28-12/8	72	Yes	No	Yes	Combined	Combined	Combined
Pennsylvania	12/26-1/11	15	Yes	Yes	Yes	99,000	7,000	8,638
Rhode Island	11/7-12/27	37	No	Yes	Yes	3,750	Not allowed	474
South Carolina	10/1-10/10	9	Yes	Yes	Yes	Combined	Combined	Unknown
South Dakota	12/12-12/20	9	Yes	Yes	Yes	500	15	320
Tennessee	10/17-12/13	30	Yes	No	No	55,000	2,500	17,032
Texas	11/7-1/10	58	No	Yes	No	Combined	Combined	Combined
Utah	10/31-11/9	10	Yes	Yes	Yes	12,654	200	3,150
Vermont	12/5-12/13	9	Yes	Yes	Yes	8,679	1,641	168
Virginia	11/9-1/2	20	Yes	Yes	Yes	42,000	2,500	7,360
Washington	9/30-1/15	35	Yes	Yes	Yes	7,118	46	2,169
West Virginia	12/14-12/19	6	Yes	Yes	Yes	80,000	7,300	11,485
Wisconsin	11/30-12/6	7	Yes	Yes	Yes	Combined	Combined	Combined
Wyoming	10/1-11/30	61	No	Yes	Yes	Combined	Combined	Combined

1--Dates for the muzzleloader hunting season as listed here are in the broadest context due to space limitations. When the muzzleloader season runs concurrently with the gun season, the gun season dates are used. These dates reflect the first day to the last day of muzzleloader hunting activity within the state. While some states have statewide seasons, others have varying seasons for different management units within the state.

2--Length of each season is the total available hunting days in each state. Some states do not allow hunting on Sundays, while some states break seasons into "early" and "late" seasons. If the muzzleloader seasons runs concurrently with the gun seasons, then the number of days in the general firearms season is used.

3--States having a designated black powder or primitive weapons season.

4--Rules of the regular firearms season will usually apply. Use of blaze orange, and getting a special permit may be required, among other restrictions.

5--Restrictions usually involve barrel length, bore, caliber size, sights and powder type.

6--"Combined" means that the number of resident muzzleloader hunters is combined with the number of resident firearms hunters. The grand total may be found in the chart entitled "Firearm Hunting Information."

7- "Combined" means that the non-resident muzzleloader hunter figure is combined with the resident muzzleloader hunter figure.

8--"Combined" means that the deer harvested by muzzleloaders are combined with the number of deer harvested by regular firearms. This number may be found in the chart entitled "Firearm Hunting Information."

■ STATE DEER HUNTING TRENDS
Broken Out By Trend Type

DEER-VEHICLE COLLISIONS	DEER CROP DAMAGE	NUMBER OF YOUTH HUNTERS	NUMBER OF FEMALE HUNTERS	HUNTING WITH RIFLES
INCREASED	**INCREASED**	**INCREASED**	**INCREASED**	**INCREASED**
Delaware	Kentucky	Alabama	Delaware	Alabama
Illinois	Louisiana	Iowa	Georgia	Colorado
Kentucky	Maine	Michigan	Michigan	Connecticut
Maine	Maryland	Montana	Montana	Georgia
Massachusetts	New York	Oregon	New York	Idaho
Minnesota	Oklahoma	Pennsylvania	Pennsylvania	Michigan
New Hampshire	Oregon	Utah	Wisconsin	Missouri
New York	Rhode Island			Montana
North Dakota	Virginia	**CONSTANT**	**CONSTANT**	North Carolina
Ohio	Washington	Connecticut	Arkansas	North Dakota
Oklahoma	West Virginia	Delaware	Connecticut	Vermont
Rhode Island	Wisconsin	Georgia	Indiana	
South Carolina	Wyoming	Indiana	Kentucky	**CONSTANT**
Utah		Minnesota	Mississippi	Arkansas
Vermont	**CONSTANT**	New Jersey	North Carolina	Kansas
Virginia	Arizona	New York	Oregon	Kentucky
Washington	Arkansas	North Carolina	South Dakota	Louisiana
West Virginia	California	North Dakota	Texas	Maine
Wisconsin	Connecticut	Rhode Island	Utah	Maryland
Wyoming	Florida	South Dakota	Virginia	Mississippi
	Georgia	Tennessee	Washington	New Hampshire
CONSTANT	Iowa	Virginia	West Virginia	Oklahoma
Alabama	Massachusetts	Wisconsin		Pennsylvania
Arizona	Mississippi		**DECREASED**	South Dakota
Arkansas	Montana	**DECREASED**	Arizona	Tennessee
California	Nevada	Arizona	Wyoming	Texas
Connecticut	New Hampshire	Arkansas		Utah
Florida	New Jersey	California	**UNKNOWN**	Washington
Georgia	North Carolina	Kentucky	Alabama	Wisconsin
Iowa	South Carolina	Maine	California	
Kansas	South Dakota	Maryland	Colorado	**DECREASED**
Louisiana	Tennessee	Mississippi	Florida	Arizona
Maryland	Texas	Texas	Idaho	California
Mississippi	Utah	Washington	Illinois	Nebraska
Missouri	Vermont	West Virginia	Iowa	Nevada
Montana		Wyoming	Kansas	New Mexico
Nebraska	**DECREASED**		Louisiana	Oregon
New Jersey	Alabama	**UNKNOWN**	Maine	Virginia
North Carolina	Indiana	Colorado	Maryland	West Virginia
Oregon	Kansas	Florida	Massachusetts	Wyoming
South Dakota	Michigan	Idaho	Minnesota	
Tennessee	Missouri	Illinois	Missouri	**UNKNOWN**
Texas	Nebraska	Kansas	Nebraska	Florida
	North Dakota	Louisiana	Nevada	Minnesota
DECREASED	Pennsylvania	Massachusetts	New Hampshire	New York
Michigan		Missouri	New Jersey	South Carolina
Pennsylvania	**UNKNOWN**	Nebraska	New Mexico	
	Colorado	Nevada	North Dakota	**NOT ALLOWED**
UNKNOWN	Delaware	New Hampshire	Ohio	Delaware
Colorado	Idaho	New Mexico	Oklahoma	Illinois
Idaho	Illinois	Ohio	Rhode Island	Indiana
Indiana	Minnesota	Oklahoma	South Carolina	Iowa
Nevada	New Mexico	South Carolina	Tennessee	Massachusetts
New Mexico	Ohio	Vermont	Vermont	New Jersey
				Ohio
				Rhode Island

■ STATE DEER HUNTING TRENDS
Broken Out By Trend Type

HUNTING WITH HANDGUNS	HUNTING WITH MUZZLE-LOADERS	HUNTING WITH BOWS	COYOTE PRESSURE ON HERD	ANTI-HUNTING PRESSURE
INCREASED		**INCREASED**	**INCREASED**	**INCREASED**
Alabama		Alabama	Alabama	Alabama
Colorado	**INCREASED**	Arkansas	Georgia	California
Georgia	Arkansas	California	Kentucky	Colorado
Louisiana	California	Colorado	Massachusetts	Connecticut
Michigan	Colorado	Connecticut	Michigan	Delaware
Mississippi	Connecticut	Delaware	Mississippi	Georgia
Missouri	Delaware	Georgia	Montana	Kentucky
North Carolina	Georgia	Idaho	New Jersey	Maryland
Utah	Idaho	Illinois		Massachusetts
Virginia	Iowa	Indiana		Mississippi
Washington	Indiana	Louisiana	**CONSTANT**	Montana
West Virginia	Kansas	Maine	Arizona	Nevada
Wisconsin	Kentucky	Maryland	Arkansas	New York
Wyoming	Maryland	Massachusetts	Colorado	North Carolina
	Massachusetts	Michigan	Connecticut	Ohio
	Michigan	Minnesota	Louisiana	Rhode Island
CONSTANT	Minnesota	Missouri	Maine	Utah
Arkansas	Mississippi	Montana	Missouri	Washington
California	Missouri	Nebraska	Nebraska	Wisconsin
Indiana	Nebraska	New Hampshire	Nevada	Wyoming
Kansas	New Hampshire	New Jersey	New Hampshire	
Maryland	New Jersey	New York	North Carolina	**CONSTANT**
North Dakota	New York	North Carolina	North Dakota	Arizona
Oregon	North Carolina	North Dakota	Oklahoma	Arkansas
Pennsylvania	Pennsylvania	Oregon	Oregon	Florida
South Dakota	Rhode Island	Pennsylvania	Pennsylvania	Idaho
Tennessee	South Dakota	Rhode Island	South Dakota	Illinois
Texas	Tennessee	Tennessee	Tennessee	Indiana
	Utah	Utah	Texas	Iowa
DECREASED	Vermont	Vermont	Utah	Kansas
Arizona	Virginia	Virginia	Vermont	Maine
Kentucky	Washington	Washington	Virginia	Michigan
	West Virginia	West Virginia	Wisconsin	Nebraska
UNKNOWN	Wisconsin	Wisconsin	Wyoming	New Hampshire
Florida		Wyoming		New Jersey
Idaho	**CONSTANT**		**UNKNOWN**	North Dakota
Illinois	Alabama	**CONSTANT**	California	Oklahoma
Maine	Illinois	Iowa	Delaware	Oregon
Minnesota	Louisiana	Mississippi	Florida	Pennsylvania
Montana	Maine	Oklahoma	Idaho	South Dakota
Nebraska	North Dakota	South Dakota	Illinois	Tennessee
Nevada	Oklahoma	Texas	Iowa	Texas
New Hampshire	Oregon		Indiana	Virginia
New Mexico	Texas	**DECREASED**	Kansas	West Virginia
New York	Wyoming	Arizona	Maryland	
Ohio		Kansas	Minnesota	**DECREASED**
Oklahoma	**DECREASED**	Kentucky	New Mexico	Louisiana
South Carolina	Arizona	Nevada	New York	
Vermont	Nevada	New Mexico	Ohio	**UNKNOWN**
	New Mexico		Rhode Island	Minnesota
NOT ALLOWED		**UNKNOWN**	South Carolina	Missouri
Connecticut	**UNKNOWN**	Florida	Washington	New Mexico
Delaware	Florida	Ohio	West Virginia	South Carolina
Iowa	Montana	South Carolina		Vermont
Massachusetts	Ohio			
New Jersey	South Carolina			...Continued
Rhode Island				

POACHING

INCREASED
Maine
Michigan
Rhode Island
Utah

CONSTANT
Arizona
Arkansas
Colorado
Connecticut
Delaware
Florida
Georgia
Idaho
Indiana
Iowa
Kansas
Kentucky
Louisiana
Maryland
Massachusetts
Mississippi
Missouri
Montana
Nebraska
Nevada
New Hampshire
New Jersey
North Carolina
North Dakota
Ohio
Oklahoma
Oregon
Pennsylvania
South Dakota
Tennessee
Texas
Virginia
Washington
West Virginia
Wisconsin
Wyoming

DECREASED
Alabama

UNKNOWN
California
Illinois
Minnesota
New Mexico
New York
South Carolina
Vermont

■ STATE DEER HUNTING TRENDS
Alphabetical Order By State

STATE	DEER VEHICLE COLLISIONS	DEER CROP DAMAGE	NUMBER OF YOUTH HUNTERS	NUMBER OF FEMALE HUNTERS	RIFLE USE	HANDGUN USE	MUZZLELOADER USE	BOW USE	COYOTE PRESSURE ON HERD	ANTI-HUNTING PRESSURE	POACHING
Alabama	C	D	I	U	I	I	C	I	I	I	D
Arizona	C	C	D	D	D	D	D	D	C	C	C
Arkansas	C	C	D	C	C	C	I	I	C	C	C
California	C	C	D	U	D	C	I	I	U	I	U
Colorado	U	U	U	U	I	I	I	I	C	I	U
Connecticut	C	C	C	C	I	NA	I	I	C	I	C
Delaware	I	U	C	I	NA	NA	I	I	U	I	C
Florida	C	C	U	U	U	U	U	U	U	C	C
Georgia	C	C	C	I	I	I	I	I	I	I	C
Idaho	U	U	U	U	I	U	I	I	U	C	C
Illinois	I	U	U	U	NA	U	C	I	U	C	U
Indiana	U	D	C	C	NA	C	I	I	U	C	C
Iowa	C	C	I	U	NA	NA	I	C	U	C	C
Kansas	C	D	U	U	C	C	I	D	U	C	C
Kentucky	I	I	D	C	C	D	I	D	I	I	C
Louisiana	C	I	U	U	C	I	C	I	C	D	C
Maine	I	I	D	U	C	U	C	I	C	C	I
Maryland	C	I	D	U	C	C	I	I	U	I	C
Massachusetts	I	C	U	U	NA	NA	I	I	I	I	C
Michigan	D	D	I	I	I	I	I	I	I	C	I
Minnesota	I	U	C	U	U	U	I	I	U	U	U
Mississippi	C	C	D	C	C	I	C	I	C	I	C
Missouri	C	D	U	U	I	I	I	I	C	U	C
Montana	C	C	I	I	I	U	U	I	I	I	C
Nebraska	C	D	U	U	D	U	I	I	C	C	C
Nevada	U	C	U	U	D	U	D	D	C	I	C
New Hampshire	I	C	U	U	I	C	U	I	I	C	C
New Jersey	C	C	C	U	NA	NA	I	I	I	C	C
New Mexico	U	U	U	U	D	U	D	D	U	U	U
New York	I	I	C	I	U	U	I	I	U	I	U
North Carolina	C	C	C	C	I	I	I	I	C	I	C
North Dakota	I	D	C	U	I	C	C	I	C	C	C
Ohio	I	U	U	U	NA	U	U	U	U	I	C
Oklahoma	I	I	U	U	C	U	C	C	C	C	C
Oregon	C	I	I	C	D	C	C	I	C	C	C
Pennsylvania	D	D	I	I	C	C	I	I	C	C	C
Rhode Island	I	I	C	U	NA	NA	I	I	U	I	I
South Carolina	I	C	U	U	U	U	U	U	U	U	U
South Dakota	C	C	C	C	C	C	I	C	C	C	C
Tennessee	C	C	C	U	C	C	I	I	C	C	C
Texas	C	C	D	C	C	C	C	C	C	C	C
Utah	I	C	I	C	C	I	I	I	I	I	I
Vermont	I	C	U	U	I	U	I	I	C	U	U
Virginia	I	I	C	C	D	I	I	I	C	I	C
Washington	I	I	D	C	C	I	I	I	U	I	C
West Virginia	I	I	D	C	D	I	I	I	U	C	C
Wisconsin	I	I	C	I	C	I	I	I	C	I	C
Wyoming	I	I	D	D	D	I	C	I	C	I	C

C = CONSTANT I = INCREASED D = DECREASED U = UNKNOWN NA = NOT ALLOWED

■ STATE DEER HUNTING REGULATIONS
Alphabetical By State

STATE	MINIMUM HUNTING AGE[1]	GENERAL HUNTER EDUCATION MANDATORY[2]	BOW HUNTING EDUCATION MANDATORY[3]	BOW HUNT FROM TREE STAND	GUN HUNT FROM TREE STAND	BLAZE ORANGE REQUIRED	USE FOOD BAIT	HUNT SALT/MINERALS	SHINE FOR DEER
Alabama	None	Yes	No	Yes	Yes	Yes	No	No	No
Arizona	10	No	No	Yes	Yes	No	No	Yes	No
Arkansas	None	Yes	No	Yes	Yes	Yes	Yes	Yes	Yes
California	12	Yes	No	Yes	Yes	No	No	No	No
Colorado	14	Yes	No	Yes	Yes	Yes	No	No	No
Connecticut	12	Yes	Yes	Yes	Yes	Yes	No	No	Yes
Delaware	None	Yes	No	Yes	Yes	Yes	No	No	No
Florida	None	Yes	No	Yes	Yes	Yes	Yes	Yes	Yes
Georgia	None	Yes	No	Yes	Yes	Yes	No	No	No
Idaho	12	Yes	No	Yes	Yes	No	No	No	No
Illinois	None	Yes	No	Yes	Yes	Yes	No	No	No
Indiana	None	Yes	No	Yes	Yes	Yes	No	No	No
Iowa	None	Yes	No	Yes	Yes	Yes	No	No	Yes
Kansas	14	Yes	No	Yes	Yes	Yes	Yes	Yes	No
Kentucky	None	Yes	No	Yes	Yes	Yes	Yes	Yes	No
Louisiana	None	Yes	No	Yes	Yes	Yes	Yes	Yes	No
Maine	10	Yes	Yes	Yes	Yes	Yes	No	No	No
Maryland	None	Yes	No	Yes	Yes	Yes	Yes	Yes	No
Massachusetts	12	No	No	Yes	Yes	Yes	No	No	No
Michigan	12	Yes	No	Yes	No	Yes	Yes	No	Yes
Minnesota	12	Yes	No	Yes	Yes	Yes	No	Yes	No
Mississippi	None	Yes	No	Yes	Yes	Yes	No	No	No
Missouri	None	Yes	No	Yes	Yes	Yes	Yes	Yes	No
Montana	12	Yes	Yes	Yes	Yes	Yes	No	No	No
Nebraska	14	Yes	Yes	Yes	Yes	Yes	Yes	Yes	No
Nevada	12	Yes	No	Yes	Yes	No	No	No	No
New Hampshire	16	Yes	No	Yes	Yes	No	Yes	No	No
New Jersey	10	Yes	Yes	Yes	Yes	Yes	Yes	No	Yes
New Mexico	None	Yes	No	Yes	Yes	No	No	No	No
New York	14	Yes	Yes	Yes	Yes	No	No	No	No
North Carolina	None	Yes	No	Yes	Yes	Yes	Yes	Yes	No
North Dakota	14	Yes	No	Yes	Yes	Yes	Yes	Yes	No
Ohio	None	Yes	No	Yes	Yes	Yes	Yes	Yes	No
Oklahoma	None	Yes	No	Yes	Yes	Yes	Yes	Yes	No
Oregon	14	Yes	No	Yes	Yes	No	Yes	Yes	No
Pennsylvania	12	Yes	No	Yes	Yes	Yes	No	Yes	No
Rhode Island	12	Yes	Yes	Yes	Yes	Yes	No	No	No
South Carolina	None	No	No	Yes	Yes	Yes	Yes	Yes	Yes
South Dakota	12	Yes	No	Yes	Yes	Yes	No	No	Yes
Tennesee	10	Yes	No	Yes	Yes	Yes	No	Yes	No
Texas	None	Yes	No	Yes	Yes	No	Yes	Yes	No
Utah	14	Yes	No	Yes	Yes	Yes	Yes	Yes	No
Vermont	None	Yes	No	Yes	Yes	No	Yes	No	No

STATE	MINIMUM HUNTING AGE[1]	GENERAL HUNTER EDUCATION MANDATORY[2]	BOW HUNTING EDUCATION MANDATORY[3]	BOW HUNT FROM TREE STAND	GUN HUNT FROM TREE STAND	BLAZE ORANGE REQUIRED	USE FOOD BAIT	HUNT SALT/MINERALS	SHINE FOR DEER
Virginia	None	Yes	No	Yes	Yes	Yes	No	No	Yes
Washington	14	No	No	Yes	Yes	Yes	Yes	Yes	No
West Virginia	None	Yes	No	Yes	Yes	Yes	Yes	Yes	No
Wisconsin	12	Yes	No	Yes	Yes	Yes	Yes	Yes	Yes
Wyoming	14	Yes	No	Yes	Yes	Yes	No	Yes	No

1--In many states youths must be accompanied by an adult, or pass a hunter education course to qualify.

2--Usually applies to first-time hunters, or all those born after a designated date.

3--Bow hunting education is mandatory in only seven states, but it is briefly covered in the general hunter education course in most states.

4--Restrictions usually apply in states that permit shining for deer, such as time restrictions and no weapon in possession, or private property.

❖ CONTACTS FOR HUNTING INFORMATION ❖

STATE	DEPT/ADDRESS
Alabama	Dept. of Conservation & Nat. Res. District Wildlife Office P.O. Box 993 Demopolis, AL 36732
Alaska	Alaska Dept. Fish and Game P.O. Box 3-2000 Juneau, AK 99802
Arizona	Arizona Game & Fish Department 2222 W. Greenway Rd. Phoenix, AR 85023
Arkansas	Game and Fish Commission HC 71, Box 171 Mountain View, AR 72560
California	California Game Commission P.O. Box 944209 Sacremento, CA 94244
Colorado	Dept. of Natural Resources Division of Wildlife 6060 Broadway Denver, CO 80216
Connecticut	Dept. of Environmental Protection Wildlife Division 391 Route 32 N. Franklin, CT 06254
Delaware	Delaware Fish and Wildlife Division of Fish and Wildlife P.O. Box 1401 Dover, DE 19901
Florida	Game & Fresh Water Fish Commission Division of Wildlife 620 S. Meridian, Farris Bryant Bldg. Tallahassee, FL 32399-1600
Georgia	Dept. of Natural Resources Game and Fish Division 205 Butler St., SE, Suite 1362 Atlanta, GA 30334
Hawaii	Dept. of Land and Nat. Res. Hawaii Div. of Forestry & Wildlife 1151 Punchbowl St. Honolulu, HI 96813
Idaho	Dept. of Fish and Game 600 S. Walnut St, Box 25 Boise, ID 83707

STATE	DEPT/ADDRESS
Illinois Division of Wildlife Resources	Director 600 N. Grand Ave., W. Springfield, IL 62706
Indiana	Dept. of Natural Resources Division of Fish and Wildlife 300 West First Street Bloomington, IN 47401
Iowa	Wildlife Manager Chariton Research Center Rt 1, Box 209 Chariton, IA 50049
Kansas	Wildlife & Parks P.O. Box 1525 Emporia, KS 66801
Kentucky	Dept. of Fish & Wildlife Res. RR 1, Box 309 Williamstown, KY 41097
Louisiana	Dept. of Wildlife & Fisheries P.O. Box 4004 Monroe, LA 71211
Maine	Dept. of Inland Fisheries & Wildlife 284 State St. Station 41 Augusta, ME 04333
Maryland	Dept. of Natural Resources Tawes State Office Bldg. Annapolis, MD 21401
Massachusetts	Division of Fish and Wildlife 100 Cambridge Street Boston, MA 02202
Michigan	Wildlife Division, Michigan Box 30028 Lansing, MI 48909
Minnesota	Dept. of Natural Resources Division of Fish and Wildlife Box 7, 500 Lafayette Rd. St. Paul, MN 55155
Mississippi	Dept. of Wildlife Conservation P.O. Box 451 Jackson, MS 39205
Missouri	Dept. of Conservation 1110 S. College Avenue Columbia, MO 65203
Montana	Montana Dept. of Wildlife 1420 E. 6th Ave. Helena, MT 59620

STATE	DEPT/ADDRESS
Nebraska	Game and Parks Commission Bassett, NE 68714
Nevada	Nevada Dept. of Wildlife P.O. Box 10678 Reno, NV 89520
New Hampshire	NH Fish & Game Dept. Region 1 Office Rd 2, Rte 3N, Box 241 Lancaster, NH 03584
New Jersey	Div. of Fish, Game and Wildlife Bureau of Wildlife Management Nacote Creek Res Stn, P.O. Box 418 Port Republic, NJ 08241
New Mexico	New Mexico DNR Villagra Bldg. 408 Galisteo Santa Fe, NM 87503
New York	Dept. of Environmental Conserv. Wildlife Resource Center Delmar, NY 12054
North Carolina	Wildlife Biologist NC Commission, Wildlife Mgemt 512 N. Salisbury St. Rollie, NC 27604-1188
North Dakota	Game & Fish Dept. 100 N. Bismarck Expressway Bismarck, ND 58501
Ohio	Waterloo Wildlife Experiment Stn Division of Wildlife 9650 State Route 356 New Marshfield, OH 45766
Oklahoma	Dept. of Wildlife Conservation 1801 N. Lincoln Blvd. Oklahoma City, OK 73105
Oregon	OR Dept. of Fish & Wildlife P.O. Box 8 Hines, OR 97738
Pennsylvania	Pennsylvania Game Comm. 2001 Elmerton Avenue Harrisburg, PA 17110
Rhode Island	Dept. of Environmental Mgemt Box 218 West Kingston, RI 02892
South Carolina	Wildlife Resources Dept. P.O. Box 167 Columbia, SC 29202

STATE	DEPT/ADDRESS
South Dakota	Harvest Surveys Coordinator Division of Wildlife Sigrud Anderson Bldg, 445 E. Capitol Pierre, SD 57501
Tennessee	Tennessee Wildlife Res. Agency P.O. Box 40747 Nashville, TN 37204
Texas	Parks & Wildlife Dept. 4200 Smith School Rd. Austin, TX 78744
Utah	Utah Div. of Wildlife Resources 1596 W. N. Temple Salt Lake City, UT 84116
Vermont	Fish & Game Dept. Agency of Environmental Conser. 103 S. Main St., 10 So. Waterbury, VT 05676
Virginia	Comm. of Game & Inland Fish. P.O. Box 11104 Richmond, VA 23230
Washington	Washington Dept. of Wildlife 600 Capital Way N. Olympia, WA 25305
West Virginia	Dept. of Natural Resources 1800 Washington St. E Charleston, WV 25305
Wisconsin	Wis. Dept. of Natural Resources Bureau of Wildlife Mngmt Box 7921 Madison, WI 53707
Wyoming	Game & Fish Dept. 5400 Bishop Blvd. Cheyenne, WY 82006
Canada	Energy & Nat. Res. F&W Div. Main Flr. No. Tower, Petroleum Plaza 9945-108 St. Edmonton, ALB CAN T5K 2 GS
Canada	Ministry of Environment Fish & Wildlife Branch Parliament Buildings Victoria, BC CAN V8V 1X5

❖DEER HUNTER'S CHECKLISTS❖

GEAR

❏ License
❏ Permits
❏ Maps
❏ Compass
❏ Hunting Knife
❏ Butcher Knife
❏ Hacksaw/Meat Saw
❏ Drag Rope
❏ Matches
❏ Watch
❏ Alarm Clock
❏ Game Carrier
❏ Game Bag
❏ Packet Knife
❏ Walkie Talkie
❏ Extra Battery
❏ Ear Plugs
❏ Binoculars
❏ Sporting Scope
❏ Range Finder
❏ Belt Shell Holder
❏ Gun Cleaning Equip.
❏ Back Pack
❏ Tent
❏ Sleeping Bag
❏ Air Mattress
❏ Air Pump
❏ Cot
❏ Blankets
❏ Pillow
❏ Camp Chairs
❏ Camp Heater

❏ Camp Stove
❏ Stove Fuel
❏ Mess Kit
❏ Kettles
❏ Coffee Pot
❏ Can Opener
❏ Ice Chest
❏ Camp Axe/Saw
❏ Water Jugs
❏ Rifle (lg.bore)
❏ Rifle (sm. bore)
❏ Shotgun
❏ Pistol
❏ Ammunition
❏ Clips or Magazines
❏ Bow/Arrows
❏ Arm/Finger Guards
❏ Deer Tags/Back Tags
❏ Back Tag Holder

CLOTHES

❏ Cap
❏ Face Cap
❏ Coats
❏ Gloves
❏ Mittens
❏ Shirts
❏ Trousers
❏ Suspenders
❏ Underwear
❏ Insul. Underwear
❏ Boots, Leather

❏ Boots, Rubber
❏ Felt Liners
❏ Dress Shoes
❏ Dress Clothing
❏ Mosquito Netting
❏ Camo Face Mask
❏ Sweaters
❏ Vests
❏ Blaze Orange Clothes
❏ Handkerchiefs
❏ Rain Wear
❏ Camo Clothes

MISC. EQUIP MENT

❏ Money
❏ Hunting Chair
❏ Tow Rope
❏ Grunt Calls
❏ Rattling Horns
❏ Tree stand
❏ Extra Bow
❏ Extra Bow Strings
❏ Came Calls
❏ Scents/Lures
❏ Decoys
❏ Brushcutter
❏ Camo Paint
❏ Plastic Cloth
❏ Carcass Cloth
❏ Deer Buggy
❏ Camp Lantern

- ❏ Flashlight
- ❏ Penlight
- ❏ Spotlight
- ❏ Toilet Articles
- ❏ Port. Toilet
- ❏ Camp Matches
- ❏ Tools
- ❏ Tire Chains
- ❏ Gas Can
- ❏ Scissors
- ❏ Safety Pins
- ❏ Needle/Thread
- ❏ Tape
- ❏ Pencil/Pens
- ❏ Notebooks
- ❏ Logbooks
- ❏ Shovel
- ❏ Flares
- ❏ Glasses
- ❏ Sun Glasses
- ❏ Shooting Glasses
- ❏ Gun Cases
- ❏ Extra Gun Cases
- ❏ Deer Bag
- ❏ Hunters Hoist
- ❏ Knife Sharpener
- ❏ Snake Bite Kit
- ❏ First Aid Kit
- ❏ Insect Repellent
- ❏ Boot Dressing
- ❏ Camera/Film
- ❏ Video Camera
- ❏ Sling Shot
- ❏ Thermos
- ❏ Playing Cards
- ❏ Radio

- ❏ Money
- ❏ Credit Cards
- ❏ Handwarmer
- ❏ Water
- ❏ Canteen
- ❏ Lunch Pail
- ❏ Tobacco Products
- ❏ Gum
- ❏ Reference Material
- ❏ *Deer & Deer Hunting Magazine*

FOOD
- ❏ Beans
- ❏ Biscuit Mix
- ❏ Pancake Mix
- ❏ Syrup
- ❏ Bread
- ❏ Cereal
- ❏ Coffee (Regular)
- ❏ Coffee (Instant)
- ❏ Cookies
- ❏ Eggs
- ❏ Snacks
- ❏ Juices
- ❏ Milk (Dry)
- ❏ Milk (Regular)
- ❏ Soup
- ❏ Peas
- ❏ Corn
- ❏ Potatoes
- ❏ Pickles
- ❏ Hot Chocolate
- ❏ Margarine
- ❏ Butter
- ❏ Salad Dressing

- ❏ Mustard
- ❏ Ketchup
- ❏ Crackers
- ❏ Potato Chips
- ❏ Peanut Butter
- ❏ Jam/Jellies
- ❏ Candy Bars
- ❏ Pop
- ❏ Mix
- ❏ Soda Water
- ❏ Beer/Liquor
- ❏ Ice
- ❏ Donuts
- ❏ Sugar
- ❏ Salt/Pepper
- ❏ Cooking Oil
- ❏ Lettuce
- ❏ Tomatoes
- ❏ Oranges
- ❏ Apples
- ❏ Onions
- ❏ Hamburgers
- ❏ Hamburger Buns
- ❏ Hot Dogs
- ❏ Hot Dog Buns
- ❏ Bacon
- ❏ Ham
- ❏ Steaks
- ❏ Sausages
- ❏ Paper Towels
- ❏ Knives/Forks/Spoon
- ❏ Hand Soap
- ❏ Dish Soap
- ❏ Alka Seltzer
- ❏ Aspirin
- ❏ Personal Medicines